London's Pirate Pioneers

The illegal broadcasters
who changed British radio

Stephen Hebditch

LONDON'S PIRATE PIONEERS

Published by TX Publications, BM Box 9867, London, WC1N 3XX.
Web: www.amfm.org.uk / E-mail: amfm@amfm.org.uk / Twitter: @amfmldn.

First edition 2015.

Printed and distributed by Ingram Spark.

ISBN 978-0-9932652-0-4.

Contents

Intro

In 1981 as a young teenager I found myself listening to a pirate radio station for the very first time. My uncle had given me his old valve hi-fi and I was now able to make my own choice of what to listen to whenever I wanted. Tuning around one Saturday evening I stumbled upon a transmission that wasn't supposed to be there: South London Radio. I was intrigued and soon discovered that it wasn't alone: each night there were different illegal broadcasters in the gaps on the dial, each on the air for a just a few hours.

It wasn't long before I was hooked on the pirates and a large aerial was added to the wall outside my bedroom window so I could better pull in their transmissions. I liked the ordinary voices that you heard, not like the smooth DJs on Capital or Radio One who came from a completely different world. The music that the pirates played often didn't feature elsewhere on the airwaves: new wave tracks from the edges of the charts, obscure rock made when I was still a toddler, electro and dub soundscapes that seemed to point to the future. There was also the sense of community that came from being a listener, learning a little about the lives of the people putting them out, the efforts that they went to in order to broadcast and the in-jokes that made you feel a part of the station.

In 1985 I decided someone ought to be providing a guide to what was going on, so I founded TX Magazine. I learned about publishing as I went along, pasting up copy written on a Sinclair Spectrum and getting amazing help to print and distribute the early issues from Anoraks UK, who published a weekly pirate radio newsletter. From the early rough issues, TX picked up a nice team of contributors and moved to more professional desktop publishing. Over the next three years it grew to sell more than a thousand copies each month, eventually changing its name to Radio Today. Unfortunately university and a job got in the way, resulting in an increasingly erratic publishing schedule and its eventual closure at the end of 1988. The associated telephone information line lived on and continued keeping people updated on events in the pirate world through to the nineties.

For a long time it's been in the back of my mind to write the story of London's pirates. British radio outside the BBC and the offshore stations has been very much neglected in print. While it might now be a very long time ago that these events took place, the people involved deserve more recognition for what they did in helping Britain move to a more open and diverse broadcasting system.

Right: DBC prepare for another Friday night on the airwaves circa 1982. Photo © Leon Morris.

In writing this book I wanted to show the huge range of unlicensed radio that London has been home to over the years. Today people associate the pirates primarily with young DJs playing music of black origin, but in their history there have been many kinds of music and programming from people of many different ages and social backgrounds. There are over four hundred stations listed in the quarter century from 1965 to 1990 that the book covers. They vary hugely in scale, professionalism and style but all represent the city that is London.

Stations and events did not exist in isolation. I have tried to explain why London's pirates developed in the way they did and why certain kinds of broadcasters were successful at particular times while others were not.

The British political system and the actions of its politicians were undoubtedly the primary reason why pirate radio took root and prospered. In the USA the radio system opened up early, with a range of commercial and non-commercial broadcasters and a desire by the regulator to fully exploit the available spectrum space. In Europe it took the actions of pirate radio stations – particularly in France, Italy and the UK – to seize the airwaves from the state monopolies. In Britain there remained a huge fear of not just opening up broadcasting to ordinary people but to anyone that the state could not control.

From the first demands for commercial broadcasting in 1948, it took twenty-five years before its eventual introduction. It was another fifteen years before the social liberalism that defined the first independent radio stations was replaced by Thatcherite market liberalism and companies were given free rein to maximise their commercial potential. The earliest ideas around creating a new tier of small community radio stations began in 1969, but it was thirty-five years before Ofcom finally began licensing a distinct low-power, non-profit sector. The broadcasting system as it was worked well for the politicians. They consequently viewed pirate radio as a policing problem, not as a sign that the way broadcasting was organised might need changing in the light of developments in technology, culture and society.

It was technology, and the politicians' failure to keep up with its progress, that made unlicensed broadcasting viable. Here pirate radio followed a very similar path in adoption to other new technologies like the Internet. First were the initial innovators: technologists for whom refining the equipment and means to broadcast were the primary interest, while their programming was rather more conservative. Next came those closer to the cutting-edge of culture who wanted to use the technology to do things that couldn't be done before or fulfil a demand unmet by the mainstream media. Then came the entrepreneurs, building on the earlier experimentation in technology and content and utilising the holes in the law to exploit the opportunities in particular niche markets. Finally we get to a point where unlicensed broadcasting technology has been fully commoditised and the techniques widely known, so no longer are any particularly special skills required to participate. The cheapness of broadcasting illegally is what has made it so very hard to eradicate.

Changes in the legitimate broadcasting system and in the laws governing unlicensed broadcasting were to have their impact on the make-up of pirate broadcasters. In 1969 your only choice for a career in radio was the BBC and their intake was highly selective. The introduction of Independent Local Radio in 1973, its further expansion in 1981 and then the explosion in new licensees from 1989 meant that there was an alternate career path for people from a wider range of social backgrounds. Meanwhile, the 1984 Telecommunications Act and then the 1990 Broadcasting Act made operating illegally a much bigger deal – one that could now harm your future life prospects. Consequently, what had started out in the sixties as a hobby for those from comfortable suburban backgrounds had by the late eighties changed to an urban enterprise for the people most excluded from the legitimate media system: the young, the working class and those from black or other minority ethnic backgrounds.

London is a glorious melting pot. Those who came to the capital from Britain's former colonies helped mould its culture, with people from the West Indies, India and Cyprus in particular playing a big part in the development of its radio. Culture has also fractured. Under major label control in the sixties, popular music was more homogeneous. The independent label boom of the late seventies broadened the range of music and participants and then as computer technology made recording accessible to almost everyone, the range of sub-genres exploded. These changes were reflected on London's underground radio.

With twenty-five years of political, technological, social and cultural changes affecting the capital's pirates, this book is as a result rather wide ranging. Whether you were a listener or broadcaster at the time or are simply interested in radio, I hope it gives you an insight into an important part of London's radio history.

Stephen Hebditch. April 2015.

Errors and omissions

Piecing together the history of illegal enterprises from so long ago has not been easy. Some of those who could help with the story could not be located, some did not want to get involved and some had sadly already passed away. A few stations that I wanted to cover in more detail are sadly dealt with more briefly than they deserve. People also have different interpretations of events and more exciting tales occasionally displace the mundane reality of what went on.

If you can fill in any gaps, put me right on something or have an alternative view about what happened then do please get in touch at amfm@amfm.org.uk so they can corrected online and fixed in any future edition. A list of corrections can be found at amfm.org.uk/errata.

The pirates broadcasters and their names

Many of those involved in pirate radio used aliases, either to hide their real identity or to project a cooler image – myself included. This can make things confusing, especially when sources use them interchangeably. In writing this book I have stuck where possible to the on-air names of presenters, with their real name included in brackets on the first mention in a section when that name is also well-known. I have respected the privacy of those whose identities have not already been revealed through existing interviews, books or the Internet.

The anti-pirate enforcers and their names

The government team trying to stop the pirates from operating went under several different names as departments were moved and renamed. Early on the work was carried out by the General Post Office's Radio Services Department on behalf of the Ministry of Posts and Telecommunications. In 1974 that ministry was dissolved and responsibilities passed to the Home Office. The department was renamed the Radio Interference Service and in 1981 moved to British Telecom when that was split from the Post Office prior to privatisation. In 1984 it moved to the Radiocommunications Agency of the Department of Trade and Industry, where it was renamed the Radio Investigation Service. In 2003 it became part of Ofcom. People from different eras often interchangeably use these names and their initials – RSD, RIS, GPO, DTI – for the unlicensed broadcasting investigators.

1964-1969

Teenage bedroom broadcasters

Every history of British pirate radio begins with Radio Caroline taking to the air at Easter 1964. From a few hours a week of pop music on the BBC Light Programme and nightly shows fading in and out on the distant Radio Luxembourg, young people could now tune in to a powerful all-day music station. Caroline was quickly followed by a wave of offshore pop pirates, some more professional like Wonderful Radio London, some rather shambolic, like Radio Sutch. Their history, however, has been told many times before and those on the North Sea weren't the only ones broadcasting outside the law.

The earliest unlicensed stations on land were tiny hobbyist operations. While some teenage boys were directed towards getting an amateur radio licence as a legal output for their interest in electronics, others wanted to broadcast real radio. The offshore radio boom of the sixties served to encourage this – if big pirates operating from ships could get away with it then surely the authorities would have little interest in a station broadcasting to just a few neighbouring streets at random times.

Most of these nascent broadcasters would follow a similar path. First would be bedroom experimentation with low power transmitters, often using circuits modified from amateur radio transmitters designed for beginners on a low budget. Over time these would be refined and a power amplifier added, enabling the signal to get out for several miles. The buzz of getting feedback from listeners across town for something they had created would drive the broadcasters on. The transmissions would also enable them to meet up with like-minded souls who were willing to help out and to connect with other unlicensed broadcasters, with whom they could share knowledge.

Inevitably they would push things too far and there would be a day when the nice men from the General Post Office's Radio Services Department would come knocking at the door. If the offender was a minor then the most likely outcome was a stern talk and the confiscation of the transmitter. If they were of age then they might find themselves at the local magistrate's court where they were typically fined from £1 to £10 for a first offence. Many would choose to stop there, but there were always a few who would not be put off.

The same hacker mentality that drove such people to experiment in the first place would now also be applied to seeing how they could successfully broadcast while minimising the risk of being caught. Separately several groups seem to have alighted on the idea of moving their operations out to fields and woods. Vital in this move was the introduction of the Compact Cassette in 1963, which by the late sixties had developed into affordable transistorised cassette players with sound quality that was good enough for music. With the launch of the C120 cassette in 1968 the final piece came into place. Hour-length programmes could now be recorded on a Saturday then broadcast on a Sunday from out in the open, switching between shows at the top of the hour just like a legal station. London's renegade broadcasters were now here to stay.

Commercial broadcasting and free radio campaigns

Political pressure to break the BBC's monopoly on broadcasting began as early as 1948, influenced by the industry's development in America and the popularity of programmes in Britain from overseas broadcasters like Radio Luxembourg – which were often preferred by listeners to the BBC's. These ideas were, however, tempered by the still recent experience of the Second World War. In 1949 the Conservative government set up the Beveridge Committee on Broadcasting to look at the future of the BBC and whether commercial broadcasting should be introduced. It reported back to Parliament in 1951, concluding "The right of access to the domestic sound and television receivers of millions of people carries with it such great propaganda power that it cannot be trusted to any person or bodies other than a public corporation."

Keeping broadcasting exclusively in public hands was Labour party policy, while commercial radio and television found little support among traditional Conservatives, who benefited from the existing system of government control. Only a younger minority in the party, influenced by American ideas of free enterprise, favoured opening up the airwaves. When the Tories decided to introduce commercial television in 1954, they chose a public service model that would be acceptable to the patrician majority in the party – and even then party whips denied MPs a free vote in Parliament to ensure its safe passage.

The next opportunity to break the BBC's radio monopoly came ten years later with the Pilkington Committee, again commissioned by a Conservative government and concluding in 1962. Encouraged by what had happened with ITV, companies began gearing up for what they were certain was the introduction of commercial radio. Those registering an interest in running stations included Odeon cinema and dance hall owner the Rank Organisation, local newspaper

proprietors like East Midlands Allied Press (EMAP), several of the ITV fran-
chisees and Pye, who manufactured radios and transmission equipment.

They were to be disappointed: the Committee sided largely with the BBC in its
report. Committee members decided that the general public were not especially
impressed by ITV and its American imports and did not want a similar radio
service. Despite having found little interest among the public, it accepted the
BBC's recommendation that it should introduce local services. The BBC had
argued that with no dependence on advertisers its programmes were likely to
be more innovative and that local stations could only be economically viable if
some programmes were networked.

The political rejection of radio from outside the BBC did not put an end to
pressure from those wanting to see the introduction of commercial radio, who
found common cause particularly with those on the right of the Conservative
party. The Popular Television Association, who had previously campaigned for
commercial TV, renamed itself the National Broadcasting Development Committee. Chaired by Conservative MP Sir Harmar Nichols, its funding came mostly
from radio and television manufacturers. More prominent in radio was the Local
Radio Association, who represented the interests of over 120 companies hoping
for commercial licences.

The LRA was founded in 1963 by two former members of Pye's advertising
department, John Gorst and John Whitney. Gorst was now a Conservative MP but
ran a string of other groups mostly campaigning against nationalised industries
and unions. In the 1950s John Whitney had produced programmes for Radio
Luxembourg and would go on to become the first Managing Director at Capital
Radio and in 1983 the Director General of the Independent Broadcasting Authority. Strong support for commercial radio also came from the advertising industry,
especially the American agencies that set up shop for the first time in sixties
London and were already experienced in radio as an advertising medium.

Then there were the people who decided to take more practical steps towards
commercial radio: Britain's offshore radio entrepreneurs.

The public-school-educated private equity backers of Radio Caroline and
the Texan oil men behind Wonderful Radio London may have been sharply
different in their backgrounds, but both shared a belief in laissez faire capitalism.
The romantic idea of a band of young disc jockeys battling the authorities from

the high seas for the cause of freedom and the right to have their music heard gave a new and readily exploitable image to the campaign for commercial radio.

When the new Labour government decided to close down the offshore stations, young people viewed the action as censorship and an attack on their generation. A multitude of grassroots groups sprang up to campaign for 'free radio': some local, some national; some concerned more with the loss of pop from their radios, others seeing the freeing-up of the airwaves as part of a wider political project. The different groups struggled over their definitions of free radio. Should there be absolute freedom? If there were to be limits then what should they be? With a mix of right and left their members often made uneasy bedfellows.

The largest of these organisations were the Free Radio Campaign and the Free Radio Association. Nationally the FRC was considered primarily a news service, though it had local affiliates that were more involved in active campaigning. The smaller FRA began as a merger between several different offshore radio listener groups and with some station support. It was chaired by property developer Sir Ian MacTaggart, a staunch Conservative and anti-EEC campaigner, and managed by Geoffrey Pearl, a key figure in the group Free Britain.

Those on the left became concerned about the company that free radio supporters now seemed to be keeping. The International Times report on the association's May 1967 protest rally described how "The teeny-boppers in Trafalgar Sq. last Sunday really care about pirate radios and the music they broadcast. [Prime Minister] H. Wilson and his Victor Sylvester formation team had better face this, instead of driving them straight into the ranks of the British Free John Birchers."[1] When an attempt was made to merge the FRA with several groups that had no connection with radio, with the intention of forming a broader campaign for personal liberty, it served only to fracture the organisation.

While the pirates might have provided the momentum for a change in the broadcasting system, it was ultimately those with deeper ties to mainstream politics, like the Local Radio Association, who were to profit most from their actions. Although the big free radio campaigning groups might not have been immediately successful in their aims, the protests they organised did keep the issue in the public eye. Their demonstrations also served as meeting points for current and potential pirate operators. Radio Free London originated with a rally organised by the Free Radio Association in 1968 and a later event led to a meeting between two people that resulted in the founding of South London's Radio Kaleidoscope.

A small group associated with the free radio campaigns was also successful in persuading the Conservative-run Greater London Council to take an interest in radio and promote 1969's Greater London Radio Authority Bill. This would have resulted in an offshoot of the GLC licensing one or more independent stations in the London area. However, lacking support from the Labour government and with concerns from local newspaper proprietors over how it might affect their advertising, the bill did not pass beyond a first reading.

From offshore pop pirates to Radio One

On 15 August 1967, The Marine Etc. Broadcasting Offences Act came into power. All except Radio Caroline closed down the previous day rather than comply with the Act. Six weeks later, on the 30 September 1967, Radio One was born. While the BBC's new station brought in the listeners – not that they now had many options – it was a long way from the output of the offshore stations.

'Needle time' restrictions imposed by Phonographic Performance Limited, who handled payments from radio and TV on behalf of the record companies, meant Radio One was very limited in how much music it could play from commercial records. There was a view that excessive airplay harmed sales, with one former chairman of the British Phonographic Industry trade body stating "a record played on the radio is a record sale lost." For part of the day Radio One shared time with Radio Two, from whom older presenters like Jimmy Young came, and as a BBC station it was seen as a part of the establishment at a time when a counterculture revolution had taken hold. Unsurprisingly, Radio One's presence did little to discourage any land-based pirates from broadcasting and as the decade came to a close their numbers began to grow, emboldened by the cause of free radio.

While they had the technology, the operational skills and a mission to liberate the airwaves, what the earliest land-based stations did not necessarily have was the ability to create good programming. The lack of radio in the UK constrained not just listeners in their available choice but also broadcasters in their knowledge of what might be possible. Radio London and the faster-moving Swinging Radio England served as the main templates for pop broadcasters, but few if any of the new pirates had ever heard the range of radio being made in the USA or elsewhere. It took some time before land-based DJs had the experience and confidence to make radio that was truly their own.

On The Air

Radio Free London

Protesting for free radio, 1968-1970

In March 1968 the last of the British offshore stations, Radio Caroline, was forced off the air due to unpaid debts. Several of its out-of-work DJs including Spangles Muldoon (Chris Carey, later boss of Irish superpirate Radio Nova), Stevie Merike, Mike Lindsay and Andy Archer started regularly meeting at fan Robin Adcroft's bedsit in Addison Gardens in Shepherd's Bush, where they decided to put a station on the air. They got hold of a medium wave transmitter from a pair of radio amateurs, Peter Chicago and Mike Bass, though their first attempts at broadcasting were not exactly successful due to their lack of technical skills. They tried wrapping the aerial wire round and round inside the flat, which caused their transmission to appear loud and clear on an unplugged Dansette record player upstairs but failed to get out further afield.

RADIO FREE LONDON

Sundays noon to 3 p.m.   255 metres

With the first anniversary of the Marine Offences Act approaching and a rally planned in Trafalgar Square for 17 August, the group decided to put on a special broadcast. On 15 August they set up a new aerial over the railway bordering the bedsit. DJ Jason Woolfe later recalled "I climbed over the electrified railway line with a piece of wire being held by Stevie from the top of the signal box. I tied the end of the aerial to a light fixture at the top of an adjacent building and returned to the flat. As I had to go to work, I left the group broadcasting. In the evening I read in a paper that the station had been raided by the Home Office and the police, and it hit the front page of every national newspaper. This happened all because I tied the aerial to a building belonging to the BBC. I hadn't a clue who the building belonged to but it was the best piece of publicity we could have got."[2]

They returned on the day of the rally using a new transmitter operating on 204m using the name Radio Free London. This was chosen as a nod to the USA-backed station broadcasting to communist Eastern Europe and Russia. Originally the group planned to finish transmissions at 4.30 when the rally ended, but enjoying what they were doing they continued on. Unfortunately this gave the authorities time to finish tracking the transmissions and fifty minutes later they were raided for the second time. As they entered the room, Spangles Muldoon attempted to get chief GPO investigator Stanley Smith to speak on air, but he refused. However, in a lucky escape for the station, the authorities took away parts from a disassembled radiogram rather than the real transmitter.

Buoyed by the success of the broadcasts, some of the team decided to continue and on 22 September Radio Free London returned to the air with the first of its regular weekly broadcasts of pop music. In October there was a split which resulted in two stations now operating consecutively on 255m. The original group, RFL North, began at midday from Central London with former Caroline DJ Jason Woolfe, then at 2pm RFL South took over with Michael Christian.

Transmissions from RFL North ceased in May 1969 following a raid on a house in Wandsworth, for which Jason was fined £50 with £15 costs. With the building surrounded by GPO investigators and police, Peter Chicago hid in the basement as he didn't want to lose his amateur radio licence. RFL South now took over the Radio Free London name, its members including Mark Ashton, who would go on to resurrect the Radio Free London name on VHF in 1973. However, raids began to increasingly target the station, which resulted in several staff appearing in court. While the fines of around £15 a time were easily met, the loss of equipment hit the station much harder and transmissions became less regular. RFL finally came to an end in 1970, when the loss of key people to new offshore station Radio Nordzee International meant that it was unable to continue.

Radio Helen
An early broadcasting network, 1968-1969

Radio Helen was a medium wave station operating for short periods of time out of houses in South London. Later it helped organise the Helen Broadcasting Network. This scheduled thirty minute programmes on 197m from different operators, each transmitting out of a different location – thirty minutes was believed to be the longest time a station could stay on air before there was a risk of a raid. Stations in the network were initially numbered, but eventually they switched to using more recognisable names. These included Radio Apollo, Radio Avenger, Radio Codswallop, Radio Freedom, Radio Rose, Radio Spectrum and Radio Jackie. Initially just on Sunday, programmes also began to be carried on Saturdays too. Unfortunately, with many stations broadcasting from the same location each week the authorities soon learned to continue their tracking where they left off the last time. The growing number of prosecutions and the inevitable problems of coordinating broadcasts resulted in the network falling apart.

The official closedown of the Helen Broadcasting Network came on 1 April 1969, though there was a very short-lived attempt at a station called Radio Helen International involving broadcasters from several member stations. Others from the network, like Jackie, chose to continue on their own using new frequencies.

Radio Invicta

London's very first soul station, 1969-1984

The first sporadic broadcasts from Radio Invicta began in 1969. Peter St Crispian had acquired an old VHF transmitter used by a taxi office and with his friend Tony Johns (Tony Irons), who had a bigger music collection, they began putting out late-night shows from Tony's bedroom in Mitcham. Tony was primarily inspired by an absence of the music he liked on the airwaves: "When I was young I loved the American soul music of the time, but by the time I was of age that type of music wasn't being played in the clubs. Annoyed by what they were playing I started collecting the old soul music I liked – Motown, Atlantic and Stax. And in the course of hunting these down, I heard much new soul, which was just as good, but which you couldn't hear anywhere. There was just no outlet for it."[3]

SOUL OVER LONDON
RADIO INVICTA
92·4 F.M. 12-3 pm EVERY SUNDAY

The first broadcasts used AM, rather than FM, and were right at the edge of the VHF broadcast band so not many people were actually able to receive them. One person who did was Roger Tate (Bob Tomalski), who tracked the station down and realised he already knew Peter after they met when Roger was photographer for a story on a pirate station in the local paper. Sharing the same music taste, Roger joined the station and using his greater electronics expertise they built a new VHF FM transmitter so Invicta could begin more orthodox broadcasts.

For much of the early seventies transmissions went out only on bank holidays. Posters would go up in the local area to announce when the broadcasts would take place. There were times when they tried more regular weekly broadcasting, putting out an hour-long show at 7pm every Sunday, but this was difficult to keep up. After one period off air Roger Tate explained "We have had problems in getting enough staff to put out broadcasts. Our two girl deejays have left. Two others have been prosecuted and one of our DJs has gone to America. That leaves us with only a few people and no transport."[4]

Broadcasts were now taking place from the tops of tower blocks – the first station to do this – giving them much better coverage and mains power outlets where they could hook up their hefty valve transmitters. At a time when London was on alert for attacks from IRA bombers, this was not without other risks. On one occasion in 1973, Invicta's transmission site was descended upon by armed police after its staff were spotted setting up equipment on top of a block close to the Thames. The police soon realised their mistake, but Invicta still lost their gear.

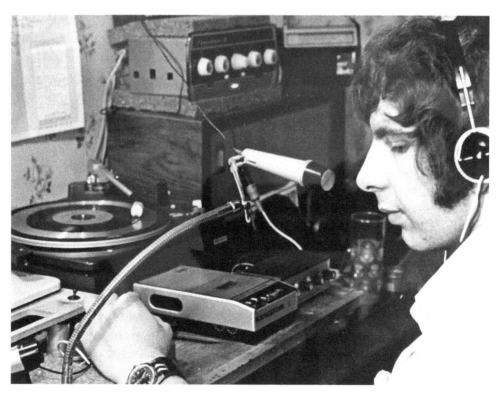

Tony Johns in an early Invicta studio. Photo courtesy of Radio Invicta.

Despite such setbacks, the station always managed to attract a substantial following of listeners for whom it was the only place they could hear soul music. A high quality studio was built in Roger's house where programmes were recorded, and he was a regular presenter alongside Tony Johns, Andy Jackson, Dave Sinclair, Steve Marshall and Steve Chandler. At Christmas 1976 they put out live programmes, but were tracked by the GPO investigators and several of the staff ended up in court and were fined.

• • • • • • • • • • • • • • • •

The story of Radio Invicta and its move to regular programmes continues in 1977.

Radio Jackie
The sound of South-West London, 1969-1985

One of the longest-running and best-known unlicensed radio stations, Radio Jackie first took to the air on 19 March 1969 on 194m medium wave. It was founded by Mike Knight (Nick Catford) with Mike Hayes, Dave Owen, Roger Allen, Tony Simms and Eddie Lloyd. The station was named after Jackie Kennedy – whose daughter had been the inspiration behind the naming of Radio Caroline.

The early years

After a few initial broadcasts under the name Clandestine Radio Jackie, the station became a part of the Helen Network on 197m. When that network fell apart not long after, they decided to continue broadcasts on their own. The early transmissions came from the flats and houses where Jackie's members lived, but they were soon running out of locations that hadn't been raided. Consequently Jackie became one of the first stations to move transmissions out to open spaces. Although this meant that they couldn't broadcast live and no longer had access to mains electricity, it did make operations considerably less risky.

Gradually Radio Jackie refined its mobile broadcasting. From initial broadcasts in Sutton's Nonsuch Park they began moving around to different sites in South West London, sometimes switching between different locations in the same broadcast to minimise detection. Transmissions moved to 227m, where Jackie would continue for all its pirate life.

In 1970 the team began experimenting with VHF transmissions. On 26 October, the opening day of the BBC's new local station Radio London on 95.3 FM, they broadcast as Radio Free London on 94.8. The new BBC service's station manager, Peter Redhouse, described the stunt as a "minor irritation"[5] but their twelve hours of programmes gained the pirate most of the press coverage. They followed up with broadcasts to coincide with the opening of other BBC local stations in Oxford and the Solent. Jackie started regular VHF transmissions every Saturday night from 1971, at first on their own and then as part of the London Transmitter of Independent Radio group.

The problem years

Following the launch of South London's Radio Kaleidoscope in March 1973, Jackie was severely short-staffed. Action by the authorities was also taking its toll. In its first four years Jackie believed there had been 81 raids attempted on the station while eighteen staff were successfully prosecuted and fined a total of £715. Now Mike Knight and future JFM founder Brian Anthony found themselves running the station almost on their own and were forced to cut hours on the Sunday service and abandon VHF altogether. Without enough people to keep a lookout for the arrival of the authorities it made broadcasting considerably riskier. A move to sites closer to South East London, away from the homes of some of the key GPO investigators, helped reduce what had now become more frequent raids, but it became a struggle to get on the air each week. Lacking the resources to continue regular broadcasts, Jackie collapsed in November 1974 and was not to return for nearly a year, bar a special broadcast for Christmas.

While Jackie was off the air, Mike Knight did a show as Radio Aquarius for a special Easter broadcast by a group of stations under the name London Stereo.

Left: Radio Jackie broadcasting out in the fields circa 1973. Right: Mike Knight in the studio

Unfortunately on the Easter Monday the main transmission site was raided by the GPO's Eric Gotts and when Mike left the remote studio to investigate he was recognised and also caught. With a suspended sentence already imposed from the previous conviction, he was sentenced to 28 days in prison by the magistrate. An appeal was lodged, but the sentence hung over him for the rest of the year.

Radio Jackie eventually returned to the air in the autumn of 1975, with Mike now keeping a safe distance from the transmitter site and with help from new and returning supporters to keep the station on the air. It was now Kaleidoscope that was having trouble finding enough people to help with its broadcasts as Jackie began to pick up lost ground.

The appeal against Mike Knight's conviction was heard in January 1976. Defending barrister Christopher Tailby described how the 23 year old had "no source of income. He does some work helping his parents and writes the odd article to buy necessities but like other artists he leads a very precarious life"[6] The judge had no sympathy, telling Mike "The situation is that you have been in exactly the same trouble four times before in the last six years. You quite deliberately set out to defy the law." He was sent to Pentonville Prison to serve his sentence. The rest of the team ensured Jackie was on the air the following Sunday.

A community return

With programmes from experienced presenters, Radio Jackie returned to a more professional sound. The station had long professed a commitment to its local area, though in practice this had often been more talk than reality. It wasn't helped by the sheer effort it often faced just in staying on the air. Now Jackie repositioned itself as 'The Sound of South West London' and began to more strongly identify with its broadcast area – even if at first this was still largely confined to local listings.

From 1978 Radio Jackie was greatly helped by reduced activity on the part of Radio Interference Service investigators. At a raid by the Hogsmill River in Tolworth, engineer Mike Barrington (Mike Dunkerton) was physically assaulted by investigator Eric Gotts. Mike pressed charges and Eric was successfully convicted, although he kept his job. In the subsequent fall-out from the case there was a dramatic drop in raids on unlicensed broadcasters and even after they resumed in 1980 Radio Jackie was still avoided. This allowed it to embark on a new expansion: hours grew to cover the whole of Sunday and more resources were available to go into programming rather than replacing transmitters and paying fines. After previously switching between different sites, they could now regularly be found every Sunday in a corner of Beddington Sewage Works.

. . . .

The story of Radio Jackie and its move to seven day broadcasting continues in 1983.

Radio Kaleidoscope

The original from Southend, 1967-1972

The first Radio Kaleidoscope operated from Southend on Sea. It was founded by Steve Taylor with his friend Tony Mendoza, who broadcast as Jolly Roger and Double D. From early test broadcasts in Steve's bedroom the station expanded to regular weekly transmissions, with a team of helpers – including a few people associated with Radio Caroline – getting it on the air from a different location each week.

The early transmissions on 223m medium wave used a 10 watt transmitter built by a local radio amateur. Unfortunately they soon attracted the attention of investigators at the Post Office's Radio Services Department in Southend. During one broadcast Steve's sister opened the door to find two officials standing outside. She refused them entry as their parents were not home, giving Steve enough time to hide the transmitter in the loft and lower other equipment onto his neighbour's oil tank. When the investigators returned to speak to his father the transmitter was surrendered and Steve's father was later issued with a written warning, although no court action was taken. The letter suggested that he took up amateur radio instead.

It was through his driving school instructor, John Langton, that Steve established links with Radio Caroline. John was involved in making clandestine trips out to the station's ship with supplies and staff, and Steve helped out with sourcing equipment that was needed. He was also introduced to Roland 'Buster' Pearson who ran the offshore radio magazine 'Monitor', who let them use his home as a studio. With these new contacts and with help from college friends the station resumed regular transmissions in 1968 using a more powerful 50 watt transmitter on 219 or 226m.

Transmissions now switched between different friends' houses each week, setting up an aerial in the garden which they hoped others would mistake for a washing line. Usually they broadcast live using portable disco decks, though some DJs – occasionally anonymously – submitted shows on reel-to-reel tape. Steve remembers "Toward the end of the planned broadcast schedule, the host house owners would be invited to try their hand as a radio DJ. Some were actually very good and the Kaleidoscope team would deliberately overrun the schedules to allow extra air time, others were not so good and the equipment would mysteriously break down! At some weekend events it was not uncommon to broadcast all night long with the host throwing a party and inviting some of their friends to join us"[7]

Up to a thousand records would be taken along for the broadcast, which gave ample scope for doing requests. According to Keith Southgate, who helped out behind the scenes, "I remember taking calls in a phone box probably about a quarter of a mile from the transmitter and then requests would be taken round to the site. I don't know if anybody considered that the GPO must have known the location of the phone box from the phone number! We were all very young at the time."[8]

With the arrival of Mike Baker, who was slightly older than the others, the station began to sound more professional and he supplied the station with a new set of jingles. Mike (who broadcast as Captain Blue or James Rakocy) also put out some separate transmissions using Kaleidoscope's transmitters in the Brentwood area. Others on the station included Caroline's Andy Archer, Andy Bowman (Roland Pearson), Kathy Jeanette (Pam Bird), Robin Banks (Robin Adcroft), Archimedes (Nigel Goulding) and Zebedee (Jim Randall). Programmes were primarily pop-based, but also covered the underground music of the day, especially on shows from Admiral Johnny Benbow (John Covill) and Steve W, who became a road manager for the rock band Supertramp.

In 1969 Radio Kaleidoscope expanded to Short Wave using a former military transmitter, the Canadian Army Wireless Set 43. These reached across the North Sea, bringing the station an audience in the Netherlands, Belgium and Germany. The unit was sold to Steve by Roger Allen so he could make more space for his

Andy Archer in the Radio Kaleidoscope studio. Photo courtesy of Steve Taylor.

Spangles Muldoon (it's believed) working on a transmitter. Photo courtesy of Steve Taylor.

new mail-order electronic components business, which later became Maplin Electronics – supplier of parts and studio gear to many later pirates. In 1970 the transmitter was sold on to Radio Jackie's Mike Knight. To try and deflect attention away from Kaleidoscope the team also set up another station, Radio Universe. This operated at different times on the same day as Kaleidoscope, using separate locations and mostly different DJs.

The final broadcast from Radio Kaleidoscope was on 27 December 1972, closing with the station's theme tune, Kaleidoscope by Tangerine Dream.

• • • • • • • • • • • • • • • •

Steve and some of the others continued doing local discos, including work for later ILR station Essex Radio. Mike Baker went on to do shows on South London's Radio Kaleidoscope before entering commercial radio. Andy Archer and Robin Banks continued shows on Radio Caroline while Australian Jim Randall went into radio back in his home country.

Radio Thames / Britannia Radio
South London's other early broadcaster, 1968-1975

Started by the 16 year-old Phil Crosby, Thames Radio began intermittent broadcasts in 1968 from a shed in his parents' garden in Coulsdon using a 15W transmitter that he had built. The station gradually became a more regular Sunday fixture but, after attempting an all-day transmission while his parents were out, it was raided by the Post Office. Phil was made to cut wires inside the transmitter and hand over the valves then the inspectors returned the following day to talk to his father. They took what they thought was the transmitter, but was actually a dummy, though he was not prosecuted because of his age.

Thames Radio returned to the air but at the suggestion of a friend's father who had been involved in wartime intelligence began moving locations each week. However, as the equipment was still mains powered this necessitated hooking into whatever outlets they could find, such as telephone boxes or railway station waiting rooms. Later they began using ex-military batteries and DC converters to enable them to operate from fields. They managed to escape future raids, though occasionally had to finish early when GPO staff were spotted.

For a while they changed the station name to Britannia Radio and moved to a more middle-of-the-road format with some local advertising support to help cover costs. After later reverting to the Radio Thames name they added shortwave broadcasts as well. Regular transmissions continued until 1973 and they returned for occasional broadcasts until 1975.

Telstar 1 / Radio UK
North London's progressive station, 1965-1979

After some test transmissions that started the previous year, Bear Freeman began regular broadcasts from Telstar 1 in 1966: "I chose 208 metres as this was where people would have been listening to Radio Luxembourg the night before and, I hoped, might have switched their radio on before retuning and heard Telstar 1 on a Sunday morning."[9]

As well as the Sunday shows, Bear would also chat to other station operators after midnight on other nights, particularly school friend Number 6, who started Radio UK in 1967 with a similar album rock format. Regular transmissions from both ended in the spring of 1970 when they were raided. Despite this setback, they continued occasional broadcasts under the Telstar 1 name throughout the early seventies, with both Bear and Number 6 presenting.

Telstar 1 returned to regular broadcasts on 14 August 1977, the tenth anniversary of the Marine Offences Act that outlawed offshore radio. While most stations at this time were still in fields playing pop music shows on tape, Telstar operated live with an album rock format on 1278 AM. Although the transmitter was only 10W or so, they were sometimes able to use a vertical aerial which meant it got out far better than the others. This wasn't appreciated by some of the other operators, who might have been able to use nearby channels had it not been for Telstar's much stronger signal. There were also some later experiments broadcasting on 90.4 VHF.

Other stations didn't always believe that a rock station could be so popular: "Someone told us we were 'wasting our time playing album rock, as nobody listened to that old hippy rubbish anymore.' Our neighbouring pop pirates, playing the supposed popular top twenty format, got about five calls a week, we got about 70 or 80 calls per week, so not bad for a bunch of hippies playing old hippy rubbish at the height of punk."[10] Telstar 1 closed in the spring of 1979.

• • • • • • • • • • • • • • • •

Telstar's AM transmitter was used by Radio Amanda. Bear joined Alice's Restaurant and both he and Number 6 appeared on Radio Andromeda.

1970-1972

Transmitting in the open

Medium wave broadcasting from a field might not be many people's idea of fun but it certainly tested station members' devotion to the cause of free radio. It also served as a bonding ritual. By the early seventies this model for pirate broadcasting was set and changed little during the decade.

First an aerial had to be put up, a quarter of the transmitter's wavelength long, meaning anywhere from 50-70 metres of cable that needed to be strung up in the trees. Expert tree climbers were much prized, although many used catapults to fire lightweight fishing line over high branches that could then be used to raise the aerial cable. One or more stakes needed to be placed in the ground to earth the transmitter – without a good earth transmissions would be less effective. These conducted better when they were wet, so some stations preferred sites beside streams or lakes.

Power came from car batteries. Constructed of heavy lead and filled with acid that could leak, these made site staff easily recognisable by the crotch-level burns on their trousers from carrying them. In order to convert from the low voltage of the battery to the high voltage needed by the transmitter's valves a DC-DC converter or inverter was needed. In the early days these were bulky items, particularly the electromechanical models some picked up cheap from army surplus stores.

The transmitters themselves were pretty hefty too and needed to be tuned each time to match the condition of the aerial. Andy Richards of later medium wave broadcaster Radio Floss explains: "Tuning the transmitter to the aerial and earth system required the adjustment of two capacitor knobs on the front of the transmitter by small increments and in turn whilst watching the needle on an amp meter on the front of the transmitter chassis. As you turned the first capacitor the needle would rise and on turning the second one, the needle would dip. What we were looking for was what we called 'Maximum Dip' which was when the needle dipped but rested at the highest level on the meter. To help us, there was a bulb connected in line to the aerial which glowed slightly each time the meter dipped, but if you hit 'Maximum Dip' it would glow brightly so we knew we were putting out maximum power."[11]

Cassette players needed to be isolated against radio interference from the transmitter and the whole lot needed protecting from the elements. Throughout the broadcast there had to be staff on hand to change over the tapes at the top of each hour and to step in when there were technical problems or if members of the public inadvertently stumbled upon their operations.

In the event of the GPO investigators turning up, whistles would be blown by lookouts and if there was time the most valuable equipment would be spirited away or hidden until it could be safely retrieved. Once transmissions were complete, the gear needed to be packed up, taken away and stored at a location unknown to the authorities – the aerial and earthing rods were sometimes left behind till next time. Having your own car or van was pretty much essential, though Jackie made do with a pram before Brian Horne joined their team. Unlike Jackie's founders he was old enough to have his own vehicle.

Not all the stations operated this way. Radio Concord broadcast at nights from bedsits and squats across West and North London, relying on lookouts and the squatter network to alert them to the arrival of GPO investigators. There were others who received little or no attention despite operating the same way. If you were north of the Thames you could expect fewer raids, perhaps because several key investigators lived in South London.

At this time unlicensed stations also began to be heard for the first time on the

Radio Floss' transmitter site in 1981 with Tim Allen (right) tuning up. Photo by Ian Stewart.

VHF band. Radio Invicta had been carrying out test transmissions and occasional broadcasts since 1969 and Radio Jackie launched a regular service every Saturday night from January 1971. Later in the year they joined other stations as part of the London Transmitter of Independent Radio network on 94.4. VHF piracy was slow to take off, however, as most of the listeners were still on medium wave and transmitter construction was more challenging. However, it did have one big initial advantage: these broadcasts were very difficult for the Post Office investigators to locate. By late 1972 this had changed and the VHF stations began to be regularly raided. Pirates could no longer joke that VHF stood for Very Hard to Find.

Progressive music and freeform radio

Most of the earlier stations had been scrappier in their presentation, often reflecting the young age of the participants and the minimal equipment at their disposal. Alongside those that were broadcasting actual programmes there were a large number of what were called QSO stations, named after the amateur radio code for establishing contact with another amateur. These were essentially just people chatting with each other, but illegally over the broadcast bands rather than legally with an amateur radio licence. QSOing drew considerable scorn from those broadcasting real programmes. It did, however, serve as an entry point for people to get experience with transmission techniques and real stations formed from those who had originally met this way.

From the mostly pop-based programmes of the earlier stations, newer broadcasters began to reflect the developments that were now happening in music, and in particular the widening split between 'credible' rock on albums and 'throwaway' pop on singles. From the late sixties the album began to grow in popularity not just as a format for collecting together singles, but as a long-form musical medium in its own right. Mainstream radio, however, was still all about the 7" single and the top forty charts, leaving an audience of album music fans unserved.

In the USA this gap was filled by the FM broadcasters: station owners made their money on AM where most of the listeners were still to be found so they were more willing to try other minority formats on FM. 'Freeform' radio shows emerged that played an eclectic mix of DJ-chosen music across different genres and these led to the birth of specialist progressive music stations. The higher quality FM stereo transmissions were also ideal for the new album sound.

John Peel, fresh from working in American radio, brought the concept to Britain in 1967 with his late-night Perfumed Garden shows on the offshore Radio London and then on his Night Ride shows on early Radio One. However, freeform radio ran up against the BBC's need for control and there was further distaste from its management – and many listeners – for the associated counterculture and its politics. Although John Peel was to be pushed into more conventional forms of programming, his show did still serve as a model for future broadcasters.

The new land-based pirates had none of the control issues of the BBC, but their technical constraints made it difficult to do the kind of radio familiar to progressive stations in the USA. Recording hour-long programmes onto tape required more careful planning, forcing presenters to make the most of their short time on air. There was, however, a more risky option as Telstar 1's Bear Freeman explains: "Broadcasting live let us do off the cuff freeform shows. The knowledge that a knock on the door could happen at any moment was forever present, with a few 'ers' and 'ums' from time to time, but we just got on with it."[12]

Radio Concord operated in the same way. According to Tommy Arnold (Arnold Levine), "I suppose you could call us deeply influenced by freeform radio. We knew about KSAN [San Francisco progressive rock station], and we played whole albums, or concept pieces. Many of the other established pirates ran tight production programming, with well formatted shows, but that wasn't our objective. Content ruled supreme on Concord, which I think made the other pirates look askance at us, even apart from the political stuff."[13]

For most budding presenters, knowledge of American radio was scant, so it was Radio Caroline's return in 1973 and its repositioning as 'Europe's first and only album station' that provided the biggest source of inspiration for rock presenters. Medium wave, however, was not exactly suited to more delicate material and it was only with the arrival of VHF stations like Radio Free London and Radio London Underground that the music could be heard sounding closer to how its original artists intended.

When Capital Radio launched in 1973, much of the same spirit could be found on Night Flight, which ran from 12-6am every Sunday. This featured live jam sessions from musicians playing rock, jazz, folk and everything in-between, filling both a requirement that Capital spent 3% of its advertising revenue on live music and solving the lack of any needle time remaining for overnight programmes. Station management axed the show in 1975 after deciding it was a bit too 'free'.

Growing control was becoming a common theme in the USA too, the early experimentation giving way to growing monetisation. After the initial flurry of musical invention in the early seventies, stations were now super-serving an audience of older music fans with ever narrower playlists that ended up featuring only the most popular tracks from rock's golden years.

Jamming, the election and the Sound Act

In January 1970 a new offshore radio station began broadcasting, Radio Northsea International. Initially operating off the Dutch coast, in March RNI moved closer to England where it hoped to be more financially successful. This prompted the Labour government to begin jamming the pirate the following month. Not only was the government concerned by the re-emergence of offshore radio, but also by the favourable support that the well-funded RNI was giving to the Conservative party, who had a commitment in their election manifesto to introduce commercial radio.

The Free Radio Association's 1970 protest.

The jamming served to provoke RNI and supporters of free radio into a flurry of activity. A dozen land-based pirate stations formed the Pirates Protest League and on Saturday 18 April at 11:30am they all jammed BBC Radio Two on medium wave. Although they could muster only a very small power in comparison to the BBC's massive transmitters, the protest did make the local press and further enraged the government.

In Southend the home of Buster Pearson was raided by MI5, removing equipment used by local station Radio Kaleidoscope along with material for Buster's offshore radio magazine, Monitor. Other pirate stations found themselves facing a crackdown and many chose to leave the air voluntarily until the election was over. Radio Kaleidoscope returned for a brief broadcast, encouraging its listeners to vote for free radio, only to find its own transmissions jammed by the authorities within ten minutes of switching on – the first and only time this has happened to a land-based station.

Five days before the June election, RNI changed its name to Radio Caroline International and began overt campaigning for the Conservatives. This was the first election at which the voting age was lowered from 21 to 18 so there was a new generation of young voters who might be swayed with this issue. The sacking of Enoch Powell after his 'Rivers of Blood' speech on immigration also helped the party seem more hospitable to those who might otherwise have voted Labour. A rally was held in London and Caroline boss Ronan O'Rahilly toured marginal constituencies in a campaign bus covered in posters depicting Labour leader Harold Wilson as Chairman Mao. The jamming stepped up with a second transmitter near Southend, which was so powerful it was picked up on all the telephone lines in the nearby village of Canewdon.

Prior to the election, opinion polls gave Labour a comfortable 12.4% lead, but when the votes were in the Conservatives had won by 3.4%. How much this was influenced by the free radio campaign is disputed. The transmissions were largely wiped out by the jamming taking place but there was a noticeable swing to the Conservatives in East Anglia. However, the jamming continued under the new government and it wasn't until July, when RNI moved back to the Dutch coast, that it finally stopped.

In the House of Commons MPs started to become concerned about land-based pirates for the first time. On 22 December 1971, Christopher Chataway MP, the minister in charge of radio, answered a question about what efforts were being made to shut down Radio Jackie: "Post Office investigating officers, acting on my behalf, are diligent in tracking down the many transmitters used by this illegal station. Nine transmitters have been tracked down and there have been twelve successful prosecutions." [14] In early 1972 Jackie sent promotional material to MPs as part of its campaign for legalisation, resulting in further questions in the House. Despite some outrage over its flouting of the law, on 7 March 1972 a recording of the station was played to a parliamentary committee as an example of what local radio could sound like should it be licensed.

Progress towards commercial radio was slow as the proposals made their way through the long parliamentary process. There was still nervousness from MPs and Lords that it might let in American-style jukebox radio with no redeeming social virtues. In 1970 a paper entitled Home Town Radio was published by the Bow Group, a think-tank that believed in conservatism with a social conscience.

Following the 1970 election seven of the group's members joined the cabinet, including Christopher Chataway, and consequently the Home Town Radio ideas became the blueprint for the new Sound Act. It proposed not outright commercial radio but local public service radio delivered by commercial contractors. This was to be the BBC with adverts, rather than the radio familiar to fans of the offshore pirates or Radio Luxembourg.

Although pleased to see progress at last, those lobbying for commercial radio retained reservations over the way it was being implemented. The Local Radio Association complained that stations would be regional, rather than local, and this would limit their success. There were also concerns about whether an operator could ever be financially viable given how much money went in payments to the IBA for transmitter rental and in copyright fees.

Stations that made more than 5% of their turnover in profit were to pay a 'secondary rental' to fund programme sharing between stations and community projects. This was intended to avoid a repeat of the situation in Independent Television where stations had become cash cows for their owners. However, it made radio one of the highest-taxed industries, putting off many investors. The Act also left many decisions at the discretion of the new licensing authority, leading to concerns about the unaccountable and centralised power that it would hold. Labour's broadcasting spokesman, Ivor Richard, attacked the plans as "Conservative theology designed to satisfy an ill-considered and half-baked election pledge."[15]

On 12 July 1972 the Sound Act received Royal Assent and the previous Independent Television Authority was renamed the Independent Broadcasting Authority. It immediately set about advertising the first licences, with two for London: for a news and information service and for a general entertainment service. Having regained power from the Conservatives in 1974, Labour chose to limit the number of stations to an initial 19, pending an enquiry into the future of broadcasting to be conducted by Lord Annan.

On The Air

Radio Concord
Squat scene radio, 1972-1976

For over four years Radio Concord broadcast from around West and North London, moving from an early output that was typical of pirates at the time to more radical live programming as it became a part of London's squatting scene. Several broadcasts took place from a squat at 101 Walterton Road in Maida Vale where Joe Strummer and the rest of his pre-Clash group The 101ers lived. Concord was very much a counterculture station, which set them apart from the others on the air. The Daily Mail complained that it was "one of the few pirate stations which has tried to influence opinions on political issues. They have plunged into controversial territories such as the situation of Northern Ireland, deserters and squatters in North London. They have even been critical of the Queen."[16]

Radio Concord launched in May 1972 on 230m medium wave with pro-grammes every Sunday from 11am to 3pm. Shows were up to the individual DJ but included chart material, oldies, rock and progressive from presenters El Supremo / Tommy Arnold (Arnold Levine), Matt Black (Jeff Schwartz), King Kong (engineer Graham Barnes) and Rhoda Orange. They also carried news, listings, stories, poems, comedy and phone-ins – one of the very first stations to regularly do this, legal or illegal. In the autumn of 1972 they switched to Saturday nights from midnight to 4am, until a raid took them off air on New Year's Eve. In court Tommy Arnold was given a conditional discharge but had to pay £1 costs.

Returning in March, they began switching regularly between different build-ings, with lookouts that would enable them to spot the approach of the GPO investigators, switch off and quickly recommence transmissions from a new site. On one occasion when the investigators did successfully track them down, Concord put a microphone through the letterbox and attempted to question their pursuers live on air. Using sites with mains electricity allowed them to run higher powered transmitters – up to 500 watts – which meant their signal reached well across London.

Confrontation with the law

Over time the line-up of presenters grew, with new regulars including Joe Lung, Len Deevish (Keith York) and Don Stevens, and they added shows covering soul and Motown, blues, folk and live music from guests in the studio. It wasn't just music, as Arnold Levine explains: "We became the only openly 'political' land-based pirate station when we connected up with the squatting movement and moved into covering many social justice issues. Our programming included squatting news, legal issues, interviews, police actions, free speech, political poetry and prose. Concord never espoused any political affiliations, and was made up of very differing viewpoints, but we all agreed on free speech, as that's what we were doing it for."[17]

These are the D.J.'s working on Radio CONCORD +

TOMMY ARNOLD........ROCK, PROGRESSIVE, OLDIES, CLASSICAL, FOLK
                                                          & INTERVIEWS.
RHODA ORANGE........OLDIES, SOUL & MOTOWN.
PHILIP DAY..........POP, NEW RELEASES AND OLDIES.
JOE LUNG............BLUES, LIVE CONCERTS & FOLK.
ANNE NIGHTINGALE FORCE 5... ROCK (& ROLL) AND COMMENTS.
ROBBIE RYAN.........TOP 40, OLDIES & POP.
MATT BLACK..........ANYTHING THAT COMES TO MIND.

Do you wanna buy or sell something? Well, Radio CONCORD runs a Classified Ads section so ring the number below.
     We are also running a Lonesome Corner for anyone who needs someone to talk to, again, ring the number below for details.
     If you would like more information about us, then please ring or write to us. PLEASE ENCLOSE A STAMPED ADDRESSED ENVELOPE WITH ALL LETTERS!
     Our phone number is Philip at 01-202 7140 from 6.30pm to 8.00pm.

             FIGHT FOR FREE RADIO.

sira	lrfrc
Southern Independant Radio Association- publish the'worlds largest free radio magazine' every 3 months for 25p + SAE to	London Region Free Radio Campaign, publish a bi-monthly magazine 'Script' send SAE for details to-
■, Park Street, Horsham, Sussex.	■, Glenmore Road, London N.W.33.

Radio Concord information sheet from 1972. Courtesy of Arnold Levine.

Unsurprisingly, the political content brought them into a confrontation with the authorities. "We were bringing up sensitive national and local political issues, so that is why the authorities didn't like us, and wanted to stop us, and so we were raided again and again, always with dozens of coppers with dogs, battering rams, and axes. They actually feared us in a way; because of our underground connections they thought they'd be attacked by drug-crazed hippies, so the GPO always brought along a big posse." One raid on a flat in Camden resulted in nine people being held for questioning, though only one was subsequently charged.

In 1975 some of the younger presenters decided to join with Radio London North to form daytime album music station Dynamite 235. They also hoped the name change might take the heat off them. Concord then became Concord NTS – Nite Time Service – operating for twelve hours through the night into Saturday morning. When there was no let up in the raids broadcasts resumed under the Radio Concord name. Several presenters were also involved in their own stations, and there was assistance in keeping Concord on air from Celebration Radio and Radio Free London's Andy Allman.

Concord eventually closed in late 1976. According to Arnold, "Ultimately, the raids got to us. Losing the equipment, records etc. got expensive to replace, and we had no money. My last raid was at an old squatted mansion next to Hampstead Heath on a late bank Holiday in 1976. A big one, I was tackled by police and GPO'ers as I stood watch outside. I only sporadically helped with Concord after that, before it shut down for good in late 1976."

. . . .

Founders Arnold Levine and Jeff Schwartz both moved to the USA, with Arnold presenting a radio show and Jeff doing occasional acting, including a part in an episode of Seinfeld. Don Stevens spent time on Radio Caroline and he and Keith York went on to offshore station the Voice of Peace near Israel and then several Irish stations.

Radio Kaleidoscope
It's what radio's all about, 1973-1975

The second Kaleidoscope was founded by Colin King, a member of the committee of the Free Radio Association, whose facilities the original Radio Kaleidoscope in Southend used to sometimes use. At the campaigning group's rally in August 1970 he met Maurice Ogden and they decided to work together

to get a station on the air. Twenty years his senior and the director of a film processing lab that made a lot of its money from the 'glamour' industry, Maurice
dabbled with electronics in his spare time. However, it took a while for him to get
to the point where he had a transmitter suitable for broadcast and so it wasn't
until Boxing Day 1972 that the first proper transmission went out. The name
Kaleidoscope was chosen at the suggestion of Colin's brother Phil Hazleton
(Robin King), believing that the Southend station had now disbanded.

RADIO KALEIDOSCOPE

Coincidentally there was a split at Radio Jackie, where several of the DJs
wanted to try different ideas but felt this was not achievable at the station. Unlike
Colin, they had practical experience of keeping an unlicensed station on the air
each week and the tricks that were needed to escape from the GPO investigators.
Deciding they could work together, the two groups began to turn the new station
into a more practical operation.

The first regular broadcast from Kaleidoscope went out on 3 March 1973. Shows
were recorded at a studio built in Pat Edison's bedroom, which had originally
been set up to record programmes for Jackie's VHF broadcasts. An audio com-
pressor was used to give the programmes a powerful, fat sound, which further
differentiated Kaleidoscope from the other broadcasters of the time. Later in the
year they began taking time on the London Transmitter of Independent Radio
network with a station dubbed KFM. However, Kaleidoscope didn't always have
the resources needed to manage the extra service and most of the work went into
the more popular Sunday medium wave channel. Following the death of Maurice
Ogden from a brain tumour, fourteen-year-old Tony Collis took over as engineer,
introducing smaller, lighter transmitters – and with considerably cleaner output.

Upbeat sounds

Colin had been very much influenced by the upbeat sound of offshore pirate
Radio London and wanted to recreate that sound. At Jackie, presenters were
largely left to decide what records they wanted to play, while the new Radio One
had its needle time limits. On Kaleidoscope there was a much tighter format that
skewed towards new chart music with up to seventeen tracks an hour.

As they went into 1974, broadcasts expanded to 5 hours of programmes each week, with regular presenters Pat Edison, Dave Owen, Phil Hazleton, Keith Ross Jenson, Tony Rocket and Denny Tewson (Mike Baker), who had broadcast on the earlier Southend station. Early in the year Dave Owen left to join offshore station Radio Atlantis and he was replaced by a new magazine programme featuring music news, reviews and listeners' letters. After the first year the brash US-derived format gave way to their own distinctive sound, more relaxed in presentation and more confident in choosing the music that was right for them.

According to Pat Edison, "We were heavily influenced by Denny Tewson who worked as a Capital Radio engineer and had access to loads of freebee records that were sent to Capital. Many of them would never get commercial radio airplay, like Jackson Browne, the Eagles and the Allman Brothers, so we picked up on those quite quickly and built a format which included a mix of non-chart 'adult pop' and a smattering of oldies. Oldies at the time being quite a narrow field as in 1973 you could really only go back so far."[18]

Unfortunately for Kaleidoscope, Tony Collis and some of the other members had ambitions to start their own station and early in 1975 they split to form City Sounds. After a few missed broadcasts the Big K returned, but staffing issues remained a problem. Further problems came when the GPO's Eric Gotts visited Colin King's employer to inform them of his involvement in the station. Summoned to a meeting with his boss, "I was summarily dismissed and, with no chance of a reference, it was going to be extremely difficult to get back into my chosen profession ... In one very smart move I had been blown right out of the picture and onto the sidelines."[19]

At the start of 1976 it was decided that it would be better to close while Radio Kaleidoscope was still at the top of its game. The final broadcast went out on 22 February 1976 and included an hour-long history of the station.

• • • • • • • • • • • • • • • •

A number of Kaleidoscope presenters built successful radio careers. Several went on to Radio Caroline, and Pat Edison continues today on its satellite service. Mike Baker joined new ILR station Beacon Radio in Wolverhampton just a few weeks after the Kaleidoscope's close, where he was the first voice on the air. It was later discovered that following a conviction for breaking the Marine Offences Act in September 1975 he had been forced by the authorities to inform on his pirate colleagues. Dave Owen and Tony Collis both returned to Radio Jackie, playing major roles in the 24-hour pirate and later legal operations.

London Transmitter of Independent Radio
The local VHF network, 1971-1975

After some initial experiments with Saturday night VHF transmissions by Radio Jackie in 1971, the station's Abie Cohen (Brian Horne) put together the London Transmitter of Independent Radio in 1972. The intention was that each night of the week there would be a different station on 94.4 FM, drawn mostly from existing medium wave operators. The individual stations would help out on site duties and contribute to the costs of the transmitters.

High up sites in wooded areas across London were found for the broadcasts, which all took place at night when most medium wave stations were off the air. They were helped early on by the authorities' inability to track VHF transmissions. When the GPO had overcome that hurdle the investigators still had to contend with crashing around in the dark in search of broadcasters who knew the terrain rather better than they did.

A power of 100 watts was used for the transmitters, but directional aerials boosted that power in the broadcast area. Each transmitter cost around £75 to build, with some designs fully transistorised and others using a valve power amplifier. Another £50 was spent on the battery, aerial and cassette recorder.

After it was decided to introduce commercial radio, Abie Cohen decided that "when Capital Radio starts up there will be no [need] for the service we provide."[20] The LTIR put out what was intended to be its final broadcast on 21 October 1973. Disenchanted with how Capital had turned out, they returned briefly in 1975.

Seven stations broadcast at different times as part of the London Transmitter of Independent Radio network:

Radio Jackie

Jackie's first VHF transmission under that name was on 6 February 1971, although it had done a one-off broadcast as Radio Free London to coincide with the launch of the BBC's Radio London. Initially there were ideas to use the higher quality of VHF to do documentaries or plays, but this turned out to be too ambitious and they settled on standard pop music programming. Mike Baron, who was previously involved with Radio Free Caroline and wrote for free radio magazine Script, was programme controller. Early presenters included Pat Edison and Dave Owen.

Radio Aquarius

Radio Aquarius, 'The station of the stars', broadcast on Friday nights from 10pm with three hours with easy-listening music. This was Abie's own station with shows also coming from Pete Murrell and Mike Knight.

Radio Classic

When Radio Jackie became unable to continue with their Saturday VHF broadcasts Radio Classic took over their slot from 9pm to 12am. After Radio Odyssey left the LTIR it shifted transmissions to Sundays so Radio Jackie could return. Radio Classic played mostly music from the fifties and sixties.

Radio Kaleidoscope

Kaleidoscope took over from Radio Star in 1973 on Thursday nights. Programmes were similar to Sundays. Kaleidoscope also put out later test transmissions on 96.3 FM following the LTIR's closure.

London Underground

London Underground was a freeform radio station that broadcast for two hours from 10pm every Sunday night. It came out of a programme originally featured on Radio Jackie's VHF service the previous year and joined the LTIR in April 1972. The output covered a wide range, from documentaries and stories to progressive rock, classical and some pop, presented by Peter Allen and Rick Martin.

Rick described some of their programmes in an interview at the time: "We're into electronic music and we've got a sizeable collection of recordings, some of which have been produced specially for us. We have produced a documentary on electronic music synthesisers ... another programme traced the Apollo XI moonflight in words and music; we frequently produce short sections of 15-20 minutes on various subjects for inclusion in our normal music programmes. We've read sections of books with musical backing, for instance a chapter from the book '2001' to name but one; others being on poetry, aspects of music, silly things like our concerto for foghorn and symphony orchestra and very serious subjects like drugs or mysticism."[21]

Unable to provide sufficient staff to help out on site with transmissions, its last broadcast went out on Christmas Eve 1972 with an announcement at the end of the broadcast that it had been the final programme.

Radio Odyssey

Radio Odyssey operated a progressive rock service on medium wave on Sundays from North London, one of only a small number in that part of London at the time. A raid on the station in February 1972 put three of its members in court where they were fined a total of £120 including costs. That prosecution and four of its staff leaving to form Radio Tranquillity brought an end to its medium wave transmissions.

After London Underground closed, Odyssey then took its place and continued up until the LTIR's own closedown in September. These broadcasts were for two hours, with the first hour covering new music, reviews and listings and a fifteen-minute alternative news segment, while the second was a concert recording.

Radio Star

After intermittent broadcasts from August 1970, Putney's Radio Star began regular Saturday afternoon transmissions from fields in March 1971 on 227m medium wave. It then became a part of the LTIR, broadcasting on Thursdays until the summer of 1973 when due to insufficient resources Radio Star decided to concentrate on its medium wave service. These broadcasts continued intermittently through until 1974. Shows on Radio Star played pop and progressive rock.

RADIO STAR 227 M

★ ★ THE YOUNG SOUND IN LONDON ★ ★

Radio 259 / Radio 242

Started by Don Stevens, 259 began in July 1969 and continued 24 hours a day until September when it was raided. Although fined £10 for illegal broadcasting, he returned with another station, Radio 242 which continued until February 1970. Don went on to work on Radio Concord and later Caroline and several Irish stations.

Radio Anonymous

Radio Anonymous broadcast from South West London from 1972 to 1973 with a mixture of pop and rock programmes. Presenters included Mark Ellis (later of London Music Radio and Skyline Radio), Steve Ellis, Bruce Howard, Paul Richards and Richard Johns. It was also where Thameside Radio founders Bob Edwards and Tony Lloyd gained their first broadcasting experience while still at school.

Radio Aphrodite

An earlier station founded by Radio Concord's engineer King Kong (Graham Barnes).

Radio Free Caroline

A station broadcasting from 1968 in South London. The team included Mike Baron, Mark Ashton and Mike Watts. Transmitters were built with parts stripped from three Canadian Army Wireless Set 53s found in a military surplus store.

Radio Jennifer

Broadcasting on 260 AM for two hours every Sunday afternoon between 1972 and 1973 from North East Surrey. The station had problems from frequent raids by a local policeman, who would track the broadcast each week and attempt to apprehend the culprits. One such raid managed to net six of the site staff – a rather more successful operation than the Post Office usually managed. Some of the Jennifer team went on to join Radio Kaleidoscope.

Radio Nelson

Broadcasting to West London from 1969. It closed in March 1972 following a raid on the house it was broadcasting from – which required three Post Office inspectors and six policemen. The inspectors described the fifty watt transmitter as one of the best constructed that they had seen. With raids on stations less common at that time, the station received coverage on the BBC and ITV news and in the Daily Mirror.

Radio Neptune

Twickenham's Radio Neptune took to the air in 1970. Its local newspaper reported it "churns out pop music and anti GPO jingles." Although it had a rather makeshift transmitter, a good aerial system at the house it broadcast from resulted in listeners across West London.

Radio Samantha

This name was first used by a medium wave station in 1972, which operated from Croydon until its young members ended up in court after a park keeper spotted their set-up in the corner of Shirley Woods and called the police. The name was later used by some of the team involved with Radio Tracy who went on to relaunch Radio Free London in 1973.

Radio Sheila

An early bedroom station founded by Dave Reading in 1971. Although regular transmissions ceased following a raid in 1971 it made occasional reappearances throughout the early seventies.

Radio Tracy

Founded in 1972 by Radio Free London's Mark Ashton, Radio Tracy was intended as a South East London complement to Jackie.

Radio Trident

An early station run by Radio Free London's Kenny Myers while still at school in 1972.

1973-1976

Capital Radio's problem birth

On 8 October 1973 Britain's first licensed commercial radio station, The London Broadcasting Company, took to the air on 719 AM and 97.3 FM with its news and current affairs programmes. A week later on 16 October Capital Radio followed on 557 AM and 95.8 FM as a general and entertainment station.

At its launch, Capital's programmes were nothing like the commercial radio of the offshore pirates or even Radio One. The music policy was under the direction of Beatles producer George Martin (who also produced the jingles) and he explained "We decided to go for the best of all kinds of music, chosen to suit the time of day, but with a considerable variety of pace. You may hear Mozart next to David Essex for example. We shall be playing plenty of good pop which doesn't get time on other stations simply because it doesn't get in the charts."[22]

During the week there were fifteen-minute dramas four times a day and extensive London news. Shows targeted different audiences at different times of the day: features for housewives in the afternoons and a rock show aimed at young people in the early evening. At night there was a phone-in followed by a range of specialist music and minority-interest shows at 10pm.

The new station turned out to have only partial control over the programming it carried. Programme schedules for ILR stations had to be submitted quarterly to the IBA, who exercised power over the tiniest of changes. IBA officers also closely monitored stations, sometimes even sitting in on programmes, and would regularly send through notes to programme controllers about things they liked or disliked. They were particularly concerned about commercial activities: after just a few weeks on air they insisted on jingles before every ad break so listeners didn't think they were part of the programmes, had Kenny Everett reprimanded for saying "And now a word from our sponsors" and limited the swap shop feature on the morning show to items under £10. They also wanted listeners taking part in competitions to have to apply in writing first, rather than simply phoning in.

With a precedent having long been set by the BBC for music copyright payments and needle time, Capital had no choice but to accept the same terms. Music from commercial releases was limited to just nine hours per day by Phonographic Performance Limited, who handled copyright on behalf of the record companies. To get round this limit stations began to make use of material that didn't count against the PPL quota: film soundtracks, albums from outside the UK, 'Radioplay' compilations with specially-licensed material from record companies and library music cover versions. Lengthy jingles (which the Musicians' Union insisted be made in the UK) also helped make it seem like more music was being played, but there was still an awful lot of chat.

It very quickly became clear that Capital's programme format was not working and listeners were not tuning in. Over Christmas it switched to playing oldies and then as 1974 began it introduced a new chart-based format, seemingly designed to be the least objectionable to the widest possible audience. At breakfast time, Kenny Everett and Dave Cash were brought in to recreate their double-act from the offshore pirate Wonderful Radio London and the drama and late-night specialist shows were axed.

Even with more populist programming, getting listeners to tune in remained a challenge: one survey early in 1974 showed 60% of Londoners didn't even know there was a commercial radio station on the air. The problem was compounded by the recession and the introduction by the government of a three-day working week in response to a dispute with electricity workers. Advertising revenue was severely hit and in the evenings there were sometimes few, if any, ads. The majority of those that did take time on the station were local businesses, rather than national brands.

In November Capital Radio staff were called to a special meeting with Managing Director John Whitney. It was announced that the station was close to bankruptcy and there were to be 28 redundancies, the majority from its news team. Chairman Richard Attenborough had to use items from his art collection as security to guarantee the station's overdraft. LBC were also hit by severe financial problems and a lack of advertiser interest, forcing them to cut back on original news and features in favour of cheaper phone-ins. It was to be some years before commercial radio reached a point where stations were profitable.

Although there are things to be commended about the programming on the early ILR stations, the fundamental problem in London was that one music station and one talk station were never going to be able to satisfy everyone. London was diverse not only in geography but in its people too. This was now a city of seven million people from a variety of different origins and, as popular music progressed and diversified, with increasingly disparate musical interests. It didn't help that the IBA had only experience of television and tried to fit radio and the way that they managed it to what they were already familiar with.

The men from the ministry

The arrival of Independent Local Radio at first resulted in a slight lull in pirate activity. Believing their job to be done, some broadcasters such as the London Transmitter of Independent Radio decided to shut down. Others, like Radio Jackie and Radio Invicta, were finding it difficult to recruit enough staff to keep their stations on air. The authorities also seemed to be having rather more success in getting people into court, making some of those who had been involved rather wary of continuing.

At this time, the control of broadcasting policy and the issuing of licences was the job of the Ministry of Posts and Telecommunications, based in Waterloo Bridge House on the South Bank. The work to take the pirates off the air was handled on their behalf by the General Post Office's Radio Services Department. This dealt with interference and reception problems and also ran the fleet of detector vans to root-out people watching TV without a licence. Local offices for the department were usually placed in major telephone exchanges around the UK and it was in one of these, in Bunhill Row in the City of London, that you could find the squad whose job it was to shut down the pirates.

Early on, most of the department's work was spent dealing with misbehaving radio amateurs, badly set-up private mobile services such as taxi radios and even with problems from model plane and boat enthusiasts. However, as pirate radio broadcasting took off it was to become one of the biggest parts of their job. Unlike most of the other issues they dealt with, there was not such an easy solution either. Even if their transmissions were easily traceable, many people involved in pirate radio refused to be put off their mission and their ingenuity made permanently removing them from the air considerably harder than for the other offenders.

New stations quickly got to know the team trying to shut them down. In the department's earliest days it was led first by Stanley Smith and then William (aka 'Jim') Crow. The main members of the investigating team were Eric Gotts, Brian Williams and Victor Frisbee. Eric became especially well-known for taking a more forceful approach with illegal broadcasters and stayed with the department from 1966 right through to the end of the eighties. Many pirates who encountered him in person felt he was on a personal crusade, although the Ministry's press office insisted "Engineers of the Post Office act for the Ministry not as a vendetta against 'pirates' but for the total elimination of interference."[23] Stations preferred to be raided by Jim Crow, who was felt to have more sympathy for the changes to the system that the stations were trying to achieve – if not how they went about doing it. Later on, pirates became familiar with Brian Holder, John Garlic and David Mason.

The names and faces of the inspectors became familiar to the people they were raiding. Some pirates when they appeared in court would try and snap photos of the officers arriving or departing – Radio Invicta even had a mug-shot sheet to help new recruits become better at recognising their opposition. At times there were special clampdowns on stations when staff from elsewhere in the country or from other jobs in the department would be drafted in to help. However, from the sixties right through until the late eighties, most of the work in London was done by the same small team.

To find a station the inspectors would begin by taking bearings from different locations to try and determine where the signal was strongest. Equipment to more efficiently carry out this first stage was soon built into the department's vans. Once inspectors had narrowed down on the map where a station was likely to be broadcasting from and then driven to the area they would switch to hand-held direction finders, with members of the investigation team often splitting up and communicating over mobile radios as they tried to figure out the exact location.

Knowledge soon spread amongst the pirates about how the investigators worked, helping to mitigate the risks of raids. Unsurprisingly for a group of radio enthusiasts, the mobile radios that the investigators used to communicate with each other were intercepted quite early on, giving broadcasters advance warning that a raid might be imminent. The investigators moved channels and systems

Left: inside one of the tracking vans. Right: using direction-finding equipment.

on more than one occasion when it became clear from the way some illegal stations were reacting to their presence that their communications had been compromised.

The more popular pirates encouraged their fans to join in on site duties. With more people available they could secure a larger area around the transmitter site. This role could make the new lookouts the most vulnerable people in the event of a raid, leading some of the Jackie team to unkindly label them 'site fodder'. However, having learned the techniques this way, many then went on to form their own stations.

While the pirates improved their transmission equipment and their techniques, it was still strictly for the hardcore: medium wave broadcasting out in the fields was a fiddly enterprise and few yet had the skills to build VHF equipment. However, once those people were hooked it was hard to dampen the buzz they got from pirate broadcasting for very long. Even when Radio Jackie founder Mike Knight (Nick Catford) was sent to prison for 28 days after his fifth offence, it was not enough to put off him or the rest of the team. His own defence lawyer described his interest in pirate radio as "fanatical," but it was only because of people like him that radio moved forward and the pirates did not die out.

Neighbourhood radio

The launch of Capital Radio gave London's pirates a new competitor to define themselves against. In the sixties the fight had been for pop radio, then after the launch of Radio One it had changed to a fight for commercial radio. Now those continuing with unlicensed broadcasting needed to decide what it was that was now different about what they brought to the airwaves. For some it was a different kind of music; for many it was simply enough to want to present pop radio a different way. A few, however, sought to define their difference as their localness.

Radio Jackie had a difficult time in the middle of the decade, as internal differences, staff defections and heavy action by the authorities disrupted its broadcasts. After the close of Radio Kaleidoscope in 1976 it finally began to regain its former strength and now repositioned itself as 'The Sound of South West London' – even if initially this didn't mean much more than reading out late chemist rotas and cinema times.

Across town, East London Radio began broadcasts in 1977. Norman Spencer

(Phil Troll), who was to become involved in talking newspapers for the blind, helped develop weekly programmes that mixed music with local community information, news and short interviews. Radio Free London also experimented with local programming for South East London before deciding it was not where their strengths really lay.

When ELR closed, Norman got together with Christopher England and Paul Allen to form Radio AMY. This was Britain's first community access radio station, putting listeners from the north of London on the air with what they wanted to broadcast, rather than simply presenting information already available else-where in a different medium. AMY was an ambitious project for an unlicensed station and its illegality was a significant constraint in how well it could interact with its local community. The lack of a licence meant many local organisations that might otherwise have been strong supporters of its programmes instead felt they were unable to participate. Those groups with a strong political agenda had fewer qualms, which led to arguments as the station organisers sought to provide a balanced service that they felt ordinary listeners would be able to relate to. It closed after a year on air, the team having decided they had proved the validity of open access broadcasting.

In the summer of 1976 the Labour government gave the go-ahead for five neighbourhood radio stations to broadcast via the early cable television networks, with the proviso that they could not carry advertising or sponsorship. To be able to tune in to these stations you needed to be served by the cable company and to hook up your radio to their service (although transmissions did leak a little from the cables in their areas so non-customers could pick them up). First on the air in London was Radio Thamesmead in 1978, founded by a local vicar to help counteract the isolation that many felt living in the new town's high rise blocks. It was followed in 1980 by nearby Greenwich Sound Radio.

While both stations had a core of DJ-driven programmes much like Independent Local Radio, the localness of their operations made them far more relevant to the people they served. Thamesmead was the more ambitious of the two in involving listeners in its programmes, although it found that most volunteers got involved because they wanted to be DJs rather than because they cared about issues of interest to the local community. Thamesmead did, however, run a wide variety of specialist programmes, from particular music genres to panel discussions and a weekly programme for the Vietnamese boat people who had been settled in the area.

Although the cable stations' legality meant that they could work with community organisations in a way that was not possible for those without a licence, they looked on jealously at the pirates with their free-to-air transmissions, especially after the pirates began seven-day operations in 1983. Station manager Bob Smith was not happy with his rivals: "If it weren't for them, we'd be on the air by now. For 10 years, we've resisted the temptation to put a transmitter up on the roof. I think that should be rewarded."[24] In practice, presenters crossed backwards and forwards between London pirate radio stations and Radio Thamesmead, while Greenwich Sound Radio was staffed by several ex-members of Radio Caroline.

Radio Jackie's transition to a full-time broadcaster in 1983 hadn't been planned – it didn't even know how long it was going to be able to get away with it. Scrambling to fill its airtime, it did the best it could. For news they rebroadcast the Independent Radio News bulletin from LBC at the top of the hour, Teletext provided travel and weather, while local papers were used for nuggets of community information that the DJs could drop in. Jackie were well aware of the criticisms others had over how committed it really was to serving those in its local area.

Presenter Dave Stevens explained "We would like to involve the local community far more in the programmes we do. Financially this is a problem we have at the moment, because we have very low advertising rates. If we were a recognised radio station with a licence we'd be able to charge more – not to such a point where we wouldn't be able to take in all the local businesses."[25] As it became a more permanent feature on South West London's airwaves, Jackie did gradually increase the amount of original material that it carried. However, Radio Thamesmead's Grant Pearson was still dismissive of its efforts, claiming "Jackie are just there because of the music – to them information is a secondary thing"[26]

As Skyline Radio in South West London and Radio Shoestring in East London followed Jackie onto to the air, they followed a similar path of rewriting content from elsewhere rather than originating their own material. When keeping a station on the air all week, there simply weren't the resources available to do much else. While there was a ready supply of DJs who saw the pirates as an entry point into the radio business, those who were more interested in journalism took the well-established routes via local papers or the BBC instead.

The harsher broadcasting laws in 1984 followed by the aborted 1985 community radio experiment did for further attempts at broad-based stations aimed at particular London neighbourhoods. Greenwich Sound Radio and its associated local TV channel closed down after the cable company changed hands in the mid-eighties. The axing of the Greater London Council resulted in Radio Thamesmead losing its main source of funds. With debts of £8,000 it was taken over by the Community Service Volunteers organisation in 1987. It was granted a licence as part of the incremental radio scheme in 1989 but what had started out as a non-profit company was then sold on to a succession of commercial radio groups who never succeeded in making it a financial success. As Time Radio it finally closed in 2009.

For the media and politicians the arrival of Independent Local Radio meant that the job was done. While the local and alternative press continued to report on the pirates, they rarely made it into the nationals and in Parliament there was now little interest too.

Pirates did occasionally still make the headlines though. On 1 April 1976 transmissions from the VHF transmitter at Rowridge on the Isle of Wight shared by Radio One and Radio Two were interrupted by a pirate station playing a number of records banned by the BBC. Radio Invicta's Roger Tate (Bob Tomalski) had figured out that the relay transmitter took its audio off air from London and it wouldn't need much power to easily overpower that signal with a small transmitter nearby. The BBC later introduced additional security measures to prevent this happening.

On The Air

Dynamite 235
Concord's younger brother, 1975

Dynamite came out of Radio Concord, mostly involving its younger members along with new recruits from Radio London North. There was also hope that the change in name would take some of the heat off the station after Concord was heavily targeted by the authorities.

Unlike its parent, Dynamite broadcast during the day on Sundays and carried more album rock and less of the political content. Presenters included Dave Robbie, Phil Bendall, Simon Newbury and future Radio Caroline DJs Don Stevens, Steve Kent and James Ross / Kelvin Carter. Eventually they returned to the Radio Concord name when there was no let-up in the raids. Some of the team also felt that the Dynamite name was inappropriate in the light of the situation in Northern Ireland and the bomb attacks by the Angry Brigade.

Radio Free London
The capital's original FM rockers, 1973-2014

In 1972 as the parts needed for building a VHF transmitter began to become more widely available and at a price that enthusiasts could afford, Mark Ashton began testing a new VHF transmitter. He then restarted Radio Free London on 17 March 1973 on 94.8 FM.

Programmes were a mix of styles though biased towards the rock music of the day. As well as Mark the presenters included Kenny Myers, Jane Ashton and Dave King, with Andy Walker and Dave Reading joining later. Guest shows included Jackie founder Mike Knight and Kid Johnson, who went on to co-found Radio Telstar South. When BBC Radio London moved frequency to 94.9 they moved down to 92.8 before finally settling on their familiar 92 FM spot.

Several transmitters had been constructed for RFL's broadcasts, but one by one they lost them to raids by the Post Office's anti-pirate team and then in November 1974 four members of staff were caught at the open-air transmitter site after neighbours reported them to the police. They borrowed a transmitter from another group and put out a final broadcast on 24 November, unsure if they would be able to continue.

Returning to the airwaves

It wasn't until March 1978 that broadcasts resumed, in part due to seeing the response to the recently-launched Radio Telstar South. Initially they came back on the air for just one hour a week, before adding a second transmitter at another site for the second hour. For a while the first hour was in stereo as they only had the money to add an encoder to one of the transmitters.

The end of the seventies saw a lull in the number of pirate station raids, which they took advantage of to gradually increase hours. They also moved from fields to the roofs of tower blocks, which as well as height gave the convenience of access to mains electricity. Programmes continued to be taped, mostly recorded as live the previous day onto low-speed 10" tape reels so they didn't need so many risky changeovers. These tapes were responsible for RFL's unique bass-

Steve Ego in the 1980s RFL studio. Photo by Kenny Myers.

heavy (or perhaps that should be treble-light) sound.

The Peak period

The new broadcasts were incredibly popular, showing just what a demand there was for their music. There was often a full mailbag of letters each week with requests and entries in the hourly competitions. They also hosted pub crawls, with support from the Campaign for Real Ale, which were well attended by ordinary listeners, not just radio anoraks. As well as the original team of there were new shows from Steve Ego and Andy Allman, who contributed a number of the station's classic jingles. Everyone knew the part they had to play in getting the station on the air each week so little advance planning was required.

In 1980 the station experimented with a split service, the first half covering local news and activities in South East London, while the second half was more music oriented. After a few months the former was dropped as they felt it was outside their core skills and they reverted to their traditional format. New DJs continued to join the station, including Debbie Smith (later with Alice's Restaurant), Mike Burnett, John Dawson, Andy Mason, Jerry James and Nigel Grant. At its peak they broadcast for 15 hours on a Sunday, though more usually they were on the air for ten hours.

Broadcasting seasons

In 1981 John Dawson decided to move to South London Radio and some of the more pop-oriented DJs joined him. RFL then settled into its familiar classic rock format, which has changed little since. Nothing too intense, just relaxed, personable DJs enjoying themselves and playing the music they like to a group of dedicated fans.

From 1980 raids began again in earnest, with a raid involving the Special Patrol Group on 27 January resulting in members of RFL appearing in court in June. RFL left the air in 1983 after losing several transmitters in quick succession. Mark

Ashton became involved with local South-East London station Skyline Radio and other DJs also drifted away.

It wasn't until 1987 that RFL properly returned to the air under the auspices of Kenny Myers, beginning a pattern that would continue into the nineties of a season of broadcasts followed by a year or two away from the airwaves. Each time they came back you knew exactly what you were getting and they seemed happy to continue chugging along doing their usual thing. Their listeners always seemed happy to have them back too. In 1997 RFL's equipment, hidden in wood-land near junction 4 of the M25, was spotted by a passer-by, who reported it to the police. The motorway was closed for two hours while it was checked out to make sure it wasn't a terrorist bomb.

As the VHF band filled up with 24-hour stations RFL moved to Short Wave, though Kenny Myers was reported to still prefer them being on VHF. These broadcasts continued, if sporadically, with some Internet broadcasts also taking place until 2014.

London Music Radio
South London pop and rock, 1974-1978

Test transmissions for London Music Radio began in the autumn of 1974, its founding team having previously been involved with Radio Anonymous. Following the closure of Radio Kaleidoscope a number of people then joined LMR and transmissions became more regular. For most of LMR's life broadcasts were on medium wave, on first 235 and then moving to 385m in order to improve night-time reception. For a while in 1976 LMR also experimented with a VHF service. Programmes were a mix of pop and rock shows.

Mark Ellis (Stuart Vaughan) oversaw the running of the station and was responsible for building its equipment. The large team of presenters and helpers included Terry Dene, Rob Lancing, Steve Hampshire, Debbie Jones, Nigel Davis,

LMR – back row: Richard Thompson, Bionic Bill and Terry Dene; front row: Bob Edwards, Tony Lloyd, Mark Ellis, Rob Lancing, Ray Lord, Cliff Osbourne. Photo courtesy of Ray Harrington.

Roger Anderson, Cliff Osbourne, John Dawson, Bob Edwards and Tony Lloyd. London Music Radio closed in 1978 after a rift between different factions. This split resulted in two different stations broadcasting under the same London Music Radio name on one day.

. . . .

LMR featured a large number of presenters who would go on to bigger things on later stations. Mark Ellis co-founded Skyline Radio; Bob Edwards and Tony Lloyd founded Thameside; John Dawson co-founded LWR while Richard Thompson, Roger Anderson and Cliff Osbourne all did stints on Radio Caroline. The London Music Radio name was resurrected by a second station in 1981.

Swinging Radio England
West London pop radio, 1974-1977
One of several stations that took their name from the sixties offshore station, SRE began broadcasts in 1974 from the Shepperton home of presenter

Roger Stevens using a medium wave transmitter. Following a raid they moved to field operations, on the air every Sunday for four hours from 10am, though they later switched to all-night Friday from the derelict Harefield House. Programmes were mostly chart-based. Swinging Radio England closed in 1977.

Presenters Bob Earl, Roger Stevens and engineer Mark King were subsequently involved with shortwave station Skyport and its VHF successor Uptown Radio. Dave Grainger went on to Celebration Radio, Allen Reeve to Radio 239 and Kid Grant (Grant Goddard), who presented a soul show, went on to be the first programme controller at the legal Kiss FM.

WFRL
Tottenham's first pirate, 1974-1975

Wonderful Free Radio London broadcast on AM from the Broadwater Farm estate in London with an aerial down the side of one of the tower blocks. The transmitting equipment was hidden in the room housing the water tank in the block below. This enabled them to put out stronger transmissions than the field-based AM stations of the time. Broadcasts were from 11pm-1am on Thursday and Sunday nights, switching to daytime on Sundays in the spring of 1975.

Founder Phil Marshall later became involved with Radio Kaleidoscope and went on to work on Radio Caroline as Phil Mitchell.

ABC Radio

One of the unluckier stations. ABC Radio began test transmissions from Enfield in April 1973 but were raided on their first broadcast and lost all four of the transmitters that they had taken along to try out. There were some broadcasts under the same name later in the seventies on 270 AM.

City Sounds

City Sounds was a split from Radio Kaleidoscope and began broadcasts in June 1975. Initially they were on medium wave before a move to 96.3 FM. Presenters included Richard Jackson, Andy Walker, Dave Sinclair and Abie Cohen with Tony Collis (AM) and Bob King (FM) on engineering duties. The station closed early in 1976.

Radio Free Atlantis

A 1975 medium wave station run by Mike Barrington. After a raid Mike was fined £50 for illegal broadcasting; the makeshift transmitter was described in court as "deadly".

Radio Globetrotter

Broadcasting on Sundays from 10am to 4pm on 223m from South West London.

Radio London North

A North London medium wave station founded by Dave Robbie in 1975. After two raids and the loss of some staff the remaining members joined the younger broadcasters of Radio Concord to form Dynamite 235.

London Stereo

A one-off station broadcasting over the 1975 Easter weekend, London Stereo put out live programmes on medium wave, short wave and VHF using presenters from stations including Invicta, London Underground and North Surrey Radio. On Easter Monday the station's separate transmitter site was raided and Tony Collis and Bob Edwards were caught, closely followed by on-air DJ Mike Knight when he turned up to investigate.

London Weekend Radio

A West London station whose presenters went on to join Swinging Radio England.

Sun Radio

Sun Radio broadcast on 92.8 FM in 1975 with taped shows made in Kenny Myers' studio and transmitted from the woods and fields of North Kent. Presenters included Dave Sinclair, Kenny Myers, Alan Ford, Mike Burnett and Andy Allman.

Radio Thameside

An early community station broadcasting to the Dartford and Erith area in 1975. Presenters included Alan Brown, Chris Taylor and Bob Parker. The station made a reappearance in 1978, complaining about the name being used by the West London station.

Radio Tranquillity

An East London rock station that began broadcasting on medium wave in 1973. It was formed by some of the staff of Radio Odyssey who were unhappy with that station's organisation.

Trans London Radio

A one-off station for the August bank holiday featuring many of the South East London names later common to Radio Free London and Radio Telstar South.

Sunkhead Radio

An 1974 station from the team that went on to launch Swinging Radio England.

Radio Sweet Grass

A small station on 222m medium wave that operated occasional Sundays in 1974 in North London and also at some of the music festivals of the time.

Radio Unicorn

Broadcast from North London on 228m AM in late 1974.

1977-1978

The move to VHF

Although VHF broadcasting was launched in South East England by the BBC in 1955, its widespread adoption was slow, particularly among young people. Radio One was still on medium wave except for a few programmes simulcast on Radio Two like the top forty. For a long time, cheap transistor radios were AM only and the BBC's horizontally-polarised VHF transmissions were designed for fixed roof aerials rather than portable radios.

Unlicensed stations had been experimenting with VHF transmissions since the early seventies, but the response from listeners had remained better on medium wave. It was only towards the end of the decade that VHF reached its tipping point. 1979's transistors were five times cheaper than 1970's and the launch of Independent Local Radio further encouraged manufacturers to bring in models at a price point that was affordable by young consumers. The IBA was keen that ILR should match the technical standards set by the BBC and heavily pushed the

The driver stage of Thameside's transmitter. Photo by Aleks Wright.

adoption of VHF. It also mandated that all output should be in stereo – on the BBC stereo was only used for some programmes.

The newer 'solid-state' technology was great for the pirates too. Valves were fragile, needed a high voltage to operate and made the equipment much heavier. In the late seventies new transistors started to become available that could deliver much higher power levels than before at the frequencies used for VHF – and each year new, more efficient models pushed that power higher. There were also new integrated circuits that could replace a number of components with a single chip, making designs cheaper and easier to construct. Thameside Radio was at the forefront of these new transistorised designs, with its first engineer Tony Lloyd significantly moving on the state of the art. Radio Free London's Kenny Myers was also a key early innovator and his original designs were built upon by a number of subsequent South London stations.

The VHF band required a much higher transmitter site than you could get away with for medium wave. Some, such as Radio Telstar South, continued to operate from suitably high open spaces on the edges of London. Most of the others made the move to tower blocks. Council-owned residential blocks had little in the way of security to get in and few people who might take an interest in someone carrying transmitting gear. They were also invariably located in densely-populated areas, while London's geography – a valley surrounded by low hills – made it an ideal location for VHF broadcasting, especially from the blocks on those hills.

Access to the roof of a tower block could be easily gained using standard keys designed for fire brigade use, which soon spread between station engineers. The room housing the lift machinery was a ready source of mains electricity for powering a transmitter and most had a convenient outlet or were adapted to give one. Unlike medium wave with its long wires, VHF just needed a simple, short aerial, which looked inconspicuous on the roof alongside existing TV and radio aerials. Setting up was much easier too: no need to wait for valves to warm up and no need for on-site tuning of the transmitter. With citizen's band radio rising in popularity at the same time, pirate transmitters now became known by a new name: rigs.

The transition to VHF was helped by the ready availability of frequencies that the pirates could use. In order to provide a good signal in the hilliest parts of the UK, where they needed extra relay transmitters to fill in gaps in reception, the BBC reserved a large part of the VHF spectrum for BBC Radio Two, Three and Four. In the large plains of South East of England fewer of these relays were needed so there were several completely free channels, notably pirate favourites 90.2, 92.4 and 94.4MHz. The BBC had also spaced out their channels at a time when receivers were much more prone to interference from adjacent frequencies and obviously they had no intention of now ever giving up their spectrum. This became a particular source of resentment to the later Radio Authority, who had no room for new independent stations while the BBC was making space for pirates.

Meanwhile, an international agreement meant 87.5-108MHz was to become a worldwide standard for VHF radio broadcasting, so emergency services and utility company communications were beginning a slow move off the band. This opened up more temporary channels for the pirates, even if the BBC were greedily eyeing the extra room for new services long-term. First to go was a space from 102-103MHz, though it was difficult for unlicensed stations to always determine which frequencies at the top of the band were clear as some of the licensed services were on low power and very localised. It wasn't until 1995 that the whole VHF broadcast band was finally clear for broadcast use.

The new Sunday primetime

For medium wave pirates, early Sunday afternoon was primetime. After dark their transmissions would be overwhelmed by high power stations from overseas, limiting them to their immediate area, so most closed down by dusk. That still left long Sunday evenings with no contemporary music. After the chart show finished at 7pm, Radio One would return to Radio Two on VHF and this would be simulcast on BBC Radio London. Sunday evening was Capital's time for its less-favoured public service commitments, with a classical music show followed by a magazine programme on the arts and then an hour of vintage 78s. With many of its Sunday shows pre-recorded during the week, there was a further lack of excitement to that day's programmes.

At this time radios still had a manual tuning knob – none of the digital tuning and presets of today's devices. To get back to Capital Radio after listening to Radio Two you would have to pass by all the frequencies in-between, hearing little snippets of other stations as you went so you could stop on something interesting. Because stations had such different programmes following each other, listeners were also in the habit of more regularly tuning around to find something that was more to their taste.

The Sunday evening void was particularly ripe for exploitation and before long 7pm was the new FM pirate primetime. According to presenter Aleks Wright, "A large number of Thameside listeners first found the station because they just grabbed the tuning dial once the chart show was finished and stopped at the first station they found with music they liked."[27] Higher up the band between Radio Three and Radio Four you'd find Radio Free London with rock and Radio Telstar South with oldies.

This period was also when Radio Invicta finally became a regular weekly broadcaster. Although it was the very first pirate station to broadcast on VHF, it was only in September 1977 that they were regularly on the air every Sunday lunchtime with three hours of soul music. Invicta were also the first to broadcast in stereo. According to engineer Roger Tate (Bob Tomalski) "It rather fascinated me that you could put a broadcast out with audio quality every bit as good as the BBC, tune across the band, and never know that it was a pirate."[28]

Like punk never happened

VHF seemed to point to the future of radio but not everyone was convinced. A 1979 Time Out article complained that "VHF's more sophisticated equipment gives it an essentially middle-class bias."[29] Medium wave stations continued to flourish and that band was where more experimental or specialist programming could be found for now. These were still stations run predominantly by young, white, middle-class males but they were becoming more relevant to their target audiences and sowing the seeds of later narrowcasting.

There did, however, remain an ingrained conservatism throughout many of London's pirate stations when it came to programming. Highlighting the split between those who wanted to be seen as responsible broadcasters, just on a different scale or with a different music, and the minority who wanted to take radio in a different direction, Geoff from Our Radio was later to complain "I flip the dial and hear pirates but they're just playing records or tapes which people are releasing anyway. If it's going to be alternative then it should be completely alternative. When you get right down to it there's not much difference between the Clash and Max Bygraves. They both have that big studio sound."[30]

To the outsider, punk might have seemed an obvious match for pirate radio – especially with the restricted airplay and bans that artists received on Radio One and Capital – but except for the big crossover hits played by the pop stations it largely passed the pirates by. More than one pirate DJ at the time suggests that while they would readily play newer, rawer styles of music in clubs and pubs, the feeling was that less traditionally 'radio-friendly' music would alienate the listenership they had worked hard to build. Being at the cutting edge of music, having the technical ability to operate a station and possessing the determination and finances to remain on air were not necessarily found in the same outfit.

A brief ceasefire

From 1978 pirates were helped by a drastic reduction in action against them by the authorities. To try and bring down inflation – then over 20% – the Labour government led by James Callaghan imposed pay restraints on public sector staff. This led to widespread strikes and employees working to rule, extending to field work by the Radio Interference Service. More specific to the department was a conviction for assault against one of its investigators that brought the way they conducted their operations to the attention of ministers.

Those involved in unlicensed broadcasting had for some time felt that there were RIS officers who went well above what was lawful in their attempts to take stations off the air. This could lead to heated situations as broadcasters increasingly asserted their legal rights, only to be summarily dismissed by officers intent on continuing as they had always done. At one raid on Radio Jackie in Tolworth, tempers were inflamed to the point that investigator Eric Gotts physically assaulted engineer Mike Barrington (Mike Dunkerton). He successfully pressed charges and in court Eric Gotts was convicted and given a conditional discharge for 12 months with £350 costs. He unsuccessfully appealed and his bosses considered his position, but with strong backing from his union managed to keep his job. Jackie founder Mike Knight believes Mike Barrington's action had a lot to do with the future success of the station: "Mike had the courage to take on the government, with the help of a handful of witnesses who saw the assault from all conceivable angles. We have a lot to thank him for."[31]

The fall-out from the case prompted an internal rethink at the RIS about how raids were carried out. The union insisted that the police should be present during raids, but the police were not keen to be involved in what was a civil matter – and one they considered a low priority at that. During the impasse, activity against unlicensed stations ground to almost a complete halt across much of

London. From a situation in the mid-seventies where non-stop raids and regular court appearances came close to wiping out them out, the pirates were in a position of growing strength. Before long a flock of new stations had taken to the air to exploit the easier environment, while those on air revelled in their greater freedom to broadcast.

It was not until 27 January 1980 that raids began again in earnest. On that day the police provided a bus of six officers from the Special Patrol Group, more used to dealing with public order offences like riots than with illegal broadcasters who offered no more resistance than trying to run away. This experiment was not repeated. Instead, having located an illegal broadcaster, the RIS investigators were now required to request staff from the nearest police station to accompany them on a raid. This slowed down how fast they could move in, while police availability in an area – often a problem, particularly as social unrest grew under the new Thatcher government – became an additional factor in determining whether or not a station was busted.

The BBC kills community radio

Meanwhile, progress had come to a complete halt in the world of commercial radio. After the initial nineteen contracts had been made there were no further new ILR stations for the rest of the decade. In February 1974 the Labour government had reconvened the Annan Committee on the future of broadcasting, first begun in 1970 but then cancelled when the Conservatives took power. It wasn't until February 1977 that it concluded, putting on hold any changes to the broadcasting system for its duration.

In radio the committee was broadly happy with how ILR was developing, although it did note that when it came to the promised public service commitments there was "a flagrant failure to provide what little they promised."[32] As a result the amount of 'meaningful speech' that ILR stations were required to carry was increased slightly, cutting music to a maximum of 49% of airtime. 'Meaningful speech' was a concept the IBA invented to cover anything that wasn't just links between records, which they hoped would dismiss criticisms that ILR output was solely music and inane DJ prattle. The committee also thought that the IBA had not developed "quite the right touch" for dealing with radio and that there were "a number of enterprising broadcasters who have ideas for new kinds of local radio which would not fit into the IBA mould."

Amongst those lobbying the committee had been the Community Commu-nications (COMCOM) group of community radio activists, who later went on to help form the Community Radio Association. They found sympathy for their ideas among the committee's members, who were very much taken with the Canadian system where small stations were run by local non-profit trusts. In their report the committee put forward the idea of a new Local Broadcasting Authority to break the duopoly between the BBC and IBA. Committee member and Labour MP Philip Whitehead recalled "We wanted a new force in broadcasting which was essentially starting at the grassroots, starting in the locality ... In the middle [between BBC and ILR] there ought to have been a positive desire to sustain and increase the local community element."[33]

Almost all of the recommendations were instead shelved by the Labour gov-ernment. Philip Whitehead later enquired of Shadow Home Secretary Roy Hat-tersley what happened: "I asked him why the then Labour government didn't introduce all of the parts of the Annan package and he said 'Quite simple, we were whitewashed by the BBC.' It's undoubtedly the case that at that moment the BBC, very nervous of losing its stake in local radio because it wanted to be in every form of broadcasting in Britain, mounted a tremendous exercise against the proposal and that pushed the government over."[34] The sole concession won by COMCOM was the introduction of the experimental radio stations on the cable TV network.

During 1977 and 1978 there were 108 cases of people prosecuted for unli-censed broadcasting, though most were for unauthorised use of the amateur radio or private mobile radio bands. In the financial year 1976-77 £539,000 was spent on the Radio Interference Service.

On The Air

Radio AMY

Community access radio for North London, 1978-1979

A split from North London Radio, AMY was started on 7 May 1978 by Norman Spencer, Paul Allen and Christopher England. AMY – Alternative Media for You – was the first community access radio station and broadcast for five hours every Sunday to Enfield, Barnet, Haringey, Hackney, Camden and Islington on 217m medium wave. The station's ethos was that radio shouldn't just be the preserve of a few chosen by The Powers That Be and that plans for more local radio shouldn't just mean Capital Radio with a smaller transmitter. As they put it: "ordinary people want a go now!"

Alternative Media for You

A nyone from their broadcast area who wanted to could broadcast programmes via AMY and they actively sought out community groups to put together programmes for the station. One popular contributor was a drama group of 7 to 11 year-olds who wrote and recorded plays ranging from traditional children's stories to their own imaginative mysteries. AMY's legal status prevented some larger organisations and the local authorities themselves from involvement in the station, however.

The main programme in its six hour broadcast was called the Community Chest – a magazine show that could switch from "a discussion on motorway plans for Barnet to light classical music to a poetry reading to heavy rock to views on the Haringey test census to Asian film music."[35] Chris explains "Each hour was balanced to shuttle back and forth between the serious or the fun and silly, between the trivial and the tragic. It was like reading a local newspaper that also included music. In a way, we were just the co-ordinators for a flow of stuff that readily came from all parts of the community, with us acting more as conductors to a symphony of a whole army of contributors."[36]

Every piece of commercial music carried on the station had to be requested and announced by a listener – either over the phone, by submitting a tape or live in the studio. AMY also carried music by local musicians, which was given a higher priority and soon began to generate listener requests as well. Music and other contributions crossed different ethnic boundaries too. Rather than segregating different groups with their own programming, they were keen to make something that would appeal to everyone and encouraged better understanding between different ethnicities.

From the beginning, AMY wanted the station to appeal to a broad audience of ordinary listeners. Their code banned politically-partisan programming and what would now be termed hate speech. While the political rules were felt by some to be too rigid – creating tension with the smaller, more overtly political groups who were often some of most fervent contributors – the code was broadly supported by the station's listeners. Meeting the needs of the different contributor groups and balancing their different viewpoints was a challenge for the station's management, made more complex by its lack of a licence.

AMY closed in May 1979 after one year of broadcasting, having felt that they had proved the viability of such a station. They were raided once during this time, Christopher England having a close escape at their transmitter site in Enfield in February 1979: "I went bounding up to them as they were looking at some medium wave equipment sitting in a field. Well, they bought my story about having DFed (Direction Found i.e. tracked) the station myself, and I got a letter some months later telling me they'd let me off this time, but if it happened again they'd prosecute me for listening. I bet they'd wished they'd known what I'd had in my pockets: spare 807 valve, crystal, programme tapes..."[37]

Christopher England believes AMY's model of broadcasting is still relevant in the current radio system. "Today's community radio is different amateurs turning up at the studio with their music collection and playing it whilst trying to sound like any other commercial radio station. What's the point? The Radio AMY format was an easy one to produce – and this was back in the days of pause-editing everything on cassette. We didn't even have open reel machines. Today's mp3 world, digital editing, scheduling, and ease of production should make it a complete doddle. So why isn't community radio doing this? More importantly, why isn't Ofcom asking community radio to do this?"[38]

• • • • • • • • • • • • • • • • •

The team continued campaigning for community radio in London. Some of its members were part of the North London Radio application in the axed 1985 community radio experiment, where they were one of the few groups with practical on-air experience. Christopher England and Ricky Stevens worked on Radio Veronica and the second London Music Radio, while Stevie Lane went on to join Radio Caroline.

Celebration Radio
Album rock from North West London, 1976-1980

Although Celebration put out their first test transmission in August 1976 it wasn't until July the next year that they began regular transmissions on 1277 AM. Throughout 1978 they were on the air most Sundays from North West London – usually for four hours but sometimes for longer – with an album rock format. Presenters on Celebration included Mark Anderson, Mark Adams, Mark Bates, Dave Grainger, Helen Davidson, Keith Jeffries, Bob Williams, Neil Kay and Andy Richards.

In January 1980 several members split to form Radio Floss. After some successful VHF test broadcasts, Celebration made a switch to Sunday mornings on 90.2 FM in August 1980. However, these weren't to last and the station faded away, although some of its team did then return on Radio Orion.

Radio City
London's rock 'n' roll station, 1978-1985

Broadcasting from Colindale on 238m medium wave, Radio City was an all rock 'n' roll station operating for four hours every Sunday.

Started by Chop and Jock, other presenters included Luke the Duke, Wild Willy West, Superman, Jivin' Jock and Tokin' Ray. Rock 'n' roll saw a resurgence in the late seventies and the station picked up a loyal listenership who also followed the DJs in the associated clubs. Radio City managed seven years of regular broadcasting – there were rumours among other pirates that the investigators felt intimidated by the tough image of its operators so left it alone. It closed in 1985, though some presenters returned on Radio Memphis. Luke the Duke also presented shows on DBC in its earlier days.

East London Radio
Britain's first community radio station, 1977-1978

East London Radio was the first unlicensed station to take a serious interest in serving an area with more than just non-stop music. Norman Spencer (Phil Troll) was particularly interested in how news, information and community features that were solely the domain of local newspapers could be brought onto the airwaves. Roger Davies was station manager and looked after the engineering side and other presenters included Paul Jones and Dave Collins.

EAST
LONDON
RADIO

A WHOLE NEW
EXPERIENCE
WITH FREE RADIO

❖❖

201m – 1493kHz
Medium Wave

Transmissions began in the summer of 1977 on first 201m and then 221m medium wave serving the East London and Essex border area. Early broadcasts were from 11am-3pm but ELR soon expanded to operate between 9am and 5pm. Although presenters based their shows around pop music, the station explained "Each programme contains community news, which consists of information on local charity events, local fetes, local government news and things of interest in the East London and surrounding areas. We also interview local groups who need exposure and give details of concerts and cinema information."[39]

Following its closure in 1978 some of its presenters went on to join North London Radio. The station also formed the East London Community Radio Campaign to push for a licence for the local area. In 1979 Meetings were held with 24 local MPs and garnered it broad political support for the concept. They continued campaigning into the nineties, operating several Restricted Service Licence stations in 1994 and 1995, but were not successful in realising a permanent station.

• • • • • • • • • • • • • • • •

Phil Troll, Roger Davies and Paul Jones now present shows on Internet radio station Big L.

Radio Invicta
London's very first soul station, 1969-1984

It took until the late seventies before Radio Invicta became a regular weekly destination for soul music fans in London.

From September 1977 it began operating every Sunday for three hours from midday. Broadcasts were initially split between two transmitter sites, though this idea was dropped as it increased the chance of technical problems without giving any more protection from raids. Soon the big club DJs were seeing the impact of the station and as hours expanded the DJ roster was augmented by several members of the 'Soul Mafia': Chris Hill, Froggy, Pete Tong and Steve Walsh. Steve's industry contacts were a particular help with Invicta's next phase of expansion, though his drive for personal success was not always aligned to the station's.

Like other pirates at the time, Radio Invicta used a regular set of public telephone boxes to take requests and get feedback from listeners. The calls showed

Roger Tate's Radio Invicta studio. Photo courtesy of Radio Invicta.

that the station was pulling in a large audience, many of them female, proving it wasn't just male anoraks who were tuning in to pirate radio. Each week Invicta would compile its Soul Poll chart of the hottest records from the calls and letters. They put on some small-scale club nights, organised coach trips to take listeners to the big soul music weekenders (in his day job Tony worked for a travel agent) and at the annual Caister Soul Festival Invicta ran the radio station. Growing music industry support enabled them to land interviews with Millie Jackson, Kool and the Gang and Archie Bell among others.

Going live

In 1981 live broadcasts were introduced, using a UHF link from a new studio to the transmitter site. A set of tower blocks in Battersea were the most popular location for broadcasts, though they occasionally ventured further afield. New DJs included Steve Devonne, Barrie Stone, Tony Monson, Nicky Holloway and RFL's Nigel Grant, who helped on site duties.

Invicta now saw its first real competition, from the newly-launched JFM and then Horizon Radio. Its founders had never considered Invicta a serious business and it only carried a few ads to cover the cost of replacing transmitters. These new rivals were different. With better organisation, longer broadcasting hours and wider coverage they began to take listeners and the occasional DJ from Invicta. Roger Tate later explained "We did it because we liked it and enjoyed entertaining people – there was no profit motive. I feel the station went downhill when we started to take adverts in the late '70s, but we had to because we were being raided more often. And when JFM and Horizon came on the air, we were having trouble from their dirty tricks department."[40]

They were additionally hampered by the valve transmitters that Roger built the station, which he couldn't always replace quickly enough after they were seized. Horizon and JFM were using transistor designs that could be constructed much faster but Invicta didn't always have the money to buy from other engineers. These problems meant it was off the air for much of 1982, falling further behind its rivals, and they began to lose heart. Tony Johns complained "Why pick on Invicta when there are a dozen other pirates who are just kids fooling around? We provide a service that London's other stations don't." A petition in support of the station had managed 20,000 signatures by the summer of 1983, but the Home Office, who were in charge of radio policy, had no interest in talking to them.

Where Invicta was different from its rivals was in its openness to different kinds of black music. As disco took over from funk in the mid-seventies it increasingly featured on the station and gained them new followers. There were also specialist programmes featuring gospel, rhythm and blues and jazz, including shows from a very young Gilles Peterson. From 1983 electro and hip-hop had more of a presence on Invicta than on its competitors. Steve Devonne was one of the earliest DJs to bring this style to the radio, at a time when it had minimal exposure in clubs, and he later presented a weekly electro chart. After guesting on his show, Herbie and the Mastermind Roadshow were invited to do their own weekly show built around their mastermixes. At the time mixing was still a novelty, rare in London's clubs, let alone on the radio, and Mastermind were at the forefront of taking the concept to a wider audience.

Competition and closure

When JFM and Horizon went 24 hours in 1984 the writing seemed to be on the wall for Radio Invicta. Having been off the air for three months they began time-sharing with Skyline Radio, operating after midnight via the same transmitter. However, this arrangement broke down due to Skyline not always remembering to switch off the link at their studio, making it impossible for Invicta to broadcast. Invicta attempted their own Sunday broadcasts but these also faded and the station never even made it back on the air for a final farewell.

While among ordinary listeners it may be less well remembered than the big 24-hour stations that followed, Radio Invicta was the one that got there first. It was the first soul station in Europe, one of the first pirates to make the jump to VHF, one of the first to introduce stereo and live broadcasting from a separate studio location, and the first to give a home on the dial to the top club DJs of its day. Invicta set the blueprint for all the dance music stations that followed.

• • • • • • • • • • • • • • • •

Tony Johns died of a heart attack in 1999. Roger Tate lamented that despite his ability as a presenter "Tony Johns never had the confidence to go 'mainstream' and therefore his broadcasting talents were largely unknown."[42] Roger went on to a career in consumer technology journalism under his real name Bob Tomalski and made regular appearances on radio and TV. In 2001 he also died of a heart attack.

North London Radio
Pop for North East London, 1977-1978

Transmissions from North London Radio began in late August 1977 from a site in Enfield on 1368 AM. The station was put together by Garry Stevens and Norman Spencer, who had both previously worked on East London Radio. Others quickly joined when they heard the broadcasts and before long NLR had a team of eleven DJs and fifteen other people helping out behind the scenes. Presenters included Dave Russell, Brian Scott, Steve James, Mike St John and Dave Christian. Local news was read out by Mike Stewart and Pete Johnson at the start of every show.

Wanting to go beyond NLR's pop format, Norman Spencer split from the others in spring 1978 to join Christopher England in a new venture. For the first week this also operated as North London Radio, before changing its name to Radio AMY. NLR continued operating for two years, escaping any raids.

. . . .

After the closure of both NLR and Radio AMY, Garry Stevens and Christopher England launched Happy Music Radio.

Radio Telstar South
Britain's first oldies station, 1976-1984

Radio Telstar South was Britain's original oldies station and one of the few regular FM broadcasters in the mid-seventies. The first broadcasts under the RTS name began in May 1976, although co-founders Roy Wass and Kid Johnson had carried out tests the previous year under the name Independent Radio London South. Kid Johnson later explained his reasons for starting the station: "In the London area during the day there were numerous [unlicensed] stations playing chart material and a few presenting specialist music formats. However, after 5 pm everything seemed to grind to a halt. Sunday evenings seemed long

and totally boring. [We] decided to 'test the ground' and see if there was a possibility of a substantive audience after Alan Freeman's 'Pick of the Pops' chart
show finished at 7pm."[43]

Although transmissions were not on high power and it was only on for one
hour a week, Telstar soon picked up a large audience desperate for music. Kid
Johnson described the listeners as "a great bunch and they really did appreciate
the service we were providing – and the great thing was that 90% of the calls were
from just ordinary people who had come across us by chance and could not wait
to participate in the greatest golden oldies extravaganza of the time."

At its peak the station could get more than a hundred letters a week and as
many phone calls. One evening in Beckenham at the phone box where Dave
Reading and Dawn Peters were taking calls they found themselves suddenly
surrounded by police. She recalled "We were all questioned and told the police
it was a meeting place and when asked why we were all carrying radios we said
we were listening to the top twenty chart show!"[44] Dave and Dawn also presented
occasional shows and made many of the jingles used on the station.

Several presenters in the early days had been involved in Radio Free London
during its 1973/74 broadcasts, including Mark Ashton and Kenny Myers. Seeing
the success of Telstar they decided to relaunch RFL. This left Telstar short-handed
and in early 1978 they considered closing the station down. However, listener
support made them reconsider. In its latter days broadcasts were generally two
hours long and usually presented by Kid Johnson and Horace Cracksman, who
also built the later transmitters.

For most of its life Telstar broadcast from woods on the North Kent border,
necessitating often cold Sunday evenings hiding in the undergrowth while the
taped shows went out. It was rather different from the "plush Golden Square
offices" where their transmissions claimed they came from (Golden Square was
then home to LBC). One broadcast near the Biggin Hill RAF base alerted the sus-

picions of the military police who thought they were attempting to jam aircraft transmissions. From the start of the eighties Telstar began using buildings in the Crystal Palace area, considerably improving their reach into North London. RTS was one of the victims of the anti-pirate action on 27 January 1980, when a rooftop raid involving six members of the Special Patrol Group resulted in site staff being arrested and an appearance in court in June 1980. Towards the end of their life Telstar were back in the outdoors in Kent once more.

Radio Telstar South finally closed in March 1984, when the rush of broadcasters to operate seven days a week made it impossible for a station only on the air for a couple of hours each week. According to Kid Johnson "We were faced with a situation where you never really knew whether your frequency would be occupied. These circumstances had made our operations untenable and we reluctantly decided that it was no longer viable to continue with a service if it was to become unreliable."[45]

Thameside Radio

Pioneers in radio technology and audience interaction, 1977-1983

Thameside Radio was founded in 1977 by Bob Edwards and Tony Lloyd. While still at school the two brothers had been involved with medium wave station Radio Anonymous and then both worked for the original London Music Radio from South London. When that closed in 1977 they began preparations for a new station, eventually settling on the name Thameside Radio. Unlike the earlier stations, Thameside was to operate on VHF, using an innovative new transmitter designed by Tony Lloyd.

The first broadcast went out on 11 December 1977 and for the early months included just a one hour show presented by Bob Edwards. He played a mixture of album tracks and singles, though like Capital at this time it was fairly safe in its musical style. Sometimes Tony Lloyd would do a second hour of broadcasting, which was more album rock based.

Getting close to your listeners

Where Thameside was different was in the level of audience participation, fostering a real sense of community among their listeners. Soon the audience were helping to direct the programmes, with regular competitions, lots of requests and even phone calls to listeners. Sometimes they would go round to their listeners' houses to deliver prizes or even to record whole shows using a mobile setup.

In its second year, programmes were extended to three hours. Having for some time featured jingles sent in by listener Dave Birdman, they invited him to present the final hour. His best shows were fantastic radio, melding Dave's own sketches and jingles with comedy records and carefully-chosen music. This period from '79 through to '81 was the station's peak years. Musically they had also become less safe, reflecting an incredibly creative time for music by adding more new wave and synthpop, the occasional demo from young bands, and with tracks often played ahead of chart success rather than simply reflecting what was at the top.

In 1979 Thameside went one step further in its audience interaction, hosting a party in Hyde Park from which they broadcast live – the first time that had ever been done by an unlicensed station. Aleks Wright and Sarah (Bob and Tony's sister) joined to present a music news roundup, with Aleks also initiating the popular Thameside Fast Food Survey, where they would invite listeners to meet at a different restaurant each week. There were also parties on the Circle Line and a mystery coach trip to Brighton. Dave Birdman extended his wings to produce two serials: The Nasties, the story of a no-hope punk rock band and their attempt to get to the top, and Norman Normal, the everyday story of a hypochondriac.

Thameside goes live

The station's technology was evolving too. From 1979 Thameside began using a low power VHF band III link transmitter to send programmes to its main transmitter. Once the technology and security had been proved they moved into regular live broadcasting. Taking advantage of a lull in activity by the Post Office investigators they installed a permanent broadcast transmitter setup at the top of Paddington's Trellick Tower, which lasted for nine months. As components became more widely available they also increased power, first to 100W and eventually 200W, allowing Thameside to reach most of London.

Live broadcasting enabled them to introduce new features. There was the Phantom Phonebox where they would give out the address of a phonebox somewhere in West London before ringing it in search of a Thameside listener. To help people find other Thameside fans in their area they started the Thameside Radio Flashing Light, where listeners would flash their house lights along to a track. A chart was introduced, with people phoning in to vote in the first hour and then the top tracks played in the second. For their fourth birthday they even broadcast live from a cruiser on the River Thames, though this was almost jeopardised when the captain set off in the opposite direction to what they had planned.

Switching sites

Eventually the authorities began stepping up their action against unlicensed stations and from 1981 Thameside found it harder to stay on the air, especially when new VHF doppler tracking technology was brought in that let investigators locate stations much faster. In order to broadcast while minimising the risk of losing transmitters, Thameside devised an elaborate system using multiple locations for the nights when they knew investigators were out tracking the station. Every fifteen or twenty minutes they would switch between tower blocks in different West and North London locations. Modified amateur radio rigs were used to communicate between the different teams while Tony Lloyd monitored the investigators' radio channel from his home and gave warnings in the event of trouble.

While the switching made it harder for listeners, who for one segment might get great reception and then the next completely lose the station, it did mean that Thameside could at least be on the air on nights when other stations were taken off or decided it wasn't safe enough to broadcast. Sometimes it was the only pirate broadcasting – and the only London radio station playing contemporary music. After many weeks of attempting and failing to get Thameside off the air – the only Sunday station not hit – the investigators were highly frustrated. Engineer Ian Stewart recalls "Thameside became the main thorn in Mr Gotts' side – we knew we were because we used to monitor his radio-telephone channel and listened to him getting more and more irate. It was great fun and sometimes quite hairy."[46]

Thameside's Dave Birdman. Photo by Aleks Wright.

Court appearances

Thameside's technology and methods did usually enable them to stay one step ahead of the authorities, but on 25 April 1982 Bob Edwards and Dave Birdman were finally caught. Bob had dropped his amateur portable so he wasn't able to hear Tony's warning that the block for their part of the broadcast had been located by the investigators. Deciding to take down the aerial at the end of their segment, rather than come back for it later, gave the authorities sufficient time to return with the police. Just as the duo opened the door to leave, Eric Gotts arrived with the officers. They were arrested and spent the night in the cells at Paddington Green police station. A transmitter was also seized at another site, though luckily nobody else was caught.

Dave and Bob were subsequently convicted of illegal broadcasting, though neither received an especially large fine given the trouble the authorities had gone to get the station off the air. However, they were also charged with a criminal offence of stealing electricity from the local council. According to Dave, "When the magistrate was told exactly what it was we were being charged with – theft of electricity – and exactly the amount we were charged with stealing – it was an incalculable fraction of a penny – his eyebrows shot to the ceiling, his face fell and he gave a little speech on how much it costs to bring a prosecution to court and wondered at the incompetence of someone who would bring such a case, answering the charge of the theft of less than half a penny of electricity."[47] More vindictively, Eric Gotts notified the BBC that the transmitter had been found with a BBC mains plug on it, resulting in Bob losing his job at the corporation. Thameside never carried advertising or appealed to listeners for funds so any equipment seized had to be rebuilt and paid for from their own wallets.

Departures, arrivals and farewells

Through this time Bob Edwards and Dave Birdman were still the backbone of the station, but there were a couple of important departures. Co-founder Tony Lloyd left frontline duties in 1980 and then in the autumn of 1981 Aleks Wright left for Hilltop Radio with two of the behind-the-scenes crew. New shows were added from Paul James, Uptown Radio's Terry Anderson and the Curly Man, who went on to pioneer premium rate telephone information lines. There were also occasional shows from Ian Stewart, who handled Thameside's engineering after Tony Lloyd left.

Annie and Eric kill Thameside

By the end of 1982, weekly broadcasting was taking its toll on the station's regulars. Thameside had also been hit hard in listener numbers when Radio One finally began Sunday evening broadcasting, remaining on Radio Two's VHF transmitter network after the top forty with a request show presented by Annie Nightingale that aped Thameside's.

While hours were extended to 1am and sometimes started earlier too, shows no longer got the listener support they had before and the presenters no longer seemed to be so actively seeking it. There were fewer of the fun interactive ideas and the music policy also became more safe. After a raid on 15 May 1983 the station never returned to the air. Dave Birdman later admitted "It had gone on for too long. It was a jolly good station but it ran out of ideas. It also started getting badgered rather too much by the authorities and when they'd finished badgering us the internal struggles were becoming pointless."[48] No other pirate station has managed the depth of listener involvement since.

• • • • • • • • • • • • • • • •

In 1984, Bob Edwards and some of the team put out two broadcasts from pirate television station Thameside TV. In January 1987 Dave Birdman, Terry Anderson and Aleks Wright returned with a new station, The Clockwork Wireless Broadcasting Company. The rest of the Thameside team disbanded, though more than a few ended up in broadcasting or audio engineering in some capacity.

CHANNEL 28 THAMESIDE TV

Uptown Radio
Rock and talk, 1978-1983

The founders of Uptown Radio had previously been broadcasting on shortwave as Skyport Radio but wanted to make a move to the VHF band where listeners stayed for longer than just to identify a station and move on. One Sunday night in the pub with the Radio Jackie crew they met David Valentine who had the VHF gear they needed and, following a few test transmissions, regular Sunday night broadcasts began in the autumn of 1978. At this time Uptown put out just two hours of shows and began broadcasts at 9pm, when West London Radio on the same 94.4 FM channel closed down. Early on they operated from open grounds in South West London before moving to tower blocks in 1982, with Dave Bowman then taking over as engineer from Mark King. An increase in power enabled them to get out much better than before, but throughout its life Uptown's transmitter sites usually limited reception to the western side of town.

When West London Radio closed down, Uptown moved to a 7pm start with a schedule that remained little-changed throughout their time on air: Terry Anderson to open the broadcast, leaning more towards alternative rock; Bob Earl with a punkier sound and finally Robin 'Topper' Lindsay with heavy metal. Terry's shows were always very speech based, with readers' letters and discussions of the issues of the day – which on some nights could limit the music to a handful of tracks in the show. Later on he added phone interviews to a number of famous people of the day, who usually assumed Uptown Radio was a commercial station they had never heard of rather than a pirate.

By 1983 the number of raids on the station increased and there were several extended gaps between broadcasts. After losing some members of the station

Terry Anderson circa 1977 in the studio used for Skyport and early Uptown. Photo by Mark King.

and then their channel to Horizon Radio they decided to call it a day. The last broadcast went out around March 1983. According to Terry, "It had gone as far as anyone could take it and it had got to the point of turning up on a Sunday and saying 'Well, here we go again.' It ended at the right time really, there wasn't any further for it to go within the structure that it had. There were more things that I wanted to do, but because of the restrictions on clandestine radio at that time, you simply had to face up to the fact that you couldn't do them. You couldn't risk having live guests in the studio, not people you wanted anyway. By then I'd been doing programmes for 4-5 years without a break and it just reached its natural time to fade away and did."[49]

• • • • • • • • • • • • • • • •

Terry did some later shows on Thameside Radio and in 1987 joined Clockwork Wireless. Under his real name, Terence Dackombe, he went on to a career as a writer for a number of radio and TV comedy shows and music documentaries as well as working as a journalist for several papers.

Back Street Radio

A punk station on 226m medium wave from North London in 1977.

Radio Galaxy

A medium wave station on 1133 AM in 1977.

Music Radio 270

A short-lived station operated by former members of London Music Radio in late 1977 following that station's closure.

Radio North Kent

Although formed in late 1977, Radio North Kent broadcast mostly on public holidays for its first year with a 10W transmitter on 92.8 FM. Following the August bank holiday in 1978, regular transmissions started each week, with DJs David Saint, Dr Derek, Frank Martin, Mike Robinson and engineer Justin Simmons. Justin also built VHF transmitters for several London stations and went on to launch Radio Weird. RNK closed in 1980.

Radio Liberty

Broadcasting from South West London, Radio Liberty first appeared in 1978 on 90.4 FM with a mostly pop format. After a long period off air it returned in 1980 with monthly broadcasts. DJs included Alan Brown, Chris Hennessy, Bob Adams, Kylie Richards and Radio Invicta's Roger Tate.

Parkside Radio

Parkside operated from South West London with six hours of programmes on 89.9 FM every Sunday afternoon from 1978. The final broadcast was at the end of January 1983.

Take Five

A holiday station from Radio Floss and Celebration Radio, broadcasting on 1286 AM for Christmas 1978 and Easter 1979 in North West London.

Weekend Music Radio

Broadcasting in 1978 on 1350 AM from South London.

Radio Weird

An unusual station put together by Radio North Kent's Justin Simmons which also featured Andy Allman, Hugo Leejay and some impressively strange jingles. It operated intermittently on 92.6 FM between 1978 and 1981, though it did make at least one reappearance via RFM's transmitter in 1988. Radio Weird was also responsible for putting out broadcasts from a fake offshore radio station called Radio JayBee.

West London Radio

Broadcasting in 1978 on Sunday nights to West London on 94.4 FM from 7-9pm.

1979-1980

Live broadcasting and hidden studios

As the seventies turned into the eighties the rush of pirates to the VHF band took hold. For the first time stations also began regular live broadcasts.

As far back as the mid-seventies, stations such as North Surrey Radio had experimented with hidden radio links connecting a secret studio with a separate, usually unmanned, transmitter site, but it was only now that it became a regular practice. In the past there had been uncertainty over how much safety such links provided to staff. It therefore made sense only to use them on special occasions like public holidays when there was less likelihood of being raided. Broadcasting at night from the roofs of tower blocks, however, made participants particularly vulnerable to being caught changing tapes. Using a radio link from another location where the tapes were played out was the obvious solution. When there seemed to be little risk in being tracked this way, the next step was to broadcast programmes live.

Thameside Radio were almost certainly the first to begin regular live transmissions in 1979, although Radio Invicta were also experimenting at a similar time for special broadcasts. Thameside used a Band III VHF link operating on frequencies in the band used by 405-line television. A little later, Invicta was the first to use a UHF link system operating in the same band as the newer 625-line colour television. While easier to track should the Radio Interference Service find the frequency, Band III equipment was simpler to construct and less problematic to use than UHF. Aerials for both systems would not look out of place on the roof of a building, except perhaps for pointing in the wrong direction.

Installing transmission equipment on a tower block still posed a risk. Now that programmes came over a radio link, the transmitter could instead be set up at some earlier time and then switched on remotely when the link was activated. The smaller size, increased robustness and lower heat of transistorised transmitters meant they could even be permanently installed in a hidden location. Thameside fitted theirs in a space between two floors on the top of the 45-story Trellick Tower near Paddington and later stations used similar tricks to keep their equipment away from the authorities or their rivals. Using the same location each week meant that listeners were also guaranteed a more consistent service and knew in which direction to point their aerials: when a station moved around and signals varied wildly each week people were much less likely to make a regular appointment to listen.

Live broadcasting necessitated finding new locations for studios. The authorities knew the addresses of many of the people who ran stations because of their
previous appearances in court. However, if studios at those addresses were only
being used to tape programmes then that wasn't an offence so they could not be
raided. Operating live was a different matter and meant stations did not always
have such professional equipment as when shows had been on tape.

Going live did, however, open up new possibilities for audience interaction.
Requests and dedications could now go out almost instantly and listeners could
be called by phone to take part in programmes as they went out. Invicta and
Thameside began same-day listener charts that allowed them to quickly gauge
what music was popular with their audience. Thameside went even further with
live broadcasts from listeners' homes and even outside broadcasts, announcing
a location at the start of transmissions and then holding impromptu parties with
those that turned up. These activities greatly strengthened the bonds between
the pirate stations and their audiences.

Pop pirates, talent and presentation innovation

The most common motivation of those drawn to pirate radio has always been
the opportunity to share the music they love with other people: pre-Internet,
your choices for doing this were limited outside your immediate social circle. In
a time when music on the airwaves had such a scarcity it's perfectly valid that a
love of it should be why most people wanted to broadcast. However, there were
also those who wanted to do things with the medium that you wouldn't find on
legal radio.

Stations playing pop or the more commercial side of rock music were often
derided by those covering minority genres for not doing anything different to
the legal broadcasters. Unlike their specialist music counterparts, however, they
were more likely to experiment with forms of presentation that you wouldn't
find at the time on legal radio. With less personal investment in particular music
genres it was also easier for them to jump on new music trends, even if that was
limited to the more populist material.

The earliest stations gave free rein to their DJs to present and format their
shows exactly how they wanted. While such freedom might be welcomed with
DJs who had the necessary skill and understanding of their audiences, it could
end up purely self-indulgent. In the mid-seventies, South London's Radio Kalei-

doscope broke the mould as one of the first to introduce more tightly formatted pop shows that could attract an audience outside the core pirate radio enthusiasts. According to DJ Pat Edison, "I ended up putting together playlist sheets for the jocks which they were supposed to adhere to, barring two free choices (I think) an hour. This was not as nobody was trusted to play the station sound, it was more a reaction against what happened a lot on Radio Jackie where with one hour shows, and free-for-all music picking by the presenters, it was very likely the same records would be played in every show."[50]

In 1983 and 1984 there was an influx of broadcasters seeking to take advantage of the newly exploitable loopholes in the Wireless Telegraphy Act and bringing with them a more professional approach to radio programming. Twickenham's Radio Sovereign was the first station to employ a structured format across a whole day's broadcasting, with carefully-chosen oldies that didn't just rely on the obvious hits. Programme controller Crispian St John (Howard Rose) declared his new enterprise gave "better money for me than I was earning in ILR."[51] Under programme controller Dave Owen, the new 24-hour Radio Jackie decided its success lay in becoming indistinguishable from the Independent Local Radio stations it wanted to join.

Inspired by the success and apparent safety from the law of these stations, more were encouraged to make the jump into illegal broadcasting. There were people who had been working on the Irish super-pirates – massive commercial stations that operated as if were licensed – and now saw an opportunity back home. There were people from in-store radio stations: DJs from Oxford Street's Radio Topshop, Radio HMV and Virgin Megastore Radio regularly found homes on London's pirates. There were recent graduates from the National Broadcasting School, set up as to provide training for independent radio, who bided their time on pirates while waiting for one of the limited opportunities in ILR to come up. There were also DJs who for various reasons moved out of legal radio: Dave Gregory went from Essex Radio to LWR's breakfast show and disgraced former Radio One DJ Chris Denning was to be found on Stevenage's Newtown Radio.

Then there were those who wanted to transcend conventional ideas of what music radio should sound like. On Uptown Radio, Terry Anderson's programmes might feature just four records in an hour, with the rest of the time devoted to his wry observations on events in the previous week. Thameside

Radio not only introduced many new forms of audience interaction but had the sonic wizardry of Dave Birdman, whose dry humour informed the jingles and features on his show.

In 1981 younger people involved with Thameside were responsible for two stations that built on its programme innovations. Aleks Wright, Jim Trent and Phil Graham formed Hilltop Radio, whose shows would probably today be labelled under the 'zoo' format name, though the idea was unheard of at the time. These swapped the single personality DJ for two or sometimes three presenters working together, bouncing ideas and stories off each other. Chris Miles (Pyers Easton), who had helped out behind the scenes on Thameside, founded London Music Radio. With Radio AMY's Christopher England and Ricky Stevens, LMR made the telephone and recently legalised Citizen's Band (CB) radio a big part of its programmes, putting listeners live on air and allowing them a greater input into what was broadcast, not just treating them as a prop like the legal broadcasters.

As the eighties progressed it became tougher for a part-time pop station to find a place on the dial and to make an impact on listeners. Still, alongside those who were there to get out their music or to make a business of radio, there remained people who broadcast just a few hours a week for the love of it. Clockwork Wireless launched at the end of 1986 with smart hour-long shows from Terry Anderson and Dave Birdman. Terry's programmes updated his Uptown style for the time, but it was Dave's which really stood out. These blended scripted comedy, sound-effects, cut-ups from old movies and related music to explore a different theme every week. He explained "Radio is wonderful. It's the best possible medium because it does allow the mind to work, but unfortunately a great many of the stations are not using it to its fullest potential – with the possible exception of Radio Four. Capital has become a meaningless string of things to put between commercials. Radio One is a meaningless string of things to put between adverts for Radio One."[52]

These broadcasters, however, were the last gasp of this kind of radio. The pop – or more often now oldies – pirates that managed to still exist became more concerned with serving an audience of radio anoraks with recreations of the past than with developing anything new. As they increasingly focussed on that core group they started to cut themselves off from a wider audience. Moves to medium wave or short wave to sidestep the frequency shortage problems of FM only served to exacerbate the problem.

On The Air

Radio Alpha
Rock goes to college, 1981-1983

Some one-off broadcasts from Radio Alpha went out on bank holidays from 1979 but it wasn't until 1981 that the station became a regular fixture on London's airwaves. Programmes were initially on Monday nights, but later they split into a Monday rock service and a Tuesday soul service. DJs included Gary Hughes, Tim Gordon, Phil James, Mark Davis, Nicky Dene, Ian Hutchinson, R.F. Burns and engineer Roger Barry. Both programmes and transmissions were of a high standard and usually live and in stereo too.

Some of those involved were at University College London, where they were part of the student radio station and they made use of some of the facilities for Radio Alpha. When the weekly service was launched it was from a studio set up in UCL's basement. For several months they broadcast from a transmitter on top of the Metropole Hotel in Paddington, resulting in a security investigation when it was finally raided by the authorities. The station closed in 1983.

Bromley Sound
Pop comes from school, 1980-1981

Bromley Sound was started by a group of friends while still in the sixth form at school. After purchasing an AM transmitter via Radio Jackie's Keith Rogers, they put out a few broadcasts before deciding that they wanted to be on FM. Through Keith's former Jackie colleague Mark Ellis they met engineer Roger Howe, who built them a 10W FM transmitter and in April 1980 they recommenced transmissions on 94.2. Before long they had moved to 60W power, reaching across London with pop-oriented taped shows from a hill outside Bromley.

Jonny Haywood was next to join. According to station co-founder Richard, "Jonny had big ambitions to be on the radio and when we heard his voice and professionalism the original station founders gave up their slots."[53] However, at the start of 1981 there were disagreements over the direction of the station, with Mark Ellis pushing to rename it London FM and move to live broadcasts while others were happy as things were. This led to Keith and Jonny leaving and the closure a few weeks later in March 1981.

• • • • • • • • • • • • • • • •

Mark Ellis went on to launch London FM. Jonny Haywood later became the co-founder of London Weekend Radio.

The Dread Broadcasting Corporation
Britain's first black-owned radio station, 1980-1984

DBC was Britain's first black-owned radio station. Founder Lepke (Leroy Anderson) comes from a musical family: his father was a musician and skilled in most instruments, his elder sister Rita was married to Bob Marley and two of his other sisters were in Swedish group DaYenne. Lepke himself had worked on West London's reggae sound systems and at the black music branch of Honest Jon's record shop. Many young bands at the time would get pin-on badges made at Notting Hill's Better Badges, where an old medium wave transmitter had been used to get music from the main shop down to the production room. No longer needed, the shop owner, Joly McFie, offered it to Lepke and in the autumn of 1980 broadcasts began from his home in Neasden.

Lepke's rationale for the station was very simple: "We exist because there is a need – a public demand – for a black music station. The only black music there is on existing stations is two hours a week. Before us there was nobody playing the massive amounts of independent records that were released and nobody playing calypso and soca at all."[54]

Rebel Radio

These early broadcasts on 214m, using the name Rebel Radio, didn't get out far and ran on Sundays from usually 1.30 to 3.30pm, but they still managed to pick up a loyal local audience. After a few months on his own, Lepke was joined by Chucky (Douglas Wright) and Dr Watt (Lloyd Rainford). His sister Margaret, The Ranking Miss P, was soon on the station as well: "I was forced by my brother Lepke. He asked me to sing jingles for DBC then told me there were no black women on the radio so I should get myself together to present a show."[55] During this time Lepke was caught once after a broadcast, admitted responsibility and later appeared in court and was fined.

DBC VHF

After attempts to continue on medium wave with a new transmitter didn't work out, they next linked up with Our Radio, who were sharing transmitter facilities with Radio Zodiac on 103.8 FM as none of the stations had much money. In a joint broadcast with Zodiac they came live from 1982's Notting Hill Carnival. Before long though, DBC broke ties and moved to 93.9 on their own. Every Friday night they broadcast six hours of programmes and were soon picking up a big audience over a much wider area. Shows at this time were all recorded, mostly taped in Lepke's studio in his house. In the early evening they would then head over to the transmitter site at the Edward Woods Estate in Latimer Road. According to DBC's Mike the Bike (Mike Williams), "The lifts were always full of people coming back with their shopping and they knew what was going on but they never said anything."[56]

While DBC is often remembered for effects-heavy reggae shows from Lepke, Miss P, Chucky and Daddy Mecka, it carried a wide range of black music styles. There were Dr Martin and Smiley with rhythm & blues, Luke the Duke with rock 'n' roll, G.T. and E.D. with soul and funk, Gus Dada Africa with African music, Sis C (later to become Camilla on LWR) with sixties soul, Neneh C (Neneh Cherry) with hip-hop, Dr Watt with reggae oldies, Nick Coleman with jazz, and Dark Star (Lloyd Bradley) and Lady Di (his wife Diana) with soul. Sometimes after the regular broadcasts they'd stay on into the early hours with tapes from sound systems. 1982 saw DBC at its peak – informed presenters playing music that was hard to hear anywhere else.

Lepke describes support from listeners and businesses as "instant", with the

Lepke in the DBC studio circa 1982. Photo © Leon Morris.

On top of the tower block circa 1982 as DBC prepare transmissions. Photo © Leon Morris.

station funded using a mix of ads and donations. "One of the first to support us was the company Whole Earth, who were very new at the time. Others were mostly small record labels and record shops – but we had a community policy that we read out most local events for free."[57]

Seven day DBC

In the winter of 1982, Lepke went to spend a year in the USA where his mother lived, leaving the running of the station to Miss P with help from Mike. On his return at the end of 1983 they decided to follow other stations into seven-day live broadcasting. Lepke explains "The news came through that if you took a pic of your rig and sent it to the DTI stating your intent to broadcast they could not just raid you but had to go through a long process... So we did just that, setting up live studios in Kilburn with a link to the main rig near Notting Hill Gate. The house belonged to a very rich lady whose cousin happened to be in Thatcher's cabinet, so I think the DTI had to tread very carefully. They did not know what to think or do."[58]

The new operation's music policy was more cross-generational than the part-time DBC, appealing to an older West Indian audience as well as those who tuned in to hear the more contemporary music played in the clubs. Programmes went out twelve hours a day, though transmissions were more confined to the local area than the earlier tower block broadcasts. By now some of the original members had moved on, so a number of new DJs were recruited for this incarnation of the station.

In August of '84 DBC broadcast live from the Notting Hill Carnival, with shows going out from a sound system outside the pink shop in Portobello Road, where Lepke also had a regular Saturday stall selling tapes of shows from the station and the famous DBC Rebel Radio T-shirts. They figured that with a big crowd it was unlikely the station would be busted despite the harsh new broadcasting laws that came in the previous month.

Towards the end of the year, DBC's seven-day broadcasts came to a close. "We only gave it up because basically Miss P had been offered a slot on Radio One and, as most of us were unemployed, some wanted to stop and find paid work. I wanted to carry on, so with premises supplied by one of the last DJs employed by DBC, DJ Challenger – who had a TV repair shop – I set up JBC. He and others wanted to continue as DBC but I said no as it would not be the same."

Later days

The launch of JBC was not the end for DBC: Lepke was still addicted to getting the music he loved on the radio and preferred being his own boss. There was a further broadcast live from Notting Hill Carnival in 1985 and he continued to do occasional broadcasts in the early hours through to the mid-nineties, mostly replaying classic shows from the station: "I had a 30 watt rig that I used at the time; I also used it to broadcast from Glastonbury, Liverpool, Nottingham and a few other places. I set up a smaller rig in a club called the Globe in Notting Hill that used to broadcast live from the clubs decks – again late night early morning – that caused a real buzz at the time."

● ● ● ● ● ● ● ● ● ● ● ● ● ● ● ● ●

Ranking Miss P began her weekly reggae show, Culture Rock, on Radio One in March 1985. She presented later programmes for GLR, Radio London and the BBC World Service and ran a production company. A number of other presenters also continued working in music and the media. Lepke provided advice for several later unlicensed stations around the UK, though he turned down a role helping the BBC with what became 1Xtra. He also put together two Restricted Service Licence stations, Grove Carnival FM and Grove FM, the latter with some financial help from the Clash's Mick Jones. In 2004 Trojan Records put out a compilation featuring music that was played in the golden age of DBC mixed in with their classic jingles.

Radio Floss
West London's pop and rock service, 1980-1985

Formed by previous members of Celebration Radio, Radio Floss took to the air on 13 January 1980 on 1350 AM from North West London. For a while some of the members of Celebration had been dissatisfied at that station's organisation and wanted to do shows with a broader appeal. A new studio was constructed in Steve Jay's shed, suitable sites for broadcasting found and prepared, and several transmitters built so they had enough backups in the event of raids. Transmissions were from 10am to 4pm, kicking off with a sixties music show styled after offshore radio, followed by programmes covering contemporary music, album rock, progressive rock and hard rock. With this mix they hoped to capture listeners across a range of different ages.

When Steve Jay went to join offshore station the Voice of Peace the others

quickly constructed a pair of tempo-rary studios so Floss could continue. Paul James and Ian Stewart then left intending to start their own station before joining Thameside. With more people joining they decided to split transmissions in 1981, with Radio Floss South playing contemporary and commercial music on the origi-nal frequency and Radio Floss North playing rock on 1386 AM. This split was not to last, however, and before long Floss was back to a single station playing exclusively rock.

All rock radio

Programmes were recorded as-live on Saturday in Andy Richards' flat above the shop he managed, with presenters including Ian Davidson, Tony Lee Stocker and Glen Johnson. By now Floss had picked up a strong local support, as Andy explains: "We also used to gather at a pub in West Harrow called the Apollo (now gone) on Sunday Nights and invited listeners to come and meet us, of which many did. On some nights half the bar would be filled with Radio Floss personnel and listeners. But most listeners contacted the station by phone and we regularly got over a hundred calls on a Sunday. Because there were no mobile phones back then we had to use phone boxes for this, which could prove awkward when members of the public wanted to make a call."[59]

Floss came to an end at the start of 1985 when raids became more fre-

Floss' transmitter. Photo by Ian Stewart.

quent. Before there had just been two or three a year and while equipment had been lost nobody had ever been caught even if there were some close shaves. However, according to Andy, "Once we started the Floss Rockshow gigs the Home Office started to take a greater interest in us. I think they saw that us making money, which we could then plough back into the radio, was a step too far and they started raiding us more regularly. By this time there were only three major stations in London still broadcasting on medium wave during the day on Sundays. We were forced to close down after getting raided three times in four weeks. We did one farewell broadcast with high power for which the Home Office left us alone."

Floss's rock roadshow continued for another four years after the station's closure. Several of the Floss South presenters, including Tim Allen and Bob Williams, subsequently formed Three Boroughs Radio using Floss transmitters and Tim Allen and Tony James went on to work in ILR. Steve Jay went on to start a broadcast engineering company.

JFM
First with 24-hour soul music radio, 1980-1985

JFM founder Brian Anthony began his radio career as a DJ on Radio Jackie and as the eighties began was presenting a soul show on the station every Sunday afternoon. Jackie had earlier experimented on VHF as Jackie FM, and when he started JFM in 1980 Brian appropriated the initials for his new station, though by that time the two groups were entirely separate. Many listeners instead thought JFM stood for Jazz Funk Music, while more cynical pirates claimed it was Just For the Money.

Competition for Invicta

The first broadcast from JFM was on the August Bank Holiday 1980 on 94 FM, with shows then regularly going out on Sundays and Bank Holidays. JFM were quick to sign up many of the leading DJs at the time, including a few who had been on the original soul station, Radio Invicta. Presenters paid £10 a week for a slot on the station, which allowed them to publicise their gigs and covered the costs of it staying on air.

Hours expanded quickly as they competed with new rival Horizon FM for listeners and advertising, and by 1983 they were broadcasting all weekend, following Radio Invicta in using secret links to get the signal from the studio to the transmitter installed on top of a South London tower block. In a TV news report, Brian Anthony boasted of how their broadcast-quality studio was assembled from spare equipment that the BBC had sold off cheaply.

DJs at this time included Jeff Young (host of Radio One's first dance show), Steve Walsh, Pete Tong (Jeff Young's successor at Radio One), Clive Richardson (later MD of the satellite Solar Radio) and Marc Damon (the voice behind a million pirate ads). Engineering was done by Keith Renton, who as a student had built the transmission equipment for Imperial College's radio station.

24 hour broadcasting

In early 1984 JFM began 24-hour broadcasting. They moved their VHF transmitter to a new permanent site at Crystal Palace, close to transmitters for Capital Radio and LBC, and began putting out a high power signal on 102.8 FM that covered the whole of London.

The DJ roster grew again, including drivetime with future Kiss FM founder Gordon Mac as well as shows from Norman Jay, Steve Jackson, Graham Gold, Lindsay Wesker, Tony Monson, Froggy, Gilles Peterson, Barrie Stone, Lynn Parsons, Robbie May and Mark Roman. There were specialist shows, such as Steve Barnard with reggae, Paul Dodd playing electro and hip-hop, and Clive Richardson's sixties R&B show, but JFM's bread and butter was commercial soul music. The station ran several popular gigs at the time, including the JFM and Mastermind Roadshow at the Lyceum Ballroom on a Friday night and special

Left: Dave Collins in the JFM studio in 1983. Right: station boss Brian Anthony.

events like their popular funk cruises to Holland.

When the 1984 Telecoms Act came in on 15 July, closing the loophole that allowed pirates to broadcast almost unhindered, many of the other stations closed down. However, JFM decided to continue broadcasting and at first seemed to be proved right in their decision when the threatened raids did not arrive. However, later in the year they began again to lose the occasional transmitter.

J.F.M.94 MHZ.V.H.F.
broadcasting 'JFM' to London
the Funk Capital
of the world!

The Gas Board shut JFM

At the end of 1984 JFM made a move to a new frequency of 104.4 VHF. Unfortunately this caused interference to a neighbouring mobile radio system used by the Gas Board – though JFM claimed it was a fault with the Gas Board's equipment, not theirs. With major disruption being caused, the DTI decided to put an end to JFM, even after it moved frequency. The Gas Board also took out an injunction against Brian Anthony to cease broadcasting.

In January 1985, DTI officials traced the link from the main transmitter site back to the block of flats that housed the studio. They then systematically cut the power to each floor to narrow down where the studio was, before finally locating it. Steve Jackson, who was on-air, and the Mastermind Roadshow's Herbie and Dave VJ, who were waiting to do their first show, were caught and prosecuted. Rumours came from several JFM DJs that a competitor had tipped off the DTI as to the studio's whereabouts but these stories seem to be without foundation. By this time the Radio Investigation Service was more actively looking to bust stations at their studios, not just take their main transmitters off the air, and the interference JFM had caused put it at the top of the DTI's list. Brian Anthony decided JFM would not return to the airwaves and he would wait to see what happened with the proposals for legal stations.

• • • • • • • • • • • • • • • •

After JFM's close DJs split into several different stations. Some of the bigger names joined Solar, some hung back until Kiss FM launched that autumn, a couple went to Fame FM, while out in Essex, Mark Roman and engineer Keith Stafford began Inner City Radio. Brian Anthony made just one short-lived return to the pirate airwaves, on the adult rock station CD93 in 1988. Keith Renton went on to work for Solar Radio and the legal Kiss FM.

South London Radio
South London's powerhouse, 1980-1981

The first South London Radio took to the air on 5 July 1980, a change of name for Radio Saturn. Broadcasts went out on Saturday nights from 7pm with Stuart Russell and Peter Gilbert. SLR used the same three watt transmitter as Radio Saturn, built by RFL's Kenny Myers, who described it as "An experiment that didn't quite work so I thought I'd better get rid of it."[60] The following year RFL's John Dawson was approached to build a higher-powered transmitter and they ended up working together. There were now four hours of programmes each Saturday, with Vaughan Smart joining as the other DJ. After finding Kenny Everett's phone number, Peter Gilbert persuaded him to do some jingles for the station and these were then used on all the shows.

The John Dawson era

After Stuart Russell moved away and Peter Gilbert became unavailable due to work commitments, John Dawson took over the station and a first test transmission went out on 11 July 1981 from a tower block in Addington. Unfortunately, as John Dawson explained later, "Basically everything went wrong. I had no staff – Alan was scared to go up tower blocks, Vaughan Smart was busy Saturday nights … Transmitters would blow up in the early days. The fourth week we finally got things together and got back on the air with four hours of programmes."[61]

Hours were soon extended to 6pm-12am, with shows including RFL regulars Mark Ashton, Nigel Grant and Kenny Myers together with Mark Mason and Rob Andrews from Radio Aquarius, Aleks Wright from Thameside and Ricky King and Dave Brown. Programmes were up to the individual DJ and featured a mix of styles including pop, soul, hi-nrg, alternative and rock, most recorded in a basic studio in John Dawson's bedroom. Transmitter power was increased to 200W with an aerial array pushing the effective power up even higher so the station was now covering the whole of London and out into the Home Counties. Although others might disagree, according to John Dawson, "We were the first VHF London free radio station to run really high power."[62]

SLR is believed to have left the air in the summer of 1982.

. . . .

John Dawson went on to co-found London Weekend Radio where Mark Mason and several of the other SLR presenters could also be found.

Radio Veronica
Pop and oldies for North East London, 1980-1981

Named after the Dutch offshore radio station – and also using some of its jingles – Veronica was one of the first VHF stations in North London. Started by Garry Stevens, the oldies service began broadcasts from a tower block in Edmonton in May 1980. Despite using only one watt of power, their position alongside Capital Radio on 96.3 gave a good enough response to confirm their decision to abandon AM. After acquiring a 60W transmitter they were able to get further into North London, putting out six hours of taped shows every Sunday afternoon from Christopher England, Brian Smith, Colin Weston, Mike St John and Alan Scott.

In the autumn of 1980 they moved to a new location in Dalston which, combined with higher power transmitters that Garry had built, gave them improved reception into East London. They also added Steve Anthony and former AMY presenter Ricky Stevens to their lineup, with shows now going out from 4pm to 10pm each Sunday. During this time they would average 70 phone calls an hour to their request line.

Hoping to get out better into South London they moved again to a tower block in Leyton. However, after four months of successful operation, one night the site staff were confronted by local police officers in the machinery room for the block's lift as they retrieved their equipment at the end of the broadcast. The gear was confiscated, identities checked and they were duly prosecuted for unlicensed broadcasting. There were no further broadcasts after that incident.

• • • • • • • • • • • • • • • •

Garry Stevens came back with Veronica Supergold in 1988. Christopher England and Ricky Stevens soon reappeared on Chris Miles' London Music Radio.

Radio 220
After some initial broadcasts in 1979, the station eventually became Southern Radio.

ABC Radio
Broadcasting in the Medway towns area in 1979. The station was founded by Stuart Clarke (Simon Parry) and DJs included John Dawson. Those involved also broadcast for a time as Radio Atlanta and Radio Medway Underground. ABC were raided on one occasion, when Stuart Clarke was caught and the equipment and a wheelbarrow were seized. He later went to Radio Caroline and was a founder of ABC Radio in Ireland.

Radio Atlantis
From East London in 1980 on 1587 AM every Sunday from 1-6pm.

Radio Comsat
When the original AM Phoenix Radio closed down, Steve Justin didn't join his colleagues on Alice's Restaurant and instead continued on AM with Radio Comsat in December 1980. Two-hour taped broadcasts went out on 1404 AM most Sundays from the NE London / Essex border, playing new wave and alternative music. Guest presenters included John Scott and Christopher England. Comsat is believed to have continued until late 1983.

Radio Corina
Corina broadcast from Chingford's Pole Hill on 92.55 FM for two hours every Sunday morning from 1979. After a run-in with the authorities there were only occasional holiday programmes, which finished in 1980.

Edge City
An offshoot from rock 'n' roll station, Radio City, from 1979 it broadcast on Sundays from 12-5pm on 1278 AM and included more new wave and rock in its output.

Radio Elaine
Broadcasting on 1503 AM in 1979.

Happy Music Radio
Following the closure of both North London Radio and Radio AMY, Garry Stevens and Christopher England got together with staff from both to launch Happy Music Radio. The station used one of the NLR transmitters on the same 1386 AM frequency, operating off the side of a tower block in Edmonton Green. In the studios where they taped the shows a big sign said "Bloody well sound happy!" HMR continued until December, when the founders switched to FM and Radio Veronica.

Lea Valley Radio
From Enfield on 90.4 FM, Sundays 12-3pm.

Radio Lucy / Radio Buccaneer
Early AM stations from Alice's Restaurant founders Dave Lane and Brian Marshall.

Radio Saturn
A station formed in 1980 by Stuart Russell and Peter Gilbert after they met chatting to each other on their own transmitters, Stuart on VHF, Peter on Medium Wave. Transmissions went out using both transmitters and also on short wave. They later renamed the station South London Radio.

Southern Radio
Southern Radio broadcast from South East London on 1413 AM between April 1979 and August 1983 with a rock format. Many of the presenters were then involved in South East Sound.

Radio Tranquility
Radio Tranquility (sic) operated from 1979 from the Edmonton area with low power broadcasts on 219m AM. Initially founded by Colin Weston, Garry Stevens later stepped in to help the station continue when Colin had to step down. It closed in October 1979.

Wonderful Radio Camden
Broadcasting to North London on medium wave in 1979.

1981-1982

Alternative radio and the pirates' new legitimacy

The move from the suburban parks and edge-of-London woodland used for medium wave to the more central tower blocks used for VHF marked both the start of a change in the people involved in pirate radio and how it was positioned by itself on air and in its publicity and also in the wider media. The DIY ethos that came in the wake of punk and the entrepreneurial spirit of Thatcherism were also to contribute to the new breed of stations.

Since the late sixties, many of those involved in unlicensed broadcasting had preferred to talk about 'free radio' rather than 'pirate radio', which was seen to have more negative connotations. In the new decade 'free radio' sounded rather old-fashioned and dangerously hippyish. There were also endless squabbles over how exactly 'free radio' was defined: some demanded absolute freedom for broadcasters while others accepted that there had to be some rules to prevent the airwaves descending into chaos. From the mid-seventies, the term 'alternative radio' came into fashion to describe all broadcasting from outside the BBC and IBA system. This not only sidestepped issues with definitions but it put the pirates on a par with other alternative culture, such as alternative theatre or alternative cinema.

London's listings magazines Time Out and (from 1981) City Limits – which both considered themselves as part of the 'alternative' – began including major unlicensed stations as though they were any other kind of trendy cultural activity that their readers might want to engage in. This not only publicised the pirates but helped further legitimise their operations: listening was now something anyone could feel comfortable doing rather than it just being a hobby for anoraks. You could talk about things you heard on the pirates with your friends at school or college or down the pub after work and it was no longer something unusual.

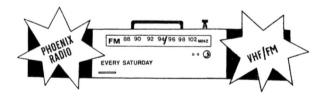

The programming on the pirates, too, was becoming increasingly alternative. West London's DBC became Britain's first black-owned radio station, playing everything from Jamaican roots reggae to lovers' rock, soca, soul, hip-hop and rock 'n' roll. Radio Zodiac and Phoenix Radio brought alternative music from the nation's independent labels to the airwaves, while new wave bands found their way onto Thameside, South London Radio and the new London Music Radio. Our Radio mixed programming for minority groups with agitprop, leading to an sometimes uneasy relationship with those pirates who were fearful of upsetting the status quo.

The business of soul music

After twelve years of an almost complete monopoly on soul music, in 1981 Radio Invicta found itself with two new rivals: JFM and Horizon Radio.

As rock had become king in the early seventies, soul had found itself increasingly marginalised in both the record industry and on the airwaves. Radio One had tried a soul music show with Robbie Vincent but it had been pulled when ratings across the country were poor. London was more amenable and from the late seventies to mid-eighties Robbie Vincent presented a very popular Saturday lunchtime show on Radio London playing the music. From its launch in 1973, Capital Radio had success with Saturday night soul programmes first from singer Marsha Hunt and then Greg Edwards, whose Soul Spectrum show ran on the station for fourteen years. At 10pm there was Capital Night Out Live from the Global Village nightclub in Villiers St (later to become Heaven) and from the late seventies the station carried occasional live broadcasts from Capital's Best Disco in Town at the Lyceum in the Strand. Soul music fans, though, wanted more than just two or three hours a week – and there was a new generation of club DJs who thought they could be equally as good on the radio and were itching for the chance to prove it.

Although many people at the time labelled them jazz-funk stations, JFM and Horizon played a wider variety of contemporary black American dance music than people today might associate with the name. And it was almost all music from the USA: while Britfunk made some small inroads, jazz-funk's adherents were obsessed by American artists and releases. Being the first to have a new single was incredibly important for both DJs and the hardcore fans: they wanted the vinyl the moment it landed from the States, not on a re-release by a British label several months down the lane.

In the face of minimal interest by the mainstream music industry – primarily because they didn't feel they could make a decent profit – the soul scene had developed its own independent network of vendors, media and venues. Fresh imports came direct from the USA to shops like City Sounds, Groove Records and Bluebird, usually bypassing the conventional music distributors. News and reviews were carried in the monthly Blues & Soul magazine and the weekly Black Echoes newspaper.

Each weekend thousands would visit a string of mostly suburban clubs and all-dayers to hear the latest music from the leading DJs, as popular amongst their followers as those from the radio but unknown to the wider public. Despite the music coming almost exclusively from black musicians, the clubs that played it were predominantly white. Some young black Londoners had turned their backs on soul as disco went mainstream, but they also found at clubs that the management did not always welcome them through the doors, even if the DJs and most other punters didn't have a problem.

Early on, when all their broadcast hours were short, there was cooperation between Radio Invicta and the new stations. On the Spring Bank Holiday in 1982 Invicta and Horizon ran a joint broadcast for the whole weekend. JFM and Invicta also jointly organised meetings for all the pirates in London intended to discuss common issues and plan frequency use. However, JFM's Brian Anthony and Horizon's Chris Stewart had ambitions that went far beyond Invicta's – and the entrepreneurial skills necessary to realise them. Soon

★ **TUNE IN** ★

to

super soul sounds

on

» **Radio Invicta** «

92·4 v.h.f

All August Bank Holiday
From 10p.m. Saturday 24th.

Horizon and JFM became fully-integrated parts of the soul music system and they both sought to exploit it in a way that Radio Invicta never had before. Unable to keep up with its rivals in the new broadcasting environment and alleging dirty tricks in keeping it off air, Invicta began a slow decline.

Although the DJs on JFM and Horizon adapted their presentation to mimic legal radio, the music closely followed what was currently working for them on those dancefloors. Venues wanted DJs that would bring in a low-hassle crowd with good money in their pockets and no hesitation of spending it at the bar. That wasn't compatible with pushing at music's boundaries. While radio did give the DJs a little more leeway to indulge their personal tastes they stuck with what they knew their audience wanted.

Hip-hop and electro might have been rising in popularity, but they were hardly represented in the clubs: their fans were either too young, they weren't the kind of punters the venues wanted or – notably for hip-hop's large South Asian following in London – didn't go clubbing. This meant you were initially more likely to hear these styles played on youthful pop stations like London Music Radio or alternative music stations like Phoenix than you were on the soul stations. Just as with disco before, there was griping from some established DJs that this new electronic music lacked the musicianship, real instruments and authenticity of real soul music. Despite hip-hop's early embrace by mainstream advertising, it remained very much a minority music on the radio for now.

Amid growing media interest in pirate radio, Parliament began taking notice once more. The House of Commons was told that in 1982 across the country 62 transmitters had been located, 39 of which were unmanned, and there had been 10 prosecutions for unlicensed broadcasting.

On The Air

Alice's Restaurant
London's premier rock station, 1981-1986

Alice's Restaurant first took to the air with its rock service on 28 July 1981 – a special three-day "Rock against the royal wedding" broadcast that went out on both AM and FM. However, it wasn't until September that the station began regular broadcasts, and then for only a few weeks.

Splitting the station

Alice's broad music policy – it had after all named itself after the Arlo Guthrie song with its "You can get anything you want at Alice's Restaurant" chorus – turned out to confuse listeners. It wasn't long since punk's year zero and new wave was still seen as in complete opposition to progressive rock and heavy metal. Returning to the air on 2 January 1982 the station split in two, Phoenix Radio in the early evenings with alternative music, then Alice's through to the early hours with rock.

ALICES RESTAURANT
──── ROCK MUSIC RADIO ────

Programmes continued regularly on Saturday late nights through to the start of 1984, with DJs Steve Price, Dave Collins, Dave Lane, Brian Marshall and Bear. The station supported itself with regular roadshows, notably at Walthamstow's Royal Standard rock pub. With the easier environment for pirates at that time they began broadcasting through Sundays too, adding DJs Tony Warren, who championed the new progressives, and Paul Chamberlain, playing a harder rock style. This was probably the peak of the station, on the air every week with a range of presenters who knew their stuff covering the full rock spectrum from metal to progressive, contemporary to classics. You could wake up to Bear playing obscure space rock album sides from the early seventies before having your eardrums bashed in by Steve Price with the latest hard rock releases. They played a lot more contemporary material than some of their rivals and when they did play older tracks it wasn't just the obvious ones you could hear elsewhere.

Alice's Restaurant's Debbie Smith in 1986. Photo by Pyers Easton.

Chris Miles guesting on the Restaurant in 1986. Photo courtesy of Pyers Easton.

Expecting trouble when the new 1984 Wireless Telegraphy Act was introduced, the station reduced hours. When it didn't come Alice's moved back to all-day Sunday broadcasts again, before in the winter sharing with East London local station Radio Shoestring. This came to a halt on 2 January 1985 when the studio was raided while Shoestring was broadcasting – luckily Alice's had moved out their record library the previous day.

Returning from the raid

It wasn't until September 1985 that Alice's Restaurant made it back on the air again, now operating all-day Sunday on their own, with Brian Marshall joining full time from Phoenix and newcomers Colin Noble and Cliff Brooks replacing Tony Warren and Paul Chamberlain. Broadcasts continued through until September 1986 but with increasing problems from raids and other stations.

Operating only one day a week became increasingly difficult as more pirates crowded onto London's wavebands. At times the music policy also sounded a little tired, in part reflecting an industry that at the time was more interested in selling old rock classics back to fans on CD than investing in new talent. Although plans for a final closedown at Christmas 1986 didn't come to anything, they did eventually return for one last broadcast on the 2 and 3rd January 1988 to celebrate their seventh anniversary.

. . . .

Steve Price and Colin Noble continued touring the Alice's Restaurant Roadshow until 1988 and Steve went on to present for several commercial rock stations. Dave Lane (Martin Spencer) and Brian Marshall (Lawrie Hallett) co-founded Phoenix Communications, providing engineering support for several unlicensed stations in the UK and Ireland, including Kiss FM, and then a number of those awarded licences after 1989. Lawrie Hallett also continued his alternate career in legal radio, notably on the community radio side, and now lectures on radio. Bear Freeman returned on RFM and has continued trying to get a real rock station on the air since, even going as far as test broadcasts under the Alice's Restaurant name from a massive shortwave transmitter in Scandinavia.

Radio Amanda

Hard rock all weekend, 1982-1984

John Shakespeare's Radio Amanda served up rock and heavy metal on 214m medium wave from Wood Green. Programmes went out live and expanded from initial Sunday broadcasts to the whole weekend. The large team of presenters included Paul Harvey, Chris Thomas, The Brain Surgeon, Joe 90 and Andy Johnson, who later joined Radio Caroline.

Amanda launched using Telstar 1's old medium wave transmitter, which having been originally built at the end of the sixties carried on good service until a raid in 1984. The station closed after a second raid not long after, though presenters continued DJing at North London rock venues in the mid-eighties.

RADIO AMANDA
214 mw (1404 khz)

Broadcasting To London, Essex & Herts.

■, MORLEY AVENUE,
WOOD GREEN, LONDON. N22 6NG
✦ ✦ ✦ ✦ ✦

. . . .

John Shakespeare made a brief return to the airwaves on RFM in 1987. There were also plans to share time on the same transmitter with RFM but these never came to anything.

Radio Andromeda

Smarter rock radio, 1982-1984

Described by DJ Bear Freeman as "the Radio 3 of rock stations", Andromeda broadcast a freeform service in the early eighties. Operating from South Herts on 1278 AM with a 120W transmitter, the station played progressive rock, art rock, space rock, electronic music and more – often whole sides at a time – that you could rarely hear elsewhere on the airwaves.

Founded by Ian Strange, other presenters included Number 6, Bear, Forgotten Henry and the Milk Cart Geezer. Andromeda continued until the change in broadcasting laws in 1984, though it returned for in May 1990 on 100.3 FM for a few weeks.

Border Radio
A lifeline for the elderly, 1981-1986

Border Radio was rather different to most of the other pirates on the air. The station was begun by pensioner Harry Marshall to provide a lifeline to older, isolated people in the Twickenham area. Every Wednesday, Friday and Saturday night from 8-11pm he would broadcast from his home on 90.2 FM with programmes of easy listening music. Transmissions were on very low power and in the easier environment for unlicensed stations in the early eighties he did not attract the attention of the Radio Interference Service. Over time others began to help out at the station, with eventually ten people either presenting shows or answering phone calls.

When the community radio experiment was announced by the Government, Border Radio closed down and Harry became involved in a local group called TW Sound who wanted to apply for a licence. TW Sound managed to get a grant from the Greater London Council which helped them put together an application. However, with a different style from the professional third-sector workers involved in the bid, Harry decided to withdraw and the experiment was anyway cancelled soon after.

At this point Harry decided to put Border Radio back on the air. Test transmissions began, but almost immediately on 14 September 1986 the station suffered a massive raid. The DTI officials were reported to have caused serious damage to his home, including smashing the door down, as well as taking away several items not connected with the broadcasts and missing out items on their receipt. Not long after Harry Marshall was in hospital, suffering from a complaint thought to have been brought on by the raid. He did return with some further transmissions, but these are not believed to have continued for very long.

Hilltop Radio
The original zoo, 1982-1983

In 1982 Aleks Wright, Jim Trent and Phil Graham left Thameside Radio to start their own station, wanting to try out new programming ideas and play more of the new music that the younger Thameside members preferred. Hilltop Radio took to the air in June 1982 with regular Sunday night broadcasts on 90 FM, starting at 6pm and continuing for two or more hours.

Hilltop's programmes were different for not being based around a single DJ. As Aleks Wright explains, "members of the team would take it in turns to be the main DJ and choose the music but they would be supported by a 'zoo' where the presenter interacted with the others in the studio as well as using listener input from letters and phone calls. This was a conscious effort to be different from the other broadcasters, both pirate and commercial."[63]

The station was also different for wanting to include more women in its output. Even in 1982, Annie Nightingale was one of a very few women DJs on the radio and for most of the decade the women who did make it on air in music radio were to remain in secondary roles to male DJs as travel reporters or zoo format cast members. Hilltop ensured there was a female lead on at least one of its shows each week, with presenters including Chrissie Anderson and Mandy Wilkins.

Musically, Hilltop was oriented towards new wave and credible chart releases of the day, with favourites like the Clash, the Stranglers, Blondie and Squeeze, though it also found time for some classic rock cuts, a little punk and a weekly slot for comedy records. It also played demo tapes sent in by listeners, providing the

Hilltop Radio's Mandy Wilkins (right) and Gillian (left). Photo by Aleks Wright.

first radio exposure for Aztec Camera. Although broadcasting at a similar time to the more established Thameside, Hilltop would receive anywhere from ten to fifty letters a week. The two stations remained on good terms and Dave Birdman contributed many of the jingles.

Hilltop Radio closed in August 1983. Although their format meant that individual DJs had less pressure to be on the air each week, finding the time alongside their day jobs became an issue and there were additional concerns about the effects of prosecution at an important point in establishing their professional careers.

Horizon Radio
Soul music radio, 1981-1985

Horizon Radio first took to the airwaves on 11 October 1981 with Sunday evening broadcasts on 94.5 FM. If JFM had come on air as a more commercial version of Radio Invicta, Horizon founder Chris Stewart pushed things further, doing everything he could to make it the biggest, most successful soul music station in London. The DJs on Horizon all had club experience but most were new to radio and, like JFM, they paid £10 a week to get a show on the station.

Both Horizon and JFM closely tracked each other's moves. As hours expanded on one, so the other would follow; as JFM began live broadcasting, so did Horizon. When JFM began 24 hour operation Horizon was only just behind, launching its own service on 28 February 1984 from a high power transmitter on 102.5 FM just round the corner from JFM in Crystal Palace. At first they also simulcast on medium wave, but this was quickly dropped when it turned out few were listening.

The Horizon DJs

Musically there wasn't a huge difference between the two stations, though Horizon's sound was perhaps less wide-ranging. A few DJs appeared on both: Graham Gold, Tony Monson and the teenage Gilles Peterson – who pestered every station to try and get a show. Afternoon drivetime was the smooth CJ Carlos and there were also shows from Paul Buick, Nicky Lawrence, Lyndon T, Jude James (James Anthony), Bob Jones, Andy Bailey, Mark McCarthy, Gary Kent, Patrick Meads 'The Wing Commander' and Sammy Jay (Sammy Jacob, future founder of Q102 and Xfm). Horizon had its own gigs, but after seven-day broadcasts began was reportedly making more on ads, invoking the ire of Capital Radio when a couple of their advertisers began taking spots on the pirate.

With the new Telecoms Act looming, which closed the loophole that allowed the pirates to broadcast until a court ordered the seizure of their transmitter, Horizon began a big campaign for a legal soul station. Adverts going out in every break encouraged listeners to write to Home Office minister Douglas Hurd demanding that new stations like Horizon be licensed. While some stations closed down, Horizon decided to continue after the new law became effective on 15 July 1984.

Raid and prosecution

Transmissions came to an abrupt end on 11 October 1984 when Horizon's studio at Westow Hill was raided along with its transmitter site round the corner in Church Road. The DJ on the air at the time, CJ Carlos, was arrested, though later in court opinions differed from the RIS officers as to whether it was for causing a breach of the peace by not giving up his box of records or for not giving his name.

Legal arguments between Horizon's solicitors and the Department of Trade and Industry dragged on before finally coming to court on 6 January 1986, in a case heard by Richard Branson's father. Horizon tried to claim that they were a DJ training school called Horizon Productions and had no connection with illegal broadcasting. In court a string of DJs turned up to say they had taken lessons there and had never even seen a transmitter or noticed anything suspicious. Somehow the link transmitter had gone missing between being seized at the studio and the equipment arriving at the DTI, though Horizon's case perhaps wasn't helped when it was revealed that during the raid a neighbour came round to return the stereo encoder that had been thrown into the garden.

CJ Carlos and Chris Stewart were both found guilty of illegal broadcasting; CJ Carlos fined £500 with costs while Chris Stewart, having lost over twenty grand's worth of studio equipment, only had to pay costs – though at £1,000 these were high, reflecting the drawn-out discussions involved in settling the case. It was later reported that Chris Stewart was being sought by the police for failing to pay, though he did apparently pick up CJ Carlos' fine.

A brief return

The raid took Horizon off the air for three months. Quickly in its place came Solar Radio, with most of Horizon's DJs moving to the new station. There had been grumblings from some DJs over the perceived wealth that Chris Stewart had acquired from running the station and the lack of say that they had in its operation. Blues & Soul magazine said he had "reportedly made in the region of £60,000 for himself over the recent few months since the station began turning over healthy advertising revenue."[64] Chris later retorted: "Monson, Jackson, Peterson were in it for the money they thought they could make, I was in it for the music only ... I came out of it with very little."[65] When Horizon did return to the air in January 1985, back on 94.5 FM, it was with a largely new team and initially only broadcasting at weekends.

Following the announcement of the community radio licences, Horizon Radio went off air on 15 September 1985 with a final broadcast from a live event at Harrow Leisure Centre with over 3,000 people attending. They applied for the South London VHF community-of-interest licence under the name 'London Music and Community Radio', promising a mix of laid-back soul and some news and community features. After the experiment was scrapped they did not reapply for one of the incremental licences in 1989.

• • • • • • • • • • • • • • • •

Chris Stewart was a consultant for new black music station Fame FM, which took to the air shortly after Horizon's closure. He briefly returned to the airwaves at the end of 1986 with taped shows on TKO. In 1988 he was reported to be looking to launch a chain of soul stations on the Costa del Sol in Spain, but this didn't come to anything. In an article on his plans he complained "London pirate radio has gone to the gutter. Most of the stations try to be street cred with that obscure hip-hop, but they end up playing to the minority. There used to be healthy competition between the pirates, now there's just aggravation."[66]

London Music Radio
Youthful interactive radio, 1981-1983

Having helped out on site duties at Thameside Radio, in July 1981 teenager Chris Miles (Pyers Easton) began his own station. Broadcasting every Saturday night on 94.4 FM, London Music Radio found a mostly school-age audience and reflected their likes and interests with shows built around phone-ins and other audience interaction.

LONDON MUSIC RADIO
SATURDAYS FROM 8pm ON 94·4fm

Initially an output for his own two-hour taped shows, LMR soon expanded into live broadcasting and added other presenters. Former Radio AMY DJs Ricky Stevens and Christopher England joined and used their experience from that community station to devise new ways of involving listeners in the broadcasts. Ricky's show included requests over the recently-legalised CB radio while Chris-

Christopher England in the Euronet studio in 1992. Photo by Mike Kerslake.

topher's put listeners on the air live over the telephone and played material that they had sent in. There were also some live outside broadcasts, including one from Highbury Fields to celebrate their second birthday. More conventional DJs appearing on LMR included Steve Davies, Andy Allman, Steve Prince and Dave Robbins. It also had some rather strange guest shows from the Curly Man.

Early on LMR was more rock oriented, but as new DJs were added it moved towards credible pop, especially the emerging new romantics sound. Christopher England's show was notable for playing electro, which was very popular with teenagers but got little if any coverage on the soul music stations. His complaints about Horizon Radio's refusal to play it resulted in Horizon founder Chris Stewart devoting most of a show to slagging off Chris and the music. London Music Radio did attract some derision from media commentators who thought it should be using its listener involvement to address more serious issues (they also objected to its occasional puerility) but the station was beloved of its young audience, who were made to feel a real part of its broadcasts.

· · · · · · · · · · · · · · · · ·

Although he later presented guest shows on Alice's Restaurant and some of the other North East London pirates, Pyers Easton was subsequently more active in radio engineering. He worked for London Greek Radio and co-founded Kiss FM and in the eighties his company supplied many stations with transmitters. He then went completely legal, providing equipment and engineering services for many licensed operators. Christopher England went on to co-found early satellite radio broadcaster Euronet with Ricky Stevens and worked as studio manager for international shortwave and satellite programme distributor Merlin Network One.

Our Radio
Open access radio, 1982-1983

The second attempt at access radio on London's airwaves emerged from community radio group London Open Radio. Started by Australian Jim Beatson after he became disillusioned with the Community Communications (COMCOM) group of community radio activists, LOR began lobbying, assuming that the tactics that had already worked to get community radio on the air in Australia would also work in the UK. Like everyone else hoping for change in the radio system they were soon proved wrong. Given a gift of £2,000 by a donor, its members decided to take more practical steps. With some of the people involved in a small anarchist pirate from Tottenham called Radio Active, they formed Our Radio and in February 1982 the first regular broadcast went out.

The station's Wednesday evening programmes were put together on tape by several sub-groups and they also appealed for contributions from listeners, though with little success. Their schedule included Radio Solidarity, with news for London's Polish community; Women on the Waves, produced by Islington feminist group Women in the City; Gaywaves, made by Phil Cox with news and information covering the more political side of London's gay scene; The Message, with news and rants from a Brixton-based anarchist group; Utapia, playing alternative music and The BAG, which was cut-up / scratch radio on a different theme each week. Our Radio's 103.8 FM transmitters were also shared for a time with DBC and Radio Zodiac.

Our Radio's broadcasts were not especially successful in finding an audience. According to Richard Barbrook, who contributed to The Message, "We broadcast for about a year and got almost no response whatsoever – about ten letters! ... The lesson of Our Radio is that it had no roots beyond its membership. It was comprised of people with a particular political line who were politically naive, unpragmatic and with no contacts outside the group. We didn't have any roots in the community and weren't plugged into any existing organisation."[67]

The anarchists, who had responsibility for getting the station on the air each week, felt Our Radio's main problem was in overcoming the lack of a ready-made audience for their kind of programming: pirates putting out music had a much easier job. They believed that given enough time and with greater financial resources they would have found some success. They took exception to Richard's conclusion becoming the authoritative version, describing him as someone that "had no interest at all in the station except to lobby the GLC to give him a fat grant (in fact he never risked his nice neck or gave us a penny when we were busted)"[68]

The first raid on Our Radio happened in December 1982, when one person was caught and subsequently fined £80. Returning in February they were then targeted on every broadcast. The final broadcast went out on 23 March 1983. Spotting the arrival of investigators and police, they escaped with the equipment to a squatted flat where they had hidden before, only for their pursuers to turn up with a search warrant and bust them. In a later court appearance Our Radio was described as an "anarchist, terrorist, homosexual radio station." There were plans to get back on the air but with no money for new transmitters, and disagreements between some of the groups since it had gone off air, this never happened.

• • • • • • • • • • • • • • • •

The anarchist group went on to publish two guides to pirate broadcasting, including Radio Is My Bomb. They were later involved in Radio Interference and Radio Wapping.

Phoenix Radio
Alice's Restaurant's flip side, 1981-1985

The first Phoenix Radio was a medium wave station, broadcasting a progressive and alternative rock service on 214m to a local area on the borders of East London and Essex in 1979. Despite founders Dave Lane, Brian Marshall, Dave Collins and Steve Justin still being at school or college, they managed regular Sunday broadcasts before closing in September 1980. Steve Justin continued on AM with Radio Comsat, while the rest of the team began preparations for a new VHF station, Alice's Restaurant. When it became clear that Alice's broad rock format wasn't working, the station split in two, with Phoenix Radio being appropriately reborn as the new alternative music service and launching on 2 January 1982 on 90.2 FM.

The first transmissions were for only two hours on a Saturday night, from 9pm to 11pm when Alice's Restaurant would take over. Gradually these expanded, first moving the start to 7pm and then in the summer of 1983 to 5pm. Taped shows gave way to live broadcasts using a UHF link from its studio to the transmitter on top of an East London tower block, switching over at 11 to Alice's separate studio. With Alice's Restaurant shows continuing until three or

PHOENIX RADIO

90·2 FM

SATURDAY EVENING'S

four in the morning it wasn't really feasible to use the same studio for both stations and this also helped station security.

Alternative sounds

Initial DJs Brian Marshall (Lawrie Hallett) and Lee Cooper were soon joined by John Scott (Graham King), who became a familiar voice on the dial opening the station each week with its distinctive chimes. Its first female DJ, Gill Black, joined at the end of 1982 followed by Mark Welsh, who played the noisier side, delving into early industrial music as well as post-punk.

Phoenix's music policy covered a broad range of non-mainstream music styles. John Scott notes "As far as I can recall, for the majority of our time on air I do not recall any other station across London with the output we had and that gave us a very distinctive edge over the more 'standard' pirates. 'Alternative' did not mean playing the likes of the Jam, Siouxsie and the Banshees, Clash, Buzzcocks, Cure, etc. as the core of the output. Whilst they featured, we were overall more interested in the flip side to the major label offerings. Where else would you have been likely to hear bands such as Ellery Bop, Fatal Microbes, Inflatable Boy Clams, The Last Chant, Nightingales, Out On Blue Six or Restricted Code mixed in with bits of dub plates, jazz, industrial, African, etc – as an example from an old set of playlists? Where else would you have heard fanzines being reviewed, demo tapes being played, indie label bosses doing shows and interviews? We made a point of fitting in things sent in or supplied by bands and labels which helped vary the output."[69]

Guest presenters included Rough Trade's Scott Piering, Robert Wyatt and The Monochrome Set. Although Phoenix didn't come across as quite so well connected or sure of themselves as Radio Zodiac, you couldn't fault the presenters for their passion for music. As well as T-shirts, the station helped fund itself by selling concert bootlegs from several independent bands.

One last shot

Phoenix Radio left the air in the winter of 1984 when Brian Marshall went to Italy to work on English-language station Radio Nova. Like Alice's Restaurant, Phoenix returned in September of 1985, but as a separate operation and on a different frequency, 90.9 FM, with taped broadcasts. Several new DJs joined, including Nick & Tips and Bruce B, as well as shows from previous occasional presenter Sue Scott (no relation to John). These transmissions only continued until 1 December, when they were raided by the DTI. Phoenix Radio did not subsequently return to the airwaves.

Radio Zodiac
Alternative radio for alternative people, 1981-1983

Zodiac began as a Sussex-based short-wave pirate station in 1978, with DJs including Roger Vosene (Mark Dezzani), John Dawson, Stuart Clark, Steve Anderson and Kevin Turner. In 1981 Roger Vosene moved to London and relaunched the station on VHF, broadcasting from 3pm on Sundays on 94.4 FM.

The new Zodiac continued the mix of music and speech, fitting into the new wave DIY ethic of the time. Musicians were often brought into the Kentish Town studio – Green Gartside from Scritti Politti was a regular. Zodiac was also a founder member of the Free The Airwaves campaign, pushing for radio from ordinary people. Roger Vosene considers as his highlights from the station "a joint broadcast from the Notting Hill Carnival (1982) with Dread Broadcasting and a benefit concert (Stonehenge Festival & Free The Airwaves) from the squatted Zig Zag Club in Paddington, broadcast live. Amongst the artists performing were Misty in Roots, Nick Turner's Inner City Unit & Amazulu."[70]

Regular listings, put together for a time by Phoenix Radio's Brian Marshall, covered gigs, independent cinema, protest meetings and other events in London. Musically the bedrock was new wave, but Zodiac also carried shows featuring roots reggae, African beat, fifties rock 'n' roll and more. DJs on the station included Mike Standing, Papa Festus and Vince Cent. Sponsors of the station included Better Badges, City Limits, Alternative Tentacles and Rough Trade.

Zodiac left the air in 1983.

• • • • • • • • • • • • • • • •

Roger Vosene went on to work on Radio Nova and Riviera Radio, high-power, cross-border stations aimed at English speakers in Southern France and Northern Italy.

Radio Alison
Broadcasting in 1982.

Radio Aquarius
Run by Mark Mason who was also involved
with South London Radio and later London
Weekend Radio. In 1982 Aquarius broadcast
on 92.5 for three hours on a Monday night
with DJs also including Rob Andrews and
John Dawson. Music tended towards alternative rock.

Radio Atlantis
Atlantis broadcast in the Medway area, originally on 235m medium wave but following a
raid when it lost all its equipment it switched
to 96.3 FM. Atlantis DJs also appeared on
several North East London stations. These
included Steve Davies, Ray Magnum, Graham
Archer and Christopher England. Atlantis
had a pop and rock format and closed in
1981, although there were occasional holiday
broadcasts later.

County Radio
After the closure of London FM, Mark Ellis
and former Radio Jackie staff including Jerry
James and Dave Small returned with a new
station in 1981. Following its close, Mark
went on to launch Skyline Radio with fellow
County Radio presenter Steve Fox. County
Radio broadcast a mix of top forty and album
tracks on Sunday afternoons on 94.2 FM.

Crystal Set
Broadcasting on Sundays from 2-6pm on
90.2 FM with music and community features.
Launched in 1981, the station later moved to
102.8 FM.

DDP Radio
An earlier station from the team that went
on to start Surrey Sounds. It broadcast taped
shows on 90.5 FM in 1981.

Radio Dog Biscuit
Broadcasting in 1981 to South West London
on 92.5 FM every Friday night from 9pm-
12am.

Flashback Radio
Broadcasting mostly on public holidays to
North West London, Flashback Radio made
regular appearances throughout the early
eighties with a dance music format. Presenters included Gary Steele, Rob Richards and
Paul M. The first transmission went out on
August Bank Holiday 1981 and they continued until 1987, with occasional periods of
weekly broadcasts.

Forestside Radio
A pop station from Phil Thomas, broadcasting
from North East London between 1981 and
1982 mostly on holidays. Presenters included
members of Alice's Restaurant, Radio Atlantis
and London Music Radio. After a raid in 1982,
resulting in Phil's prosecution, the station did
not subsequently return.

Gamma Radio
A rock station broadcasting on VHF to South
East London in 1981.

Radio Gemini
A low-power station broadcasting in South
West London on and off from 1981 until 1987.
Gemini saw itself as a family station and
played a wide variety of pop music along with
carrying local information for its area.

Liberation Radio
Broadcasting on Tuesday nights in 1982 with
a mix of different music styles on 92.6 FM to
the Middlesex area.

London FM
Following the close of Bromley Sound, Mark
Ellis went on to launch London FM in March
1981. The station lasted only a few months.

London Sound

A soft rock service to South London on 92.5 FM in 1981.

Radio Orion

Started by some of those involved in Celebration Radio, Orion broadcast a hard rock service from the North London / South Herts borders on 90.2 FM. Launched in May 1981, Orion continued operating until late 1982 – although according to the station "it never closed, it just sort of faded away". Presenters included Captain Airwave, John Richard, Malcolm Rutherford and George Squire.

ORION
Every Sunday 90·2 FM.
Rock To London.

Radio Polestar

Broadcasting in 1981 on 93.1 FM on Wednesday evenings with a rock format.

Santa Sounds

A one-off station in Christmas 1981 by some of the Radio Floss team on 222m medium wave. Presenter Paul James and engineer Ian Stewart were to join Thameside not long after.

South Bucks Radio

SBR was a regular broadcaster in the area during the early eighties. It made a return in October 1986 on 90 FM but the transmitter was stolen the first week. Presenters included Dave Stewart, Radio Alpha's Ian Hutchinson and – most unusually for a station from that part of the world – Tim Allen.

South West Radio

Heard with test transmissions on 103.8 in the spring of 1982.

Radio Suburbia

After initial holiday broadcasts on 90.5 FM during 1981, Radio Suburbia began regular transmissions that summer from a tower block in Kingston. DJs included Gerry Sinclair, Brian Tharg and Martin Lewis playing mostly commercial rock, although there was some soul early on. Broadcasts went out on Saturday nights, initially on tape but later live and in stereo. Suburbia was off the air for much of 1982, reappearing in the autumn and then moving to a new 91.9 frequency at the start of 1983. It is believed to have closed that summer.

90·5 mHz VHF | Radio Suburbia Saturdays, 7.30 pm until 1 am

Surrey Sounds

Surrey Sounds began broadcasts in September of 1982 operating on 90 FM from Epsom Downs forest. The station had a permanent aerial attached to the top of a 28ft tree to which they would connect for the weekly broadcasts. Presenters included Rob James, Steve Day, Roger Hall and Martin Hill. It closed in March 1983 following a raid which resulted in two members being prosecuted.

Radio Utopia

Broadcasting in 1982 on 1520 AM on Sundays from 2-6pm with rock music.

Uxbridge FM

A small pop station operating daytimes on Sundays in 1981 on 90.2 FM to North West London.

Westway Radio

A rock service for West London in 1981 from 10pm to midnight every Friday on 104.2 FM.

1983

Small business radio and seven-day broadcasting

1983 was the year that pirate radio in London ceased being just a hobby and turned into a business.

It had become apparent to a number of those involved in breaking the radio laws that the 1949 Wireless Telegraphy Act was a flawed piece of legislation designed for a different time. This was also it seems apparent to the Radio Interference Service, although they tried to hide it. Most of the illegal broadcasters they met did not have sufficient knowledge of the law so the RIS investigators were able to bluster their way through and seize any transmitters they came across. In fact, the officers did not have the right to do this: only a court could order their confiscation.

At Christmas 1982 Radio Jackie began its usual 24-hour live holiday broadcasts, safe in the knowledge that they were unlikely to be busted at this time. These went down exceptionally well with listeners so they just continued broadcasting. Shortly after they were raided and – despite protestations – the transmitter was seized. Engineer Tony Collis and Dave Owen went to Wandsworth Police Station to protest. Successfully arguing that the law was on his side the equipment was returned and Jackie went back on the air.

The Jackie team realised they had a now or never chance to take the station to the next level and become a proper, full-time broadcaster. Tony Collis offered to put in the money that was needed to enable it to do so but on condition that he was sole owner of the new business. The rest of the team accepted, enabling Jackie to enter a new phase of its life. At first the raids continued, but each time the investigators turned up they were refused permission to take the transmitter, given the name of a different owner and by the time of the subsequent court appearance a new transmitter was already in place before the old one was handed over for confiscation in court. In fact the law didn't even require the operators of an unlicensed station to identify themselves: they had to allow investigators to inspect the equipment but that was all. Jackie's service continued uninterrupted and the authorities soon realised they couldn't win.

Almost alone among unlicensed broadcasters, Jackie sought to cultivate links to politicians that might be able to help with its cause. These connections were facilitated by station organiser Peter Stremes (who used the on-air name Pete Rivers), a former chairman of the Scottish Federation of Conservative Students. It helped that the concept for Jackie very much fitted in with the Thatcherite entrepreneurial ethos of the time, enabling it to be sold to Tory MPs as 'small business radio'. Supporters of unrestricted free enterprise in the Conservative Party saw the concept of the station as something to be supported against the old-fashioned monopolies of the BBC and IBA. Angela Rumbold, Jackie's local MP and a cabinet minister, held a number of meetings with Tony Collis and even appeared on the station. She in turn was able to get the ear of Norman Tebbit, the minister in charge of the Department of Trade and Industry.

These activities helped play their part in Radio Jackie being left alone by the RIS for over eighteen months of non-stop broadcasting. Peter Stremes explained "We feel the Home Office see us as a sensible and responsible working example of commercial community radio. Perhaps they will tolerate us in order to modify the current state of the broadcasting system"[71] In a raid on Radio Shoestring in January 1985, Christopher England was told by RIS officer Eric Gotts that during this time Jackie was treated as "phase one of the community radio experiment"[72].

Radio Sovereign was next to exploit the loophole, beginning transmissions of its 24/7 oldies service for South West London in May and with a professionalism that forced neighbouring Jackie to up their game. Programme controller Crispian St John (Howard Rose) was determined not to give detractors any ammunition: "The whole operation has to be open and above board in order to make it credible in our opinion. From the moment we began broadcasting we were in touch with the different bodies like the PRS [Performing Rights Society] and we have made it very clear to them we want to pay. We follow the IBA rules on advertising and codes of practice. We follow the normal broadcast rules on news and current affairs, balance and so on. We have to be a responsible outfit. I wouldn't be involved in a station that wasn't."[73]

Other pirates were at first confused by the medium wave stations' ability to stay on the air, especially as their own tower block transmitters were still being regularly taken away. Some thought Jackie and Sovereign had made a secret deal with the authorities, others that it was something special to do a ban by Customs & Excise on VHF transmitters. Asked about why they didn't broadcast like Jackie, JFM's Brian Anthony told one reporter "Unlike medium wave we can't claim the equipment back or say look you're not taking it, it belongs to us, because they'd just whizz us away as well." [74]

By now JFM and Horizon were London's two leading soul stations, on the air all weekend if they were lucky. Invicta had got by for years on ads for 'Hollywood

Curl' hair products and money raised from their own small-time club nights. In contrast, JFM's Brian Anthony and Horizon's Chris Stewart wanted their stations to be serious businesses. DJs on both paid a weekly subscription that covered the basic costs of replacing seized transmitters, in return for which they got to plug their own residencies. As competition intensified, the two stations became more aggressive in ad sales and in promoting their own station-branded events, financing their further expansion.

In September Skyline Radio took to the air with a similar service to Jackie but for South East London and on both medium wave and VHF. Skyline continued sowing confusion among other pirates by carrying messages about the VHF transmissions being a 'testing and developing' service, hoping to avoid a rush of other full-time operators onto the airwaves. The soul stations now desperately wanted a piece of that pie. Skyline co-founder Steve Fox revealed "I had Brian Anthony of JFM offer me five grand if I would tell him how to get around the 'Customs Law' and Chris Stewart sent a couple of his henchmen round to inform me that if I did not spill the beans then my personal safety could not be guaranteed." [75]

The move to all-weekend or seven-day broadcasting hit the part-time operations hard. For the first time since the sixties, frequencies in the UK were a commodity with a value attached to them – and those in possession of the best ones were prepared to use force to keep hold of them. One station owner even drove around with a loaded shotgun in the back of his car, threatening more than one operator that attempted to broadcast near what was now 'his' channel. The fight over scarce frequencies signalled an end to the era of friendly rivalry and cooperation between stations.

Radio for London's ethnic minorities

Although black music was now making its mark on the illegal airwaves, it took until 1983 for unlicensed radio stations targeting specific ethnic minorities to become widespread. While BBC Radio London had mostly speech-based evening programmes for the larger ethnic groups in London, the commercial stations remained uninterested. Capital Radio was especially dismissive about carrying minority programming, its Deputy Managing Director Brian Morgan complaining "London is so many minorities. If we decided to have reggae on Monday, gay programming on Tuesday, and another minority on Wednesday, first of all it would alienate all the listeners other than those that are particularly interested in that activity. It would also mean that they themselves would get very little airtime because their turn would come up perhaps once a month, once every two months. And I don't think that is really the best way of providing a service."[76]

One of the groups left without a voice were London's Greek Cypriots. There had been immigration from Cyprus since it had been annexed by Britain in 1914, with further waves of migrants, settling mostly in the borough of Camden, as a result of the unstable situation on the island which culminated in the Turkish invasion of 1974. Amongst those who had come to the UK was George Power (Akis Eracleos), who had risen to be an influential DJ on the soul scene and had then been

London Greek Radio in 1984.

pulled into pirate radio like many DJs. His first attempt at his own operation, City Sound Radio, was not a success against the established soul operators so instead he concentrated on building a station for a different community: London Greek Radio.

With a template now set for how an ethnic pirate should operate, others soon came onto the airwaves. While the Greek Cypriot community was only around 150,000 in number, it spawned unlicensed stations far beyond its size. In part this was because many Cypriots in London came from a tradition of small business ownership and in part it was due to the political positions taken by some broadcasters. Unsurprisingly, the Greeks were followed by Turkish Cypriot stations, with three rival brothers starting their own separate services in the spring of 1984.

Those in London's large South Asian community were also quick to join the airwaves. Hansmukh Patel, who ran a newsagent's shop in the Holloway Road, started Asian People's Radio at the end of 1983. As the shop closed down in the evening, APR would begin broadcasts. Unlike later Asian broadcasters, presenters on APR mostly spoke English and the music was chosen to be accessible to a wide range of ages. It also carried a daily news update focussing on events in the Indian sub-continent.

The Southall area, with the largest Indian community in London, was where in 1984 Avtar Lit founded Sina Radio, the forerunner of the legal Sunrise Radio. Sina targeted an older audience with programmes in Punjabi and Hindi and included a daily talk show as well as music programmes. Sina was highly commercial and was very successful in finding local advertisers and promoting its own events with local and touring musicians. Surprisingly it attracted few rivals in its area: Sangam Radio, which began broadcasting in 1987, was the only notable one. In 1987 listeners in the East End could receive Asian Community Radio, which focussed more on the bhangra and Indian disco that younger Asians preferred.

The late eighties saw specialist stations for London's Arabic and Irish communities, but these were less successful in consistently staying on air. Many found it hard to find a space to broadcast and were either swamped by other unlicensed operators or subject to heavy raids for coming too close to legal broadcasters. With most of the smaller stations for ethnic minorities broadcasting only in their native languages and not having much contact with other operators, their histories unfortunately remain largely hidden.

The decline of rock radio

If ethnic broadcasting was on the rise, the traditional rock music that had been a cornerstone of much of pirate broadcasting in its earlier history was now disappearing from the airwaves. Through the early eighties rock was becoming increasingly marginalised in punk's wake: fans had to be content with the two-hour Friday Rock Show presented by Tommy Vance on Radio One while Capital Radio scaled back its nightly Your Mother Wouldn't Like It with Nicky Horne before eventually replacing it with a weekly show from Alan Freeman that was more oriented to classic rock than new releases. When complaints flooded in after Radio One's axe moved on to its alternative rock shows, it responded "It's impossible to play all the new records and some of them are frankly awful anyway."[77]

London at this time still had a big traditional rock scene that was not being represented on the airwaves, from the bands that were part of the tougher, punk-influenced New Wave of British Heavy Metal to the New Progressives reinventing artrock for a younger generation. Supposedly-vanquished rock dinosaurs like Genesis and Pink Floyd were also still shifting massive amounts of albums and selling out huge stadiums.

After its pop presenters departed to form South London Radio in 1981, the longer-established Radio Free London became solidly rock. Alice's Restaurant, the elder brother to the alternative Phoenix Radio, had the widest coverage across London's rock scene and its newer bands and releases. On medium wave there were Radio Amanda, Radio Floss and Radio Andromeda, a station notable for exhuming forgotten music from rock's seventies heyday. On VHF there were Radio Alpha, Radio Orion, London Rock and Imagine. The majority of these came out of North London' suburbs, though there were spinoffs from South East London's RFL and a few others popped up on the Kent borders.

By the mid-eighties, however, rock in all its forms was disappearing from the pirate airwaves. Alice's Restaurant closed its doors and although Radio Free London would regularly return for a season of broadcasting, the gaps off air grew longer and it increasingly favoured classic cuts over new releases. RFM looked like it could be a contender, but a division in the station resulted in two diminished operations that could have done better if they'd stayed together.

There are a number of reasons for rock radio's lack of success from this period. Many of the generation who had run the earlier rock stations had moved on with their lives while those who had stayed in pirate radio were instead doing engineering for the stations with the money – Alice's Restaurant's engineers were later keeping Kiss and Solar on air. Meanwhile, for a younger urban generation rock music was out of favour, with that age group more likely to share the musical tastes of their black peers at school or college.

Both the suburban soul and the urban reggae scenes were largely excluded from the mainstream record business in the UK, which had forced them to develop their own self-sufficient ecosystems into which pirate radio later become a significant component. Rock, though, was the bread

RFM's Claire up on the roof in 1987. Photo courtesy of Dave Fuller and Claire Mansfield.

and butter of the music industry and unlike those scenes it had ample promotional opportunities without the pirates. There were two smaller rock scenes outside the mainstream, a younger independent heavy metal scene and an older one based around biker rallies and pubs, but these had insufficient clout to properly support the pirates.

Clubs and bars were the single most important part of funding for the black music stations, but their counterparts on the rock scene were on the retreat. Alice's Restaurant and RFL had both earlier run successful weekly gigs that helped fund their operations but, as the mid-eighties financial boom took hold, commercial rents were rising and it was no longer a viable proposition for many venues to put on live rock bands for a clientele of denim-clad, pint-downing punters. There was much more money to be made on cocktails and food. By the late eighties London was down to not much more than a dozen traditional rock pubs.

Rock consequently became a minority music on the pirate airwaves. With frequencies increasingly scarce, stations needed to maintain a seven-day presence if they wanted to retain their channels, and that was beyond the resources of the remaining rock stations. Even if they could find a slot, the increasing clashes between stations over frequencies and the growing transmitter thefts made many think twice about continuing. A few instead returned to the medium or short wave, where the environment was closer to the old days.

Despite this, there remained a big demand for rock music that wasn't being satisfied. In 1989 one applicant for an incremental radio licence commissioned research that showed rock was the music most Londoners would like to hear and that London's rock fans were now the most dissatisfied with their radio. The following year Xfm's pirate forerunner Q102 tapped into the younger rock audience, riding the indie resurgence in the wake of the Madchester generation of bands mixing guitars and dance beats.

In answer to a question in the House of Commons it was revealed that in 1983 there had been 97 raids across the country and 42 convictions. The House was told "We intend to continue to give action against pirate radio stations a high degree of priority." [78]

On The Air
··

Asian People's Radio
Britain's first Asian radio station, 1983-1986

Asian People's Radio was the UK's first South Asian community station. It took to the air at the end of 1983 on 90.8 FM playing a broad range of Indian music with English-language presenters. The station operated from above Hansmukh Patel's newsagents in North London's Holloway Road. Transmissions were evenings only and primarily music-based. From 1985 its broadcasts included a nightly news roundup compiled and presented by Roger Ross, who went on to run News Music Radio.

Unfortunately APR's transmissions attracted a lot of attention from the authorities, leading to several raids in the autumn of 1984 as action against pirates was ramped up following the introduction of new laws. At Easter 1985 the station's main DJ, Vijay Patel, was fined £1,000 for unlicensed broadcasting at Highbury Magistrates Court and then lost a subsequent appeal. In the weeks running up to the court case APR had lost seven transmitters and six sets of studio equipment.

Asian People's Radio closed down around this time to apply for a community radio licence. Following the axing of the experiment it returned briefly in September 1986, though transmissions did not last long.

Breakfast Pirate Radio
Pushing at the limits of taste, 1983

Comic actor Keith Allen's radio station first came to the public's attention in the June 1983 edition of The Face magazine. Transmissions were announced for every other Sunday between 10am and 1pm on 235m medium wave. Keith had previously got funding from a record company for a tape project, but when they heard the actual tapes they decided to pass. Having met DBC's Lepke while moderating a studio discussion on pirate radio for Channel 4 youth programme 'Whatever You Want', Keith persuaded Lepke to let him use DBC's transmitter.

Opinions differ on how many broadcasts went out – somewhere from one ("from a church in Islington I believe using the spire as aerial while the Sunday service was going on"[79]) to seven (using helium-filled balloons over Notting Hill according to Keith). Programmes were an envelope-pushing mix of comic characters like Jerry Arkwright 'northern industrial gay' and rasta Boots Sex Dread, malicious celebrity gossip, radio outtakes and the names of supposedly bent coppers: "We wanted to be the station which, if it was all legalised tomorrow, there was no way they could legalise us."[80]

Also performing were David Rappaport, Robbie Coltrane and Keith's then partner Alison Owen, the station's "token feminist and roving reporter". The material that was used was later turned into a set of tapes sold mainly through independent record shops and mail order.

The cover of one of the BPR recordings.

City Sound Radio
What could have been Kiss FM, 1983-1985

City Sound Radio began life in 1983, broadcasting on Monday nights from 8pm-12am on 92 FM. The station was almost a prototype Kiss FM, founded by George Power with Gordon Mac and engineer Nigel Grant. George and Gordon both worked at Kisses nightspot in Peckham while George and Nigel had met at Radio Invicta, where George had guested and Nigel had done the odd show and helped out as a member of the site crew. Transmissions only lasted a few weeks – presumably until their first raid – after which Nigel Grant was back playing rock on Radio Free London and George Power went on to launch London Greek Radio.

Nigel Grant relaunched City Sound in 1985, broadcasting from 12pm to 12am every Sunday on 90.8 FM with DJs including Debbie Gopie, but again the station did not last long.

Radio Gemma
Pop and rock for North West London, 1983-1990

Operating in North West London, Gemma began broadcasting all day Sunday on FM in the summer of 1983. Programmes were on tape and covered a range of different styles from pop to soul to reggae to heavy metal. In early '84 they vanished from the airwaves after a raid before making a comeback in the autumn of 1985. For most of their life, transmissions came from a site at Barn Hill in Wembley previously used by Radio Floss and although only using only ten watts still got out well. After the close of Three Boroughs Radio in June 1986 several of that station's DJs joined and broadcasts were extended from four hours to most of the daytime.

Presenters during the later broadcasts included Bob Williams, Phil Raven, John Silver, Tim Allen and founder Stuart Price. The final broadcast of this incarnation went out on 17 August 1986, with the pop DJs going on to relaunch Radio Duck the same day. After Duck closed, Gemma returned in February 1988, though transmissions are only believed to have continued for a few weeks. It returned again at Christmas 1990 but the broadcast was cut short after interference problems with another station, one of whose members was spotted near their transmitter site. On their subsequent New Year's Eve broadcast the transmitter was found smashed up.

Radio Jackie
The Sound of South West London, 1969-1985

The year of 1983 marked a major change at Radio Jackie as – more confident of the limits of the powers that the authorities could currently wield – they embarked on 24-hour broadcasting.

After the success of non-stop Christmas and New Year programmes, Jackie decided to remain on the air. Hit by a raid soon after, they successfully argued that their transmitters could not be seized without the order of a court, and resumed transmissions. Seizing the opportunity that the loopholes in the law offered, the members of the station agreed a plan for Radio Jackie to become a proper business. Having the finance available to facilitate this new phase in its development, engineer Tony Collis became the owner and managing director of the station while Dave Owen returned from a job in Independent Local Radio and became programme controller. One of the listeners offered them a

short-term lease on a flat in Worcester Park for the studio and a more professional transmitter and aerial system was installed at Dave's mum's house in Sutton.

Now Radio Jackie was a proper business. It was registered as a limited company and its employees were enrolled for PAYE. They began approaching local businesses with attractive – and cheap – advertising packages, and gradually built up a regular clientele who loved the new business it brought them. By the spring of 1984 it was offering packages of 13 ads every day for a week for £225. There was even a Radio Jackie shop where you could buy station merchandise and submit requests to be played on air. Before long they had outgrown the flat housing the studio and moved to bigger premises at 32A Central Road in Worcester Park. Here there was space for an on-air studio, news studio, production studio and a small office.

Weekdays at this time saw Mark Lawrence doing the breakfast show, followed by Ron Brown, Rob Randall, Dave Owen with drivetime and in the evening Geoff Rogers. Specialist shows included big band music every Friday night, Bob Halfin's Memory Lane with music from the thirties to the fifties every Saturday night, oldies with Mike Knight every Sunday afternoon and Les Adams' remix show on Sunday nights. A young Dave Pearce and Paul McKenna also passed through the station.

Campaigns and criticism

A formal campaign was begun for a local licence, with a petition signed by over 55,000 people and support from local councillors and MPs. Extensive charity work, raising thousands of pounds for local charities helped raise Jackie's profile in the community. However, the station was not without its critics too. Jackie's programmes at this time were largely – and intentionally – replicating what Independent Local Radio did elsewhere. Daytime shows played safe, mainstream music while its local coverage was heavily reliant on existing media, particularly the local press. In a letter to the Evening Standard, Radio AMY's Christopher England criticised the station for its lack of ambition in not opening up programmes to the wider community. There was also a veiled criticism from Douglas Hurd MP, who had responsibility for radio at the Home Office: "Some pirates aren't doing anything new at all. They're simply doing something on a smaller scale and hoping to get away with it without contributing anything particularly."[81]

There were also complaints from the Independent stations, first from Capital Radio and then newcomer Radio Mercury, whose boss John Aumonier issued a High Court injunction against Tony Collis alleging Radio Jackie was stealing listeners and advertising from the Sussex-based station. For six weeks Tony hid out to make it impossible for the injunction to be served on him while the legal ownership of the station was transferred to Robin King, brother of Radio Kaleidoscope founder Colin King, who lived in the Netherlands. Although this enabled Jackie to continue broadcasting, Aumonier's pressure on the authorities began to cause Jackie major problems.

The big raid

After the introduction of the 1984 Telecoms Act, Radio Jackie seems to have known it was living on borrowed time. Raids were predicted after the new laws came in, but they didn't happen. Then at the end of January 1985 Jackie were given a tip-off that the big one was about to happen. On Friday 1 February the new Radio Investigation Service launched separate raids on Radio Jackie's offices and transmitter site. They broke down the doors and stripped the studios of every last piece of equipment and all the paperwork that was needed to prove individuals' involvement in the station.

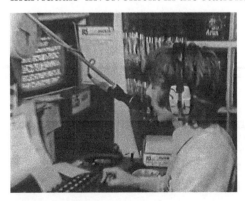 

Left: Dave Owen in the first 24-hour studio. Right: Radio Jackie's second offices and studio.

Concluding that they could not continue operating in the way they had before – and that if they didn't then it would not be Radio Jackie – the station decided to close down. They came back on the air using makeshift equipment and prepared for a final farewell on Monday 4 February 1985. Hundreds of listeners turned up outside their offices to say goodbye, with programmes also going out on a VHF transmitter from the same location to ensure they could not be taken off. Even then the DTI couldn't resist raiding the medium wave transmitter site in the last minutes of the broadcast.

Later in 1985 twelve members of staff were successfully prosecuted for offences connected with the running of Radio Jackie and fined a total of over £5,000. Programme controller Dave Owen (David Wright) was fined the largest sum, £850, with lesser fines for DJs including Les Adams, Rob Randall, Bob Matthews, Mark Lawrence and Ron Brown. The prosecution asked for £4,000 costs, including flying in investigators from Manchester.

. . . .

Members of Radio Jackie continued campaigning for a licence. When in 1996 the Radio Authority finally advertised one for South West London they applied, only to be beaten by Thames Radio. When Thames ran into financial difficulties Jackie bought the debt-ridden station for £1. It returned as Radio Jackie in October 2003, restoring full live broadcasting and local news bulletins and bringing many of the original Radio Jackie team back on air.

London Greek Radio
The original Greek Cypriot broadcasters, 1983-1988

On 8 October 1983 George Power and Chris Harmanda launched London Greek Radio, the first station in London broadcasting solely to one of the capital's ethnic minorities.

George Power and Crackers

Although not widely known outside his circle, George Power is a pivotal figure in London's underground club and radio history. Described by Jazzy B as "quite hard and a little bit militant, but very cutting edge",[82] he first came to notice in 1976 when he replaced Mark Roman as the main DJ at Crackers in Soho. Cited by later London soul DJs as one of the seminal clubs of the time, Crackers played a less commercial sound than the Soul Mafia and to a blacker, gayer clientele. In the mid-eighties George was at Kisses Nightspot in Peckham with future Kiss FM co-founders Gordon Mac and Tosca and then Camden's Electric Ballroom with Paul 'Trouble' Anderson as warm-up and Gilles Peterson in the jazz room.

George was invited to do the occasional show on Radio Invicta, but didn't get on the air regularly until founding City Sound Radio in 1983. Although it didn't last long and made little impact on the big soul broadcasters, coming from Greek Cypriot parentage George spotted a gap in the radio market for a station that targeted the Greek population of North London.

LGR launches

London Greek Radio's early broadcasts were not always easy because, claims Chris Harmanda, "The English pirates wouldn't tell us how they got away with it, so we had to find out for ourselves."[83] Having brought in engineer Pyers Easton they moved onto a more stable technical footing. LGR quickly found an appreciative audience and was followed not long after by a flood of competitors.

With the introduction of the 1984 Telecommunications Act, the station shut down in the belief that broadcasting would now be impossible. A protest meeting

One of LGR's less-salubrious later studios in 1986. Photo by Pyers Easton.

in support of LGR's legalisation was held at Camden's Electric Ballroom, with over 2,000 people attending and double the number unable to get in, necessitating a second meeting the week after. A petition garnered 50,000 signatures and they received support from the Cyprus High Commissioner and the Greek Ambassador, but to no avail: the Home Office responded that "It would be a backward step and unfair to the legal stations if we were to start licensing pirate radio."[84] Following the lead of other stations, LGR returned to the air a few months later, replacing its previous £15,000 studio with rather cheaper equipment. It left the air again in the autumn of 1985 to apply for a licence under the community radio experiment, during which time George Power co-founded Kiss FM. LGR returned to the air in the spring when it became apparent that it was not going to win a licence.

Programmes on LGR were predominantly Greek music, interspersed with ads for local businesses and community information. However, there were also some cultural programmes, a daily news report from Cyprus and every Sunday morning they carried a church service. LGR was extremely successful in attracting advertisers to the station, charging £60 for a 45 second advert running twice a day for a week. By 1987 it estimated its running costs at £4,000 per week. According to the station, 85% of all Greek Cypriots in the London area tuned in each week.

The raids get heavy

After the laws changed in 1984, action by the authorities against London Greek Radio began to get more intense. It often seemed to be targeted more heavily than other stations, although the reason is not clear. Rival Voice of the Immigrants claimed unlike them LGR was not politically neutral. LGR denied this, with spokesman Dr Zannetos Tofallis responding that the authorities "told us that they have been watching us and have established that we are not political extremists. Their only objection is that we are unlicensed."[85]

For a long time the station broadcast from the roof of a Greek delicatessen in Muswell Hill. In early 1985 a group of RIS officials backed by twenty police took down LGR's aerial mast and in May 1986 the RIS turned up with a massive crane to take them off air. The owner of the shop was successfully prosecuted for illegal broadcasting that August and was fined £1,000 plus £250 costs. After that they switched between different sites around North London. Raided 37 times in 1987, continual action forced it off the air between July and October.

The biggest attempt at silencing London Greek Radio came in 1988 when the authorities raided their offices, taking away all the paperwork related to the station. In a case heard at Highgate Magistrates Court in July, companies and staff associated with London Greek Radio were fined £13,900 plus £10,550 costs. They staggered on for a while before closing down that winter to apply for an incremental radio licence in conjunction with Afro Caribbean broadcaster WNK. While off air, George Power launched Sunshine Radio, an English-language service on the Cote D'Azur in the South of France.

A licence

After losing 151 transmitters over the years (according to DTI figures) or over 300 (their estimate), London Greek Radio was awarded the North London community licence, returning to the air legally in November 1989. Dr Zennetos Tofallis told the press "We should be in the Guinness Book of Records. At one stage we were being raided every other day."[86] There was a brief delay in the opening after Turkish groups complained that the two hours per week of programming that LGR planned to carry was not enough and warned of potential public disorder. However, a compromise was reached with WNK agreeing to carry an additional hour.

The start of the legal station was tough and it lost £300,000 in its first two years of operation. In 1992 it turned to its listeners for help in raising the £100,000 needed for the station to continue. Its fortunes began to improve after WNK went out of business and it had the 103.3 FM frequency to itself.

. . . .

LGR continues to this day, more successfully evolving their format in the face of an ageing original audience than some of the other ethnic stations. In 2013 George Power resurrected the Crackers name, launching a series of new club nights and starting Crackers Radio as an LGR side-project, broadcasting every Monday night on the station.

London Weekend Radio

London's music frequency, 1983-1984

LWR took to the air as London Weekend Radio on 1 January 1983. The station began as a joint venture between two DJs. Jonny Haywood had done shows on Bromley Sound as well as deejaying in a few small South London clubs and wine bars. John Dawson (Keith Green) had started helping out on Radio Jackie and Radio Free London before running his own station, South London Radio, where he refined higher-power VHF transmitters.

Going live

Initial broadcasts from LWR were on Saturdays only, with a mix of programmes from soul to pop to alternative to lighter rock. DJs at this time included Mark Mason, Martin James and Jerry Peters. Before long they added Sundays as well, with programmes coming live from John Dawson's bedsit in Sydenham using a VHF Band III link to the broadcast transmitters on various South-East London tower blocks. LWR had an openness to most forms of music, with DJs playing electro and alternative dance that wasn't being heard on the more conservative soul stations. It was here that hip-hop DJ Tim Westwood launched his radio career.

In early 1984 they were hit hard by a series of raids on their transmitter sites. Broadcasting from the tops of council tower blocks meant that the authorities could turn up any time and take away the transmitter. The station decided that if it was going to survive and exploit the same loopholes as other stations it would have to switch to private premises for its transmissions and to justify that it would need to be on the air every day. On 10 March 1984 the station went 24 hours as LWR – London Wide Radio. They rented space for their FM transmitter up on Crystal Palace's Church Road, near where the other big pirates could be found, put up a new aerial mast and moved into a new studio set up in DJ Pat Sinclair's house in Catford.

Going wide

Daytimes, the 24-hour station had a pop format, with Robbie May (later on BFBS and RTHK) on breakfast, Jonny Haywood mid-morning, the Marquee Club's Jerry Floyd on lunchtimes (complete with extensive racing tips), Paul Stafford (later on Kent's Radio Invicta) on afternoons and Oscar J Jennings (Peter Anthony, later on Luxembourg and Caroline) doing drivetime. During the day, hourly IRN news bulletins were taken off LBC while regular travel updates inevitably came from teletext. In the evening and at weekends they carried specialist shows, ranging from rock with Del Stevens and indie with Mark Mason to soul with Lindsay Wesker, Pete Tong, Tony Monson, Bob Jones and Nicky Holloway.

With the coming of the new Telecoms Act in 1984, LWR made the decision to close down on 14 July 1984 before the new Act came into force the following day. A special goodbye broadcast went out from Jonny Haywood and John Dawson, thanking all the fifty-one DJs that had passed through the station during this period.

• • • • • • • • • • • • • • • •

Jonny Haywood moved on to work in independent radio and was later Head of Music at Jazz FM. John Dawson and programme controller Mark Mason relaunched LWR with a specialist black music format two months later.

Tim Westwood in LWR's council flat studio circa 1983. Photo © David Corio.

Skyline Radio
South-East London's local station, 1983-1985

Skyline was South-East London's answer to Jackie – and shared a few staff and more than a few ideas in common. The station was started by Mark Ellis (Stuart Vaughan) and Steve Fox (Bob Dunn). Both had begun their pirate careers helping out on Radio Jackie, Mark moving on to Bromley Sound and London FM and then both of them working on County Radio.

When the loophole was found that prevented transmission equipment being taken prior to a court ordering its seizure, Skyline quickly assembled the £8,000 needed to get the station on the air with a seven-day operation, put together a DJ team and launched on 19 September 1983. Skyline simulcast on AM and FM, going out on 212m / 1413KHz from Knights Hill, West Norwood and on 90.2MHz VHF from Church Road, Crystal Palace, fed via multiple secret links from their studio in Camberwell. While intended as a local station for South-East London, the VHF transmissions reached well into the rest of London as well. Like Jackie, they also opened (well, shared) a shop to promote the station and sell merchandise in South Norwood's High Street.

Local days, specialist nights

Programmes on Skyline went out from 6am to midnight and several of the DJs came from Croydon's Whitgift Shopping Centre in-store radio station, which Steve Fox owned with Chris Ryder. First Steve Fox and then Ray Thomson presented the breakfast show while on drivetime was former RFL jock Mark Ashton, who had been involved in that station's own earlier attempt at local broadcasting. Other presenters included David Gates, Jill St James, Alan Jones, Ray Clifford, Steve Ego, Peter Knight, Nick Love, Mike Summers and Nick Miller. News was carried on the hour, initially taken from IRN but later read in-house. They weren't as active in the community as Radio Jackie, however, and while DJs would read details of community events they didn't carry much news for their area.

Evenings saw a number of specialist shows, including Pat French with reggae,

Debbie Smith with rock and Chris Ryder (Chris Neophytou, aka Caesar the Boogieman) with his soul show. From early 1984 they also began carrying Radio Invicta each day in the early hours, but this arrangement did not last long. Skyline ran several events, including a regular disco at the Frog and Nightgown on the Old Kent Road.

Licence campaigns and applications

Ahead of the passing of the new Telecoms Act in July 1984, Skyline Radio began campaigning for a licence. Regular adverts requested listeners to write to the Home Office demanding the licensing of stations like Skyline. When the new Act came into force and the raids started in the autumn of 1984 Skyline began increasing security, moving studios every few weeks. The medium wave transmitter proved more problematic to keep on the air and after several raids was dropped.

Broadcasts continued until June 1985, by which time they were having increasing difficulty staying on the air in the face of RIS action. Co-founder Mark Ellis said "All we ever wanted to do was to draw attention to the need for smaller scale radio stations. As soon as the Home Office announced its plans for community radio we went off air." Together with Chris Ryder he applied for the South London licence under the name Radio Croydon, hoping to do something similar legally. Mark announced "If we're one of the lucky ones then we'll be back on air next summer. If not then we won't bother."[87] After the experiment was abandoned they did not return. The station is still looked on with fondness by Bob Dunn: "Skyline remains a great memory and both Stuart and myself are pleased as punch that talented presenters were able to use it as a springboard to greater things."

Left: Skyline's eggbox-lined studio. Right: Caesar the Boogieman.

Many of Skyline's DJs progressed to careers in legal radio. Chris Ryder was the most well known, going on to work at several local stations, Talk Radio and the legal Kiss FM, though he wasn't to everyone's taste. Neil Midah became Neil Francis on Radio Caroline, Starpoint FM, Virgin Radio and now Solar. Nick Miller was part of the launch team on Talk Radio, later moving to LBC and Jazz FM. Oscar J Jennings, who also worked on LWR, joined Radio Luxembourg and then Radio Caroline as Peter Anthony. In 1987 several DJs from Skyline began a new pop and oldies service called London Town FM from the South London / North Surrey borders before regrouping as Raiders FM under the leadership of Mike Summers.

Radio Sovereign
Britain's first seven-day solid gold radio, 1983-1984

Radio Sovereign broadcast for less than a year but paved the way for the seven-day unlicensed stations to come.

Crispian St John – an experienced broadcaster who had worked on Radio Nordzee International, Radio Atlantis and Radio Caroline as well as in Independent Local Radio – wanted to start a station in South West London. He had a transmitter built by Radio Jackie's Dave Small and approached John Kenning for backing. John had interests in music and disco promotion and had also originated the offshore radio project that became Laser 558. He had just returned from the USA and saw the potential for an oldies service: "I had heard brilliant stations in the USA broadcasting all oldies. Crispian said such a format would not work in the UK. I disagreed, and as I was putting up the money, Crispian had to go along with it!"[88]

For Crispian it was important to show how a small-scale station could be done (almost) entirely by the book. Sovereign would operate professionally, follow the IBA programming and advertising codes, pay its full-time staff and DJs (£5 and up per show) and even set aside money for copyright payments. The only part that would not be legal would be the transmissions. They set up in a house in Sherland Road Twickenham, with the aerial slung between two buildings and the transmitter in a shed. Former Jackie engineer Mike Barrington lived on the premises and nursed the somewhat makeshift transmission equipment, which eventually reached 400W power, though the aerial output was rather less. Transmissions began on 10 May 1983 on 1503 AM before moving to the clearer 1494 channel.

Solid gold radio

While other pirates beat Sovereign to the title of first oldies station in the UK, Sovereign was on air live every day with a smoother sound and an updated set of the classic 1960s Pams jingles used by the offshore Radio London. Compared to today's gold stations, the music had a broader range and was less heavily formatted, with hourly 'future gold' tracks from the charts that they considered would become eventual classics. News was on the half hour, a mix of national

Kevin Turner presenting on Sovereign in 1983. Photo by Peter McFarlane.

news cribbed from teletext and stories taken from the local papers, though they had unrealised plans to move to a news agency. Weekdays saw Ron Brown on early mornings, Crispian St John on breakfast, Rob Randall mid-mornings, Kevin Turner early afternoons and Bernie Simmons on drivetime. Weekends included Paul McKenna, Joy Jameson and Paul Anthony.

Viable but illegal

Crispian was happy to be proved right on Sovereign's viability: "One of the things that was pointed out to us at the very beginning by the Home Office in different documents was the fact that small stations like this could not financially exist. That was one of many points put against this kind of radio. We have proven that financially we can exist and survive as long as we like. We spent I think about £30,000 as we took a lot of expert legal advice, which we kept under our hat on the whole thing. Running costs are well over £1,000 a week. I think we're talking about £2,000 in all at the moment. Staff, promotional expenditure, our engineering, new music."[89] At the time the cost of establishing a medium-size ILR station was estimated at £750,000.

Sovereign was visited by the authorities on several occasions. However, John Kenning always refused to allow them to take away the equipment and threatened to call in the police if they tried: "They always gave in, somewhat to my surprise, but as it stood then, the law was actually on my side and they never took our transmitter. To be honest, it was just a bluff as far as I was concerned, but it worked!"[90]

The station was taken to court twice. In the second case in November 1983 John Kenning was fined £1,000 plus £100 costs. It was inferred that the next time the investigators returned they would seize the expensive studio gear and his treasured collection of vinyl. A decision was therefore made to close. Radio Sovereign left the air on 2 January 1984 with a final closedown announcement from Kevin Turner.

Sovereign goes to Italy

John Kenning shipped the studio to northern Italy, where he relaunched Radio Sovereign as a station aimed at English speakers in the South of France. Later it was bought by Capital Radio, renamed Riviera Radio and moved to Monaco. Crispian St John returned to Caroline as Jay Jackson, where he read the news and did programmes, before founding the weekly radio magazine Now Radio under his real name, Howard Rose. In 1987 he attempted a comeback of Sovereign in Ireland, but it never got beyond test transmissions. Having successfully launched incremental station KCBC in his home town of Kettering in 1990 he then returned to writing about radio as editor of the Radio Magazine.

• • • • • • • • • • • • • • • •

Most of Sovereign's DJs went on to further careers in radio. Bernie Simmons, Jerry James and Rob Randall were all to be found on Jackie. After a brief spell on Jackie and Radio Shoestring, Paul McKenna followed Crispian to Radio Caroline before launching his legal radio career. Kevin Turner and Mike Barrington were also to be found on Caroline. Howard Rose died in 2002 after complications following routine surgery at the age of only 49.

Voice of the Immigrant
The Greek competition, 1983-1984

London Greek Radio was quickly followed onto the airwaves by another station for the Greek Cypriot community. VOI broadcast every day from 7am-12am on 93 FM. Station manager Tommy Chrysotomous described its programming: "We're teaching the history of Cyprus, the history of Greece. We do children's' programmes every day between half past five and six o'clock. We do live church services every Sunday morning. We're there to entertain them, to teach them. They can learn a great deal about their ethnic identity, their traditions, their culture."[91]

In April 1985 Tommy was fined £300 with £150 costs in the last of several appearances in court. He claimed that he had lost £10,000 while running the station.

Cityside Radio

A pop station that had three brief bursts of life. First transmissions from Cityside appeared on 90.2 FM in 1983 with programmes from Steve Bishop, Tim Roberts and future Starpoint co-founder Ben West. In 1985 it surfaced as part of the London Alternative Broadcasting network of stations before that was quickly canned in favour of Starpoint. Steve Bishop then briefly resurrected the name in '88 when things went awry with Hits FM.

Civic Radio

A soul and jazz station founded by the fourteen year old Gilles Peterson. Programmes were recorded in the garden shed of his parents' house and played out from the top of a nearby hill. Civic was on the air on Tuesdays from 8-11pm to South West London on 90.4 FM. The station only lasted a few months, though its transmitter was used later by Radio Invicta.

Radio Eclipse

Broadcasting from 5-11pm on Sunday nights from South London.

GAPP Radio

Broadcasting on 103.0 FM.

GBL Radio

Broadcasting on 92.0 FM for a few months.

Hard Rock Cafe

Another food-themed broadcaster, this South East London rock station broadcast on 92 FM on Monday nights for one hour in 1983 with sole DJ Ian Roberts. HRC made a brief reappearance in 1990.

London Basin Broadcasting Company

The cheekily-named LBBC was a holiday pop and rock station from Phil Thomas at Christmas 1983. Presenters included the usual suspects from Radio Atlantis, Alice's Restaurant and London Music Radio.

London Community Radio

Intermittently on the air between 1983 and 1987 in the Fulham and Putney area. In 1985 it changed its name for a while to Groove FM. The station was run by Adam Moore, who also deejayed at South West Sound and went on to be a producer at news station LBC and had a subsequent career as a hard house DJ.

London Rock

On the air for a few months in 1983 and run by Mike Burnett and with some other former Radio Free London staff presenting. The station broadcast live every Thursday night on 92.3 FM with the VHF transmitter on a block of flats in Sydenham Hill.

Radio Pythagoras

An occasional broadcaster playing avant-garde music to West London.

Riverside Radio

Broadcasting on 104.5 FM.

Rooftop Radio

Broadcasting Saturdays and Sundays on 89.9 FM with a soul format.

Southbank Radio

Operating weekly on 90.4 FM.

South East Sound

One of the last AM stations south of the Thames, broadcasts began as Radio 220 before becoming Southern Radio and then South East Sound in August 1983. Programmes were mostly mainstream rock from founder Ray Adams with presenters including Iain Johnstone (John Burch – the man behind offshore radio supporters group The Caroline Movement), Geoff Rogers, Keith Archer, Benny James and Dave Windsor. The station closed in early 1986 after Ray Adams was prosecuted and fined £1,000.

Radio Xanadu

Broadcasting on Sundays.

1984

The age of the super-pirates

Exactly twenty years on since the launch of Radio Caroline, 1984 was a defining year for London's radio. It was the year of the super-pirates – big new operations that broadcast twenty-four hours a day on high power across London that for the first time were influencing music in the capital, not just reacting to what was being played. It was also the year Laser 558 took to the air, an offshore station where you were 'never more than a minute away from music'. These were to form a focus for discontent in the ILR system and turn its contractors against the existing regime enforced by the IBA.

It was a while before the cat was finally out of the bag about just how limited the legal powers to shut down illegal stations actually were. Now there was a rush to begin 24-hour operation: JFM was next in February, closely followed by Horizon, and then in March London Weekend Radio relaunched as LWR. Like Skyline, these stations all took premises in either Church Road or Westow Hill in Crystal Palace. This was one of the highest spots in the capital and close to the transmitter used for Radio London, so listeners already knew in which direction to point their aerials. Tall aerial masts were erected on the roofs of shops and an unmanned transmitter installed in an upstairs room, while programmes came from hidden studios close by.

Across London other stations began seven-day broadcasting too. Radio Shoestring in Walthamstow began in March as a local station for the North East London area and DBC also began a daily service from Notting Hill. Before long the super-pirates were making serious inroads into London radio listening. Although Capital Radio had lived with competition from illegal broadcasters since birth, Independent Local Radio in the rest of the South East had previously had less to worry about. Now they were about to get seriously spooked by a new operation From the North Sea.

Backed by Irish businessman Philip Smyth, Laser 558 had not had the easiest of starts. Its early broadcasts involved an experimental transmission system that used helium balloons, which was not exactly suited to the North Sea weather. In May it finally took to the air with full programming, using American DJs and a fast-moving pop format that packed in the hits like no licensed British station could legally do. Although Radio Caroline had come back on the airwaves from the North Sea the previous year, its format was from an earlier era, gaining it few young converts. Laser was different: its DJs were brand new to broadcasting on a ship and sounded thrilled to be there, even if the reality of everyday life was less fun.

ILR turns on the IBA

Independent Local Radio's initial shock at the impact that the pirates were having turned into an action plan, amid further fears of what breakfast television and Channel Four might do to their advertising revenue. The stations' trade body, the Association of Independent Radio Contractors, held a secret meeting of station bosses at a Heathrow hotel in June that set out a manifesto to change the direction of independent radio, using the threat of the pirates to turn the system to their advantage.

They demanded more action be taken against both offshore and land-based unlicensed stations, threatening that members would withhold statutory payments if this did not take place. Many stations had a member of the House of Lords on their board and these were briefed to ensure their message was heard in government. More significantly, the AIRC sought to completely renegotiate the terms under which independent stations operated. They wanted an end to the IBA's micro-management, so stations would have total responsibility for their output; an end to restrictions on station mergers and a massive cut in the transmission fees that they paid the IBA and the extra levies that the most profitable companies paid the Treasury.

The AIRC found sympathy from the IBA's new Director General, John Whitney, the former boss of Capital Radio and a former chairman of the AIRC. Since he had taken office in 1983 the IBA had already begun to change: meetings with stations had become less concerned about programming content and more with commercial considerations. The lobbying for all the changes that the AIRC wanted would be a long process and it wasn't until the 1990 Broadcasting Act that their manifesto would come to be fully realised. They did, however, win some earlier concessions.

There was a cut in the transmission fees paid to the IBA and the profit levies paid to the Treasury. The level of monitoring of stations by the IBA was reduced, letting them make more changes on their own. Requirements for live music were axed and network programming was allowed for the first time, allowing the introduction of the Network Chart. Greater ownership from outside a station's franchise area was permitted and new franchises were given to neighbouring stations instead of the IBA seeking new companies to run them – there were anyway few takers in the remaining areas of the UK without an ILR station.

The government also finally appeared ready to deal with the pirates.

Closing the legal loopholes

The lack of action had been a major bugbear for all those involved in legal radio. Richard Francis, the BBC's Managing Director of Radio was typical, complaining "We feel that the Radio Interference Service, particularly with the greater powers that are about to become available to them, should be able to do more under those powers to apprehend the pirates. This seems to me to be a public service which may have been lacking resources but also may have been lacking in a certain impetus to get at the problem."[92]

Douglas Hurd, the minister at the Home Office with responsibility for radio, insisted it wasn't that the government had no interest: "There isn't a lack of political will. There has been a shortage of resources and there's been a shortage of evidence."[93] A combination of the progress of technology, the weakness of the broadcasting laws and the assertiveness of those prosecuted meant it was no longer straightforward to secure the evidence necessary to convict an individual of "establishing, installing or using" an unlicensed station.

In the early seventies magistrates would more readily accept the word of the investigators that an individual was involved in the illegal use of a transmitter. This started to break down when those caught began demanding greater proof that they had actually broken the law on that occasion. Abie Cohen (Brian Horne) of the London Transmitter of Independent Radio was particularly inventive, claiming in court on one occasion that a transmitter found in his possession was only warm because it had been between his legs in the car.

Now that most broadcasters knew that a transmitter could only be seized after a court case and that you didn't even have to identify yourself to the inspectors – making it harder to bring anyone to court – it gave pirates free rein to operate. Radio Sovereign's Crispian St John (Howard Rose) described what was now a typical raid: "We allow them in and let them do what they want to do, basically, which is to inspect the equipment, make notes on it and trundle off home. We close down because they need to inspect it their way. They certainly don't take the equipment away. They have no right whatsoever to do that."[94] Still sent out by the bosses to raid stations, the RIS officers appeared rather frustrated – perhaps even a little morose – at their inability to actually do anything.

In that session of Parliament, one of the flagship pieces of legislation for the Conservatives was the 1984 Telecommunications Act privatising British Telecom. Into this went amendments to the 1949 Wireless Telegraphy Act, allowing the immediate seizure of transmission equipment in use for unlicensed broadcasting, limiting sale and possession of equipment and requiring those caught to identify themselves to investigators. The Act also transferred the Radio Interference Service, which had most recently been part of British Telecom, to the Department of Trade and Industry's new Radiocommunications Agency and gave it a new name, The Radio Investigation Service. Some staff opted to stay at British Telecom, anticipating higher salaries, resulting in the new agency being slightly smaller than its predecessor.

The countdown began to the day when the Act went on the statute books: 15 July. Radio Jackie launched a petition for the station to be licensed, gathering over 50,000 signatures. Horizon Radio, Skyline Radio and others began letter-writing campaigns to MPs, with hourly adverts warning listeners that without their help they might soon leave the airwaves. On the Sunday before the Act came into force some stations closed down, with LWR, Radio Shoestring and London Greek Radio running emotional final programmes. Others continued on, still hoping for the best. In the event there were no immediate raids: the changes at the RIS meant it was occupied by internal matters for much of the summer.

It wasn't until October that the first action under the new laws took place, hitting Skyline, JFM, LWR and Horizon. The raid on Horizon also netted its expensive studio and its owner Chris Stewart (Christian Barnhurst). Although his drive played a big part in pushing the soul stations to a much greater success, Chris' desire to control all aspects of its operation – Gilles Peterson describes him as "megalomaniacal" [95] – was causing him to fall out with his DJs. Taking advantage of the situation, they hastily assembled a new operation, Solar Radio, which gave all its presenters a say in its operation and widened the range of music that it played.

Reports claimed that the raids were in response to interference being caused to the new ILR station from the Crawley area of Sussex, Radio Mercury. Unlike Capital, the newcomer wasn't prepared to tolerate pirate operators encroaching anywhere near the territory it paid so much for. At the end of November Mercury went one step further, taking out an injunction in the High Court against Radio Jackie broadcasting in its transmission area.

Mercury's managing director, John Aumonier, declared "Radio Jackie is the most dangerous example of the current airwave anarchy."[96] Jackie's owner, Tony Collis, hid out to try and avoid being served with the court papers for the injunction while Jackie's legal ownership was switched. Radio Jackie station organiser Peter Stremes told the press "We have no choice but to fight. If we go down it will mean the end of every station like us."[97] In the end, however, Jackie's demise was to come a different way and before the injunction could be implemented.

The heart and soul of Radio London

The popularity of soul music on the pirates had not gone unnoticed at Radio London. The BBC's local station had not had an easy past. Launched on 6 October 1970 and on VHF only until Capital's arrival, it was part of a chain of local stations conceived in part as the BBC's response to demands for local commercial broadcasting. However, the budget necessary for truly successful local broadcasting was not forthcoming and a minuscule four hours of needle time per day meant little scope for working with music either.

Despite the valiant efforts of some presenters, reporters and producers to make something of the opportunity it offered, much of the time Radio London relied on cheap phone-ins and repackaged news from network radio. Where it saw more success was in its programming for ethnic minorities, although sometimes this could be more worthy than entertaining. London Sounds Eastern mixed South Asian music and community features, every weekday evening there was the hour-long magazine programme Black Londoners and it had the first reggae show on British radio, Reggae Time, first with Steve Barnard and then Tony Williams.

A 1981 relaunch had changed daytimes to more of a Radio Two music format, but after an initial boost Radio London was sinking in the ratings once more. The Conservative government was not sure that the BBC should be in local radio at all – neither were some of the BBC management – and there was talk of the local stations being closed down or even privatised. When former Radio One breakfast show presenter Tony Blackburn joined and started featuring more soul music on his morning show it was a moderate success in the ratings. So in 1984, seemingly willing to try anything, Radio London relaunched again with the Invicta-aping tagline 'The heart and soul of London.'

The daytime format was now oriented towards commercial soul music, albeit not exclusively so in the breakfast and drivetime shows. Tony Blackburn played nothing else, pushing at the limits of the broadcasting rules with terrible double-entendres before quitting when BBC management asked him to tone it down: "They wanted to kill off soul and were getting nervous about all the jokes with double meanings. It was only Carry On style humour and wouldn't be heard by kids. But the governors stamped on it. I won't miss them."[98]

Radio London also heavily promoted its 'Soul Night Out' events at London clubs, which became a useful extra source of revenue. There was also a practical reason for the music format: much of the music played was from US imports that were not subject to the Phonographic Performance Limited needle time limits. To further reduce costs it signed a licensing deal with the Streetsounds dance compilation label, which again was outside the PPL restrictions. One producer was reprimanded, however, for agreeing to give mentions on air to Bluebird Records in return for Radio London being supplied with free vinyl by the shop.

Club music's move from talking to technique

The big pirates' move to 24-hour broadcasting, their need to now fill a large number of hours with volunteer broadcasters and their desire to be seen as offering some degree of public service opened up new opportunities for less mainstream genres outside peak hours. Radio Jackie, with its older audience, had big band music on Friday nights and music from the 1930s to 1950s on Saturday nights. JFM had reggae with Steve Barnard, hip-hop with Paul Dodd and vintage R&B with Clive Richardson. Gilles Peterson turned up on both JFM and Horizon playing jazz. On LWR Tim Westwood was pulling in a huge young audience for his evening hip-hop show and Mark Mason played alternative dance music that would only resurface on the airwaves in the Balearic boom.

1984 was also the year that mixing finally began to have a presence on the airwaves. Although it was a technique most club DJs knew about and Record Mirror's James Hamilton began listing BPMs for tracks as far back as 1979, beat-matching was very slow to take off in the UK. Capital Radio's Greg Edwards cautioned "Nobody's going to get a job on radio just by linking records. A DJ will never learn his craft by listening to records and finding out which ones have exactly the same beat. An engineer is there for that job." Radio London's Robbie Vincent was even more dismissive: "American bad habits are not going to catch on here. People in the UK don't want to hear three solid hours of identical music."[99]

If mixing was slow to take off in the clubs, it was even slower for the concept to cross over into radio. Dance music DJs on the pirates generally adopted the presentation style of their counterparts on legal radio even if, like Graham Gold or Froggy, they were known for their mixing in the clubs – though Froggy (Steve Howlett) did play his mixes off tape. The stations also didn't have the necessary fast-start variable-pitch turntables – the classic Technics SL1200 decks would only become an essential part of pirate studios later in the eighties.

More common early on were pre-recorded mastermixes – taking inspiration from US electro to build new extended tracks out of multiple records. North West London's Mastermind sound system did shows on Radio Invicta that featured their impressive multi-turntable mixes. The group's founder, Herbie Laidley, also mixed the Streetsounds Electro compilations and its eight-strong DJ team included later Kiss jocks Dave VJ and Max LX. Les Adams played his own mastermixes on shows on Radio Jackie and Radio Contact before going on to put out releases with DJ music service the Disco Mix Club. With James Hamilton he also assembled the non-stop party sounds for Capital Radio's New Year's Eve broadcasts.

Tim Westwood was a critical figure in pushing hip-hop as a music form on the radio and in making it something Londoners felt they could be involved in. His LWR shows pioneered the playing of short mixes and raps sent in by listeners, an idea that other hip-hop shows followed. He might not have been a scratch DJ but Tim did develop a presentation style that flowed with the music rather than treating links and music as isolated elements. In 1984 he explained, "London pirates have really missed out on the New York style of presentation, such as you find on Kiss FM. Legal radio presenters are generally staid, traditional, uninnovative and unoriginal; the pirates have none of their restrictions but they haven't moved on and they never achieved the potential. It's not enough to be a poor imitation playing different music."[100]

Although Kiss FM launched with a promise that live mixing like their New York namesake was going to set them apart from the others, for the first half of their pirate existence they were more traditional in their presentation style. There were still a few notable pioneers on the pirates in the middle of the decade, such as a Kiss's Richie Rich and LWR's Barry Bee, but for a long time those DJs were the exceptions. It wasn't until house made its presence felt on the airwaves in '87 and '88 that stations started to equip their studios with suitable turntables and beat-matching, rather than just segueing, became more commonplace. The hard 4:4 beat of house made it much simpler to seamlessly blend tracks together and by the time of the rave stations in 1989 mixing had become a cornerstone of pirate broadcasting.

Having previously always referred to the VHF band, on 30 September the BBC gave in and switched over to using FM as its official term instead. In the House of Commons it was reported that in 1984 across the country 119 transmitters had been found, 50 of which were unmanned, and there had been 43 prosecutions. Since the new Act came in there had been 60 raids on 36 different stations.

On The Air

LWR
A pop station reinvents itself as a black music champion, 1984-1990

Despite the grand closedown in July, it took only two months before LWR was back on the air. When they saw how those stations that had continued broadcasting were not subject to crippling raids, co-founder John Dawson and programme controller Mark Mason decided on a relaunch without Jonny Haywood, at the time off DJing on a cruise ship. On 15 September 1984 LWR returned with new backing from club promoter Zak & Dee Promotions, named after the two brothers that ran it: Zak (Emmanuel Offe-Burobey) and his brother Fuzzy Dee (Daniel).

Mark Mason explained "Before we met this person we were living off a shoestring. We had to scrounge as much as possible to pay for things. Every day we used to wonder where we were going to find the money to pay the rent. As long as the person we've teamed up with now keeps putting up the money, we're OK."[101] Zak got involved because "I saw the need for a 24-hour station that appealed to the street. I turned what was a pop station with minimal soul and electro into a black music station."[102]

In many ways this could be considered a different station from the earlier LWR. The new daytime schedule switched from soul with Mark Mason on breakfast, to Zak's mid-morning reggae show, back to soul with Ron Tom for lunch, reggae in the afternoon with J.J. then Tim Westwood on drivetimes with his more soul-oriented selection – except for Tuesdays when he had his massively popular hip-hop show in the evening. Westwood had first gained attention as warm-up DJ

LWR's Crystal Palace transmitter site in 1986.
Photo by Pyers Easton.

for Steve Walsh in the clubs, but it wasn't until he began playing hip-hop that he started to make a name for himself. The Tuesday show would get one of the biggest mailbags on the station, sometimes 200 letters a week.

John Dawson continued engineering duties for the relaunched station, with broadcasts still going out from Church Road in Crystal Palace while studios moved regularly around South East London. For several months they operated from a flat in the North Peckham Estate, but this was not a popular location with DJs and eventually they suffered a studio raid there; later they were above dub musician the Mad Professor's studio in Peckham, until again they lost it in a studio raid. In one raid in October 1985, apparently instigated at the request of Capital Radio, the Radio Investigation Service found the studio just round the corner from the broadcast site, connected with long cables that ran over the roofs.

More DJs were added as 1985 progressed, including future rap star Derek Boland presenting a mix of funk, electro and hip-hop; Joe Douglas (later boss of North London's legal WNK) playing reggae and soca; deeper reggae with Daddy Ernie (later a mainstay of Choice FM); jazz from Steve Edwards (later on Jazz FM and Radio One) and the underrated Barry Bee, one of the first DJs with a regular mix show. As well as more black presenters, the station also put more female DJs on air than many of its competitors, including DJ Camilla, Debbie Gopie, Angie Dee, Angie Le Mar, Sarah HB and DJ Elayne (Elayne Smith – also later on Choice FM).

Eventually John Dawson tired of the pressure and he left the station at the end of 1985 for Starpoint, followed shortly after by programme controller Mark Mason. In his place Roger Howe took over on engineering duties. Zak was now in complete control of the station. More driven than the others, the former accountant believed in doing everything he could to maximise the business. His renamed promotions company Midas Media began new LWR-sponsored club nights and acted as a DJ agency for LWR jocks.

Hiding from the law

During 1986 the raids became more sustained, not helped by LWR being one of only a few pirates on the air and for a short while the only one attempting 24-hour broadcasting. The increasing numbers of studio raids and regular court appearances were also leading to a growing paranoia amongst pirate operators. In the spring LWR switched from live broadcasting to tapes. For a while they put out just music, jingles and adverts, with the occasional live broadcast from a club. Then DJs started recording taped programmes, although often tapes went out late or in the wrong order. Just as live shows returned in summer of 1986 the DTI began big action against the Crystal Palace transmitter sites, removing the stations' tall aerial masts. It was only towards the end of the year that LWR began to get back on track with regular live programmes again. By this time Tim Westwood had left to join newcomer WBLS, replaced by Steve Harris on hip-hop duties.

By early '87 the raids had lessened, though they moved transmitter sites in the summer as their previous landlord was apparently not impressed by damage caused to the building during one of the raids. LWR's Studios remained in rough locations. DJ Lewis Dene remembers "turning up one night to find the flat next door kicked in, having been raided by the drug squad for being a crack house. The station engineers had also dismantled the studio and done a runner, without informing me of course!"[103] Another time they were on the eighth floor of a tower block where DJs were warned to use the stairs rather than the lifts if they didn't want to be robbed.

Fresh DJs and powerplays

The core DJs on the station remained much the same; though Jasper the Vinyl Junkie took over on lunchtimes with more funk and house than his predecessor Ron Tom. The Lone Ranger – former Radio One DJ Dave Gregory – was now on breakfasts, the slot most club DJs wished to avoid. Jazzy M, who'd started out presenting a more soul-oriented show, became the DJ to go to for house music with his popular twice-weekly Jacking Zone show. Maxi Jazz, later to join dance act Faithless, moved from Starpoint to present a weekly show mixing up less mainstream soul and funk, only moving onto hip-hop after 12.30 as he knew by then his boss had gone to bed and wouldn't be listening.

As '87 moved into '88, the top-of-the-hour ad breaks were getting longer, with a healthy mix of adverts for both the station's own gigs and outside events, records and shops. Advertisers could book a package of 28 spots for £200. There were also a growing number of 'powerplay' records, with reggae labels in particular prepared to pay big amounts of cash to get their acts onto the station. A profile of Zak in the Observer reported he was now driving a Porsche, albeit second-hand. However, from an original office for his promotions company in Covent Garden they relocated to cramped space above Fidel's Fashions for Men in Brixton Road and claimed to make only £700 a week at best. Asked why he did it, Zak responded "It's the satisfaction of knowing you're number one, of eroding the established stations, of being able to hear LWR everywhere in London and knowing it's something you've engineered."[104]

A second short farewell

After the announcement of the new 'incremental' radio licences in 1988 LWR remained quiet about what its plans were. It wasn't until December that they announced that the station would be closing down to apply for a licence. The final show went out on 31 December with Chris Collins and Wayne Turner in the studio while a separate LWR party took place in a London club.

When the winners of the incremental licences were announced and they weren't among them – the Radio Authority later said they never applied – it wasn't long before LWR took to the airwaves again. However, when it relaunched at the end of July 1989 it was minus many of its former jocks. Several had been headhunted by Choice FM, the black radio station that won the South London licence, while others were still hoping they might be picked up elsewhere or in the second round of licences. This incarnation of LWR continued on into 1990 but with new legal competition and changing tastes it was not as successful and eventually left the airwaves.

In the studio at LWR in 1988.

Zak was not exactly happy with his legal successors: "People who put together something on shoestring budgets that grabbed the attention of the nation – it was a revolution – and what have they got to show for it? We've done all the donkey work but it comes down to who you rub shoulders with. I'm not happy and I don't think a lot of people are. We haven't been given what we fought for. We've been bog-washed, hoodwinked, we've got no more choice."[105]

LWR leaves several legacies. The huge number of DJs that it provided a training ground for, a number of whom went on to major success on London legal radio, national radio and the charts. The space it gave to music that was not played elsewhere at the time, with its early championing of hip-hop and house as well as prominent reggae shows. Its success in its second incarnation as a black-owned station and a pioneer in putting black voices on the air. Where it was less successful was in investing in activities and building links to people and organisations that might have helped it cross over to legality.

Radio Shoestring

Eastside community radio, 1984-1987

South West London had Jackie, South East London had Skyline and, for a few months in 1984, North East London had Radio Shoestring. The station came on the air on 29 March 1984 with a studio and transmitter on the top floor of a former workshop in Walthamstow that had seen better days.

The station happened by chance. According to engineer Pyers Easton, "I was shopping with my girlfriend at Wood Green shopping centre and heard an in-house radio station that sounded way too professional so I sought out the booth and met Paul McKenna and Mitch Johnson who were running it. They then introduced me to Greg Powers who wanted to do something and we set up Shoe-string."[106] Presenters were drawn from a combination of pirates and in-store stations. These included Christopher England, Steve Roberts, Danny Dipole, Peter Davies, Steve Justin and Steve Bishop. Future Radio One DJ Gary King sang the jingles ("pride of place on my CV"[107]) with Paul McKenna voicing them and doing early shows alongside Mitch. The jingles were made for 102.5, but by the time they launched Horizon had taken that frequency so they were actually on 103.2.

Shoestring made some local impact, but the quality of presentation was mixed and it wasn't clear what it was setting out to achieve. News, sport and weather came from teletext – and not always put together very enthusiastically by pre-senters who would mostly rather be playing music. Christopher England's weekly Mega Request Show usually generated 10-20 letters, one of the larger mailbags.

The Radio Interference Service turned up once during this time. According to Christopher England: "I upset them greatly by not letting them take names or equipment. This proved highly embarrassing for them in front of the police and press who'd accompanied the midnight swoop; so Eric [Gotts] took a load of photos with a camera drawn from a belt holster, while John Garlic tried to caution and question me. Very difficult when you've got no legal power to force the person to even tell you his name. They then tried to 'inspect and test' the rig (which is all they were empowered to do). This seemed to consist of Eric grab-bing the rig and announcing he was taking it. A stand-up argument ended with me asking the police to insist that he reconnected the rig and left. Red faced, he did. According to the press who were with him (and later contacted me) he was extremely upset as they drove away."[108]

With the introduction of the new anti-pirate laws in the 1984 Telecommu-nications Act, Shoestring took the decision to close down on 14 July. The final day's programmes included a live outside broadcast from a local park where Greg Powers took requests and dedications until bad weather forced them to abandon the idea.

Like many other stations, Shoestring returned to the air in the winter of 1984 when the expected action on the stations still broadcasting did not materialise. Programmes were seven days a week once more with Alice's Restaurant sharing time late night at weekends. However, on 2 January 1985 their studio was raided just before Christopher England was due to go on air at 9pm: "They found me sitting on a sofa in a room adjacent to the studio. Whilst they were dealing with the chap in the studio, I had a chat and joke with one of the two coppers that had come with them. As a regular listener, he was very apologetic and turned a blind eye as I emptied my pockets and bags of anything slightly incriminating, and stuffed the cushions full of letters, tapes, and running orders." [109] Christopher and the on-air DJ, Paddy Jaye, were both subsequently prosecuted and fined.

Shoestring returned again for brief periods of broadcasting in 1986, 1987 and 1988, also for a time using the names Broadway FM and then Eastside Commu-nity Radio. Greg Powers continued to run the station but the radio jocks were over time replaced by local club and bar DJs so it lost its original character.

Sina Radio
Sunrise Radio's pirate mother, 1984-1988

While Asian People's Radio began its broadcasts a year earlier, their higher profile and more powerful transmissions attracted greater interest from the authorities. Sina Radio restricted their transmissions to the local Southall area and – for the early part of their life at least – were largely left alone.

Confused origins

It is hard to determine the real story of Sina Radio and its team before it successfully won one of the first incremental licences and became Sunrise Radio. According to his licence applications, founder Avtar Lit was involved with community television pioneers Greenwich Cablevision before spending time in the USA where he set up an Asian radio station and newspaper in California. He has regularly claimed that Sina was a cable radio station, although local contractor Ealing Cabletel only began broadcasting the first legal Asian station in the UK, Radio Roshni, in 1987. That broadcast for just six hours a day and was run by Satya Shivnandan, a journalist from the Community Radio Association.

When in 1986 TX Magazine reported on the broadcasts going out under the Sina name on 90.8 FM and sent a copy of the magazine to the address given out on air, Avtar called to demand that the next issue made clear that Sina Radio International – "with stations in San Francisco, Los Angeles and Utah City" – had no connection with the pirate broadcasts. "Somehow" the unlicensed station had got hold of programme material for these stations and was putting it out, complete with their address.

What is definitely known is that a station identifying as Sina Radio began unlicensed broadcasting in mid-1984 from Southall, with a combination of live programmes and prerecorded music tapes. As well as Avtar Lit, Manjit Singh Gehdu – who went on to be a news presenter on TV Asia – was key in the station and in his obituary it was reported that broadcasts often came from his house. Unlike Asian People's Radio with its English language presentation, Sina was aimed at an older audience, targeting mainly first-generation immigrants from India with programmes and ads predominantly in Punjabi and Hindi. Music shows dominated, but there was also a daily talk show with Lucky Dhillon that continued on Sunrise Radio.

From the beginning the station was extremely successful in attracting advertising from local businesses. Avtar Lit later claimed "Sina sold nine minutes an hour – the IBA limit – and there was often a waiting period of two or three weeks to get on",[110] although some listeners in 1988 reported over four minutes of ads going out four times an hour. They also ran their own music events, which were heavily promoted on the station. Despite its status, Sina was regularly used by the local council and other public sector bodies.

From the end of 1987 there were more frequent raids, with eleven reported by the RIS on Sina Radio in just the first half of 1988. In the summer the station started a campaign among listeners to raise extra funds to enable it to continue broadcasting, which received coverage in the local press. Sina Radio filled a massive demand for South Asian programming in its catchment area and very successfully served that need. One advertiser reported a drop of 50% in sales when the station was off the air.

When the community radio experiment was announced, Sina was one of the applicants, its application suggesting programmes very similar to those they were putting out already. The application did not seem to put an end to very similar local transmissions that continued on their frequency. When three years later the Government announced the incremental licences, they again applied, and again a station remained on 90.8 FM in Southall until Sunrise successfully won the licence. Sina had not been the favourite and other applicant groups demanded the licence should be reallocated as those who stayed on air were barred. The IBA responded "We investigated the allegations fully, but we are satisfied there was no substance to them."[111]

Sunrise Radio

Like other incremental stations, Sunrise Radio had a slightly rocky start. Launch costs crept up, with Avtar declaring "We originally thought it would cost around £200,000. We will be very pleased to get on air for £300,000."[112] Programmes initially came from the former studios of local cable pop station Carousel Radio before a move into dedicated premises close to Southall railway station. Although Sunrise had to go to investors for more funds to stay on air not long after its launch, it remained one of the few from the original incremental stations not to sell out to a major broadcasting group and to continue with its format intact. After successfully exploiting its core South Asian audience, Sunrise went on to acquire a number of other stations, though it did better with those serving a similar market.

In 2005 Avtar Lit was named Britain's richest Asian media entrepreneur in a survey commissioned by Sunrise. However, Sunrise's listenership was increasingly ageing and it failed to attract younger Asian people with its programming, while an attempt at starting a TV station lost the group significant sums. By 2014 his fortunes had changed. Sunrise Radio entered administration in January and was subsequently sold, then in April Avtar Lit was declared bankrupt following a long-standing dispute with a founding shareholder in the company.

Solar Radio
The black music super station, 1984-1988

When Horizon Radio was forced off air in October 1984, it didn't take long for many of their DJs to return on a new station, Solar Radio, broadcasting on Horizon's old 102.5 frequency. For a while there had been discontent among some of Horizon's DJs over the operation of the station and the level of control exercised by boss Chris Stewart. The split led to a difficult situation between the two groups in the early months.

SOUL TO THE | CAPITAL 24 HOURS A DAY

The soul station evolves

Solar – The Sound of London's Alternative Radio – took to the air with its first broadcast on 4 November 1984. Although led by Tony Monson, it was intended to be more democratic than Horizon and the DJs chipped in the £3,000 costs to get the station on the air. Tony, the younger son of a member of the House of Lords, was a journalist on the Black Echoes music paper where he compiled the Echoes Streetsounds chart carried by first Horizon and then Solar. Back in the sixties he'd been a presenter on the offshore easy-listening station Britain Radio. Well-liked and respected among his peers, Tony accepted shows on most stations that asked him, doing time on Radio Invicta, JFM, LWR and Horizon as well as occasional work on Capital Radio and later a weekly soul show on Essex Radio. He was assisted in the day-to-day running by Paul Buick.

Solar widened the core commercial soul base of Horizon, with deejays like CJ Carlos, Paul Buick, Barrie Stone and Nicky Lawrence, and also added more specialist programmes in the evenings. The format was extended to cover more contemporary electro, electro-funk and hip-hop, which Horizon's Chris Stewart barely tolerated. Steve Devonne, Chris Forbes and Paul Dodd covered this side initially and Les Adams 'The Mix Doctor' did a weekly mix show.

There were frequent raids but the station always bounced back quickly and at this time 102.5 was a clear channel that didn't interfere with anyone. Paul Buick was caught in the first studio raid in December 1984, when they also lost a large number of records in the studio library. Mark McCarthy was caught the next time on 12 June 1985 while doing the 11pm to 1am show, by which time they'd learned their lesson and what was in the studio was kept to a minimum. Solar paid his fine of £150 plus £100 costs and the DTI returned all his records except the two that were playing at the time. "I also astonishingly got back my ghetto blaster, which I had in the studio, which was recording the show at the time of the bust in Westow Hill, Crystal Palace and even more astonishingly the recorded tape was still in it. I still have that recorded show to this day, obviously the DTI did not think to use this as evidence."[113]

JFM joiners

After the January 1985 closure of JFM, several of that station's DJs made the move to Solar. By now it was looking like a who's who of classic soul DJ talent, with presenters including Marc Damon, Graham Gold, Aitch, Jude James, Barry Tee, Brian Hurst, Roger Barry, The Lone Ranger (former Radio One and Essex Radio DJ Dave Gregory), Lee Randall (Randall Lee Rose), Jim Colvin and Louie St Clair plus specialist shows from Jez Nelson, Gilles Peterson, Tomek, Clive Richardson, Steve Barnard and Mastermind's Dave VJ and Max LX.

This was Solar's strongest period on air. It had the pick of DJs from London's dance music scene, with a professional-sounding output that was populist enough to pull in a good daytime audience but also on the evening and weekend specialist shows had presenters who knew their music. In April a survey made its way to several press outlets purporting to come from the IBA and giving Solar over 1.4 million listeners at the weekend. It turned out to be a fake, but the station had become a popular choice for many listeners.

The popularity of Solar and its appearances in the press attracted some resentment, however. In July the station suddenly went off the air and when staff went to the transmitter site they found that the eighty foot aerial mast had fallen down, damaging a neighbouring roof and demolishing a wall. Tony Monson announced "At first we thought it was an accident. But, on closer inspection, we were horrified to see the aerial had been deliberately hack-sawed. It has to be one of our rivals as this sort of thing has happened before. On Friday someone broke into our studio and stole our transmitter, but we've managed to get it back. I won't name names, but I know who the culprits are."[114]

The first closedown

When the announcement of the community radio experiment was made, Solar decided to come off air to apply for a licence. The final closedown went out on 29 September 1985, with many DJs in the studio to say farewell. Paul Buick took the opportunity to explain their recent problems with the breakfast show going off air. This was apparently caused by a group of builders who every morning would stand on top of the scaffolding where they worked watching women go by below and inadvertently getting in the way of their infra-red link transmitter beam.

Solar's licence application was more interesting than Horizon's, promising coverage of a wide range of black music, with specialist music and spoken-word programmes in the evening and a structure that they said properly represented the community they intended to serve. Not all the DJs were interested in going legal, however. Louie St Clair set up TKO and was joined by a few Solar DJs, though Tony Monson announced to the press that anyone still broadcasting illegally would be banned from a legal Solar.

Solar returns to the airwaves

In the event, the experiment was cancelled and so after a couple of weeks of test transmissions they returned as a pirate on 15 December 1986 on a new frequency of 93 FM, now kept on air by the Alice's Restaurant engineers. They went straight into a full seven-day programme schedule, not radically changed since their previous appearance on air. However, this did not last for long as they were hit by a series of raids and clashes with another group that also wanted to use the 93 FM frequency. They struggled through to Christmas before disappearing from the airwaves for seven weeks.

When they returned in February '87 it was for weekends only and minus some of the specialist shows. DJs at this time included Sammy Jay, Tony Hodges, Mark McCarthy, Graham Gold, Jez Nelson, CJ Carlos, Les Adams, Tony Monson, Dave Collins, Barrie Stone, Brian Hurst, Mark Wells, Jude James and Robert Allen. After the problems at the end of the previous year they soon re-established themselves as a regular presence on the capital's airwaves each weekend. The station saw itself as London's quality soul station, with Tony Monson later explaining "If Kiss had the majority of trendy club-goers at any one time, Solar was trying to cater for the soul fans who couldn't handle the intensity of the club scene."[115]

That autumn Solar began finding it harder to stay on air, at one time losing a transmitter four weeks in a row. Solar was now broadcasting from the tops of tower blocks rather than a permanent site and there were increasing thefts of rigs by other operators. They finally managed a return to seven day broadcasting that winter, but following a studio raid in March 1988 they went back once more to only broadcasting at weekends, minus a number of the less-committed presenters. Eventually Solar called it a day as a pirate in October 1988.

SOLAR 93

We are back on 93MHz
FM STEREO with all the
familiar presenters!!

24 hours a day — 7 days a week
with the very best in
SOUL-JAZZ-FUNK and REGGAE
For further information
Call us on — 01-519 8884

. . . .

When the new incremental licences were announced, Tony Monson initially planned to apply on his own, but was persuaded by Gordon Mac to join Kiss FM's application instead. Tony was one of the launch DJs when Kiss returned legally, along with a few other names from Solar's past, but left when he decided it was not going in the direction he had hoped for. Solar Radio returned as a legal satellite station in April 1992, initially leasing chunks of time from classic rock station EKR, before in 1998 acquiring its own dedicated channel on which many of the former DJs began to appear. In 2000 they moved to Sky's new digital platform, where they continue to this day, as well as now being available on the Internet at solarradio.com.

Radio 103.4

A Monday night soul music service broadcasting on 103.4 FM.

ACE Radio

Asian Community Entertainment, broadcast daily on 96.2 FM during the first half of 1984. The station was then raided and the presenter on air at the time subsequently fined £300 plus £60 costs. It returned later in the year but a raid in February 1985 took it off the air permanently.

Radio Activity

A Radio Activity appeared on and off with low power transmissions on a variety of frequencies from the summer of 1984. It's not clear if this had any connection with the later station founded by Ben West. That Activity launched in August 1985 on 89.9 FM with a 100W transmitter from a location at Crystal Palace and began sharing time with K-Jazz as part of a planned group of stations called The London Alternative Broadcasting Network. However, this quickly fell apart leading to the birth of Starpoint Radio, though Activity was more of a pop station than its successor.

British Greek Community Radio

BGCR were originally on the air to North London in 1984. Following the axing of the community radio experiment they returned to the air in 1986, though they were hit by frequent raids and broadcasts did not continue for long.

Contrast FM

A split from Radio Shoestring by Paddy Jaye and other DJs who wanted to concentrate on playing soul music rather than being an East London community radio station. Contrast broadcast every day to North East London from Christmas 1984 to early 1985 on 90 FM. The station lost over £3,000 of equipment in one raid and one of the DJs was subsequently fined £600.

Countdown Radio

A one-off station broadcasting on 92 FM from South London in the run-up to the new 1984 Telecoms Act coming into effect.

Elvis Fan Station

A Saturday afternoon station based around Elvis Presley music and broadcasting on 92 FM.

Imagine

Broadcasting from the Epping area on 92 FM with a soft rock service from presenters Steve Martin, Pete Simmons and Dave James. Programmes were on tape, initially just two hours per week every Monday night from a 40W transmitter – or 10W after a raid. The station was particularly prone to raids or transmitter theft for some reason. One evening they did a one minute test transmission at 8pm, then when they returned to the site to start programmes at 9pm the equipment had already gone. Imagine closed in 1986 and founder Steve Martin would go on to do shows on RFM and The Music Machine.

JWR

Broadcasting on Sundays on 102.95 FM.

Radio Love

A Greek station operating on 90.2 FM in North London.

Radio Marilyn

Marilyn broadcast every night from 8-11pm with hi-nrg and gay dance music on 90.7 FM. This side of London's clubland was largely unrepresented on London's pirates. At least one of the presenters was also involved with Radio Invicta.

Radio Memphis

After Radio City closed down, Superman and Memphis Mick started Radio Memphis in 1984. The station broadcast every Sunday lunchtime with three hours of rock 'n' roll on 1260 AM. Other presenters included

Chips and DJ Murf. Transmissions continued until 1987, making them one of the very few remaining medium wave unlicensed stations at that time. Some of the presenters were later involved in the FM rock 'n' roll station Radio Embassy while others appeared on the very short-lived Radio Liberty and Cityside Radio.

Panos Radio
Originally broadcasting from the Greek restaurant of that name in North London, Panos Radio first appeared in 1984. Early programmes went out live from the restaurant each evening until a raid closed the operation down – that must have been entertaining for the diners. The station returned in 1988 on 89.4 FM, apparently now as a stand-alone operation.

Rainbow Radio
A small Essex station that was on the air every Sunday with pop and rock programming until they were tracked by people at a local BBC training centre who started to cause them problems. The station made occasional appearances through until 1988. Presenters included Dave Andrews, Andy Johnson and Mike Stone.

Radio Spinach
A short-lived operator on 90.4 FM.

Radio Venus
Broadcasting on 92.2 FM every day until a raid in February 1985 took them off the air permanently.

Voice of the Greek People
Broadcast in 1984 until a raid when station boss Aliz Giougas (described in court as a "housewife") was fined £250 with £5 costs. It had previously been raided three times and several thousand pounds of equipment seized. The station returned in 1986 on 105.2 FM for a few months.

Wandle Valley Radio
Broadcasting from near Carshalton, Wandle Valley Radio was a local station operating weekly on 90.2 FM. It was founded by Radio Invicta's Roger Tate (Bob Tomalski) with engineer Alan Rogers. Programmes were a mix of soul and pop and it also put listeners live on air to make requests over the phone. WVR had two main innovations. First, it was probably the earliest unlicensed station to make use of a microwave link to transmit programmes from the studio to the transmitter site. Second, after the end of the conventional programmes it carried thirty minutes of computer software for the BBC Micro and TRS-80 microcomputers – at this time home computers predominantly stored software and data on ordinary cassettes.

Stand by for broadcast at Alice's Restaurant in 1986. Photo by Pyers Easton.

1985

The community radio experiment

On 23 January 1985 Home Secretary Leon Brittan announced that he intended to "enable community radio to develop as soon as possible"[116].

Community radio was already a part of several other countries' broadcasting systems, a third tier alongside state broadcasters like the BBC and commercial stations such as those licensed by the IBA. They were defined as non-profit-making organisations, owned and run by the communities they served and broadcasting programmes produced by local volunteers – though most had some paid management to oversee them. Stations in Australia and Canada particularly provided a model for community radio's introduction in the UK and a number of Australians become involved in projects here.

Prior to the launch of its local radio services in 1970, the BBC had experimented with (unbroadcast) ideas involving greater community involvement in programmes. Frank Gillard, its director of sound broadcasting, argued that small, cost-effective stations could exist with just a simple VHF transmitter and a few tape recorders. In 1977 the Community Communications (COMCOM) group had been formed to push for community radio and their work helped gain acceptance for the idea from the government's Annan Committee on the future of broadcasting. Following the formation of the Community Radio Association in 1983, lobbying intensified for the government to licence this new tier. Some unlicensed stations had also experimented with forms of community access radio, notably Radio AMY and Our Radio.

Many involved in community radio came from a background in progressive politics. In 1983 the Greater London Council funded the Community Radio Development Unit, which backed six projects seeking licences as well as the community radio magazine Relay. The GLC's radical-left leaders saw this in part as a way of challenging the dominance of the right-wing press. While the community radio movement included many with a genuine interest making good grassroots radio that was relevant to those they served, there were consequently some for whom class struggle and identity politics took precedence.

On the libertarian right there were those who saw community radio funded by philanthropy or local fundraising – the American model – as a more ideologically-acceptable alternative to the BBC. Not everyone was averse to such stations being funded by advertising or sponsorship either. In 1984 free market think-tank the Adam Smith Institute, influential on the right of the Conservative Party and with input from Radio Jackie station organiser Peter Stremes, published a report on the future of broadcasting that recommended the breaking-up of the BBC and the replacement of the IBA with a new body that would only oversee frequency allocation. Others had more practical concerns: The Institute of Practitioners in Advertising heavily lobbied in favour of broadcast deregulation simply to expand the options available for advertisers.

Then there were the pirates who for lack of any alternative way to realise their broadcast ambitions co-opted the community radio name for their own, often profit-making, ventures: smaller-scale independent local radio like Radio Jackie, stations for ethnic communities like London Greek Radio or Sina Radio and those seeking specialist music formats like Solar Radio or Alice's Restaurant, who could now define themselves as 'community of interest' stations.

The Home Office (in charge of broadcasting policy matters) were also under pressure from Trade and Industry Secretary Norman Tebbit (whose department managed the broadcast spectrum) to get on with opening new services as a way of dealing with unlicensed radio. Brian West, director of the Association of Independent Radio Contractors hinted that the DTI was "harbouring the thought that it will be somewhat easier to legalise the pirates than to clamp down at them."[117] The split in responsibilities between the two departments was the cause of many clashes: the DTI thought the Home Office was too keen to preserve the status quo and defend the BBC while the Home Office worried that the DTI wanted to take over its broadcasting duties.

Three years earlier, the Home Office's Robert Hazel had told a GLC conference on community radio "We have not taken this forward as quickly as we would have wished. And this is not because of any lack of interest in community radio – quite the reverse, we are genuinely interested."[118] One year into his job as Home Secretary and in the face of intense lobbying, Leon Brittan – a more libertarian politician than his old-school predecessor Willy Whitelaw – decided to finally take action. Leon Brittan also seems to have had considerable personal enthusiasm for the project and his announcement was unusually fulsome.

Surprisingly, the Home Office decided that it would licence the stations in the experiment directly, rather than through an arms-length agency like the IBA. This wasn't completely bizarre: the cable radio stations like Radio Thamesmead, which had begun as an experiment too, were already supervised in this way.

Those had to conform to rules set by the Home Office, which even required them to submit their schedules each month for approval. The cable radio stations were desperate to be allowed real licences, even if just as an experiment. In 1981 John Cartright, the local Labour MP whose constituency covered Radio Thamesmead and Greenwich Sound Radio, outlined their case in Parliament, noting "It is, I think, typical of the official mind that such priority should be given to regulation and control and that this should be regarded as a valid reason for holding back those who are anxious to have a go in the interests of their community."[119]

Direct licensing was also seen as a way of circumventing the IBA, whose lack of entrepreneurial spirit was believed by some Conservatives to be throttling the media industry. Unsurprisingly, the IBA was furious that the experiment was proceeding without their involvement. Getting little sympathy from the Home Office they issued a press statement saying "The IBA is anxious that this new development is not introduced to the detriment of the existing Independent Local Radio system. In any case, the IBA believes that ILR already provides an effective and self-financing form of local community radio." They demanded that the new stations "should be required to operate under similar financial and general obligations to the ILR companies; otherwise they will constitute unfair competition."[120]

The idealistic community radio supporters and the more entrepreneurial pirates were soon sparring in the press over definitions. "We're not talking about get-rich-quick cowboys or giving franchises to small cliques of businessmen", said the CRA's national organiser, Ray Beatty. "We mean genuine community stations run by local people."[121] Meanwhile Peter Stremes corralled fourteen pirates including Jackie and Solar into the 'Campaign for Successful Radio in Britain', holding a meeting in Parliament chaired by Jackie's local MP Angela Rumbold and with support from other Conservative MPs. Spokesman Charles Turner from Stockport pirate KFM complained about the CRA "They don't take into account the single most important thing – and that's what the public wants."[122] For those hoping for radio free from commercial interests, Angela Rumbold made clear "There is no role at all for tax or ratepayers' money in community radio."[123]

The death of the super-pirates

The prospect of community radio licences and a newly energised Radio Investigation Service acted together to kill off most of the super-pirates. Radio Shoestring, recently back on air for the first time since July, were raided at their studio on 2 January and left the airwaves. After causing interference to Gas Board communications having recently moved to a new frequency, JFM were next for a studio raid. Station boss Brian Anthony was also served with an injunction by the Gas Board against further broadcasting.

On 1 February Radio Jackie were raided and it was made clear that they were not going to be allowed to continue as they had before. Showpiece raids the same day took out all the stations in Crystal Palace and the major operators elsewhere in town. Three days later Jackie closed down for the last time as a pirate, having decided it could not continue as before. The raids on the other stations did not let up as they had in the past and in June Skyline Radio decided to call it quits as well.

On 26 July the full details of the community radio experiment were announced. There were to be 21 licences in total, with five stations in London: three neighbourhood community stations in South East London, South West London and North London and two community-of-interest stations, one on VHF for South London and one on medium wave for North London. Unlicensed stations would be able to apply as long as they were no longer on air, but they had only nine and a half weeks to get their applications in. By the end of September London had said goodbye to Horizon, Solar and London Greek Radio.

Suburban soul meets urban reggae

Invicta, JFM and Horizon had come out of the predominantly white suburban soul scene. Former JFM DJ Smokey Joe later explained "At that time there was a big gap between the black community and the guys who were doing pirate radio. It was a 'them and us' situation. There was all these white guys doing pirate radio and when they came out they went to all the black clubs, and it was like a real roadblock. I mean, they were all good presenters and all good friends y'know, but there was just this gap – there were no black presenters as such."[124] The exception was DBC with its roots in the bohemian Notting Hill, though with limited resources that had not always been a consistent presence on the airwaves.

This was to change with each new wave of stations. LWR had returned the previous September and under its new boss Zak, a club promoter born in Britain to

Ghanaian parents, it had dropped the daytime pop programming for soul and reggae and had introduced new black presenters. Quickly filling the hole left by Horizon and Solar were Fame FM and TKO. Fame was owned by brothers Trevor and Spencer Williams, who promoted a night at the Podium Club in Vauxhall targeting black urban professionals, and they brought in Horizon's Chris Stewart to act as a consultant in setting it up. TKO was run by Louie St Clair, one of a handful of black DJs at Solar, with initial help from Solar's Paul Buick and CJ Carlos.

While still showing their origins in the earlier stations, their dominant daytime sound was starting to change to the lovers' rock and soul that appealed to an Afro Caribbean audience. Fame FM DJ Cleveland Anderson later explained how "there were two sides to the soul scene in London. There was the south; the black side. Then if you like there was the Chris Hill – Goldmine and Lacy Lady, the Caister side of soul. There was a difference in the music, it was all soul, but there was a difference."[125] These three stations can be seen as a transition between the previous generation of more broadly-appealing soul pirates and the broadcasters that followed who were solely targeting a black audience.

Club promoters turned out to be ideal cover for operating a pirate station. They were always hungry for punters for their events. They dealt with large amounts of cash taken on the door, enabling income from adverts to be easily laundered and money to be skimmed to pay engineers and rent. They had access to the club security muscle that was sometimes needed to keep their competition respectful or make their advertisers pay their bills.

Despite beginning to scale back the size of the Radio Investigation Service, the pressure did not let up on the pirates. The RIS announced that in future it would devote more resources to stopping those causing interference, rather than helping listeners and viewers with reception problems. The House of Commons was told that across the UK in 1985 there had been 136 prosecutions, only one of which was unsuccessful. This came at a cost of £600,000 for the financial year. There had also been expensive action against Laser 558, with the DTI spending £50,000 a month to hire a boat to monitor supplies to the station. In the end it was Laser's own failures – primarily an inability to successfully monetise its huge audience due to the laws against offshore radio – that sank its operation.

In July, Manchester MP Tom Pendry asked the Secretary of State for Trade and Industry "if he will give an estimate of the date by which he expects to have eliminated pirate radio broadcasting within the United Kingdom." John Butcher responded "I cannot estimate when unlicensed broadcasting will be eliminated since the individual broadcaster, not I, takes the decision on whether to broadcast. What I can ensure is that breaking the law in this way is subject to rapid enforcement action and financially is never worthwhile."[126] That was more hope than reality.

On The Air

Fame FM
Black music radio, 1985

Fame FM was the less-successful of the stations to come out of the closure of Horizon and Solar. It was started by Trevor and Spencer Williams, promoters of the Spots Club at the Podium venue in Vauxhall (now The Colosseum) and later investors in the legal WNK. Horizon's Chris Stewart was brought in to advise them on getting the station on the air, though its format was more geared towards Afro Caribbean listeners and it carried much more reggae than its predecessors.

Following test transmissions on 12 December 1985 there were only intermittent programmes on 94.5 FM over the next few weeks, due to a combination of their aerial repeatedly blowing down in high winds, lack of technical experience and at least one raid on the transmitter site. Fame eventually broadcast for three months before a studio raid on a house in Streatham took it off the air permanently and its backers decided they'd had enough. In the subsequent court case it was alleged that the station had repeatedly jammed Gas Board communications, though the defendant escaped with only a £150 fine and £50 costs.

Presenters on Fame included Nigel B (who would go on to be Programme Controller at TKO), Cleveland Anderson, Lyndon T and CJ Carlos – who was also doing shows on TKO at the same time.

A station with the same name and jingles briefly returned in the spring of 1987 and summer of 1988 operating weekends only, but on both occasions did not last long.

JBC
Harlesden's black community radio pioneers, 1985-1989

Today JBC has almost vanished from view, but it was a pioneer in black community broadcasting in the UK. The station began in the spring of 1985, moving straight into seven-day operation on 97 FM.

JBC was set up by DBC founder Lepke (Leroy Anderson) with one of the last DJs to join that station, Challenger (Stanley Crosdale). The initial team had all previously been on DBC's seven-day service. Unlike most pirates of that time, who took great steps to hide their operations, JBC operated openly from a small studio in the back of Challenger's TV repair shop in Harlesden. While this meant that there was no way for the DJs to get out of a prosecution on the occasions that the DTI did visit, it also gave the station protection because it was a lot simpler for the investigators to meet their numbers by plucking transmitters off the roofs of tower blocks.

JBC made significant efforts to provide programmes for the local area and build links with its community – including the police – rather than just being an all-out commercial operation. In January of 1986 the station held a successful protest meeting at Brent Town Hall and began a petition for it to be given a licence. JBC received the backing of the ruling Labour group on Brent council, whose leader was interviewed live on air – reportedly causing a raid planned for the same time to be abandoned. Together with broadcasting on lower power and on 104.8, a completely vacant channel, these activities may have helped them escape the near-weekly raids that others were seeing at the time. Not having to spend so much effort on evading the authorities gave them more time to concentrate on their programmes instead.

Programmes

JBC's earlier broadcasts started in the afternoon on weekdays, with a core sound of reggae, lovers' rock and a little soul. Mid-evenings they switched to specialist shows, covering soca, African beat, soul and Asian soul. On Saturday mornings they had their children's show, with a mix of discussions involving local children in the studio and some trying their hand at DJing. On Sundays there were two gospel shows: an early morning one concentrating mostly on music and a late afternoon one involving two local church ministers to which listeners could call in.

By the summer of 1986 programmes were going round the clock, with a breakfast show from Amion Zee, mid-mornings from Steve Barnard (BBC Radio London's original reggae presenter), then Princess Asha, Dimples and Challenger on drivetime. Evening programmes extended to cover roots reggae and jazz while on Sunday lunchtimes Patricia presented a programme for the big Irish community in North-West London.

Listeners increasingly appeared on the air in phone-ins and Steve Barnard and Challenger both presented shows discussing topics relevant to the local community. It was the closeness to their listeners that helped make them a success according to Challenger: "It's the way we present the programmes that makes us different and popular. We got a Caribbean flavour: the things we say, the way we talk, the records we play, the type of talk. People like it 'cos they take part in it"[127]

Raided on TV

JBC wasn't completely without raids. On 28 January 1987 a TV crew from Channel Four's Bandung File programme were filming at the station when the DTI turned up. This did not appear to be coincidental: Dilys Gane, Director of the Radio Investigation Service was present for the first time in a raid. As he walks through the TV shop to the studio behind, investigator Eric Gotts can be seen putting his hand over the camera lens to prevent them filming him. The officers can be heard on the report questioning JBC's staff that they were not hiding anything from them. This was because JBC kept the more expensive power amplifier for the transmitter hidden up a chimney. JBC returned to the air the following day. After this, raids happened more regularly, with the DTI smashing down the door of the shop on one occasion so they could gain access.

Like many other unlicensed stations, JBC opted to close down on 31 December 1988, hopeful of a future licence. However, no licence for North-West London was offered and after some initial noise in the press they returned in the summer of 1989 as a pirate. These transmissions continued up until the spring of 1990 after which they disappeared from view. Challenger is not believed to have returned to broadcasting after, though several of the DJs then went on to work for other black stations around London in the nineties. None of their successors quite got their programming mix right in the way that JBC did.

Left: in the JBC studio in 1987. Right: Eric Gotts and Dilys Gane exit the building after the raid.

Kiss FM

The bridge between seventies soul and eighties dance, 1985-1988

As the autumn of 1985 crept in, London's airwaves were a lot quieter. JFM had been silenced in a heavy raid earlier in the year while Horizon and Solar were now off the air in the hope of a licence. Gordon Mac, Tosca and George Power were the regular DJs at Kisses Nightspot in Peckham High Street. Tosca kept bugging George to start a new soul station and finally, with London Greek Radio off the air so it could apply for a community radio licence, he had the time. Gordon, former drivetime jock on JFM, was more reluctant at first to get involved but Tosca finally convinced him. The final founder – if not a soulboy like the others – was engineer Pyers Easton, who had been keeping LGR on the air.

From New York to a London squat

Kiss pirated its name, its concept and its logo from New York's WRKS Kiss FM (perhaps with a little inspiration from the club where its founders worked too). Since changing format to become a black music station in 1981, tapes of WRKS had regularly crossed the Atlantic where mixes from DJs like Shep Pettibone, Afrika Bambaataa and Mr Magic were hungrily devoured by music fans who wondered why London couldn't have radio like that. At the beginning the London Kiss didn't quite reach those heights.

The first broadcast went out on 7 October 1985. Initially with a studio in a DJ's house, they soon moved to a squatted flat in Charlton. The transmitter was in Shooters Hill, bolted with the aerial to a chimney of a shop. Gordon had sweet-talked the music fan who owned it into letting them use the roof. Kiss went into seven-day broadcasting straight away: Dean Savonne doing breakfast, then Gordon Mac, Nicky Holloway, Max LX and on drivetime, Tosca. Other shows came from Richie Rich, Tee Harris, Norman Jay, Paul 'Trouble' Anderson, Colin Faver, Dennis O'Brien and George Power. Some of the black DJs had been involved with a plan to put another station on the air, but jumped onto Kiss when it got on the air first.

When it launched, Kiss promised to the music press that it would be the first station in the UK with regular live mixing. In practice, the studio gear didn't really enable this, though some gave it their best. Musically Kiss was still to find its feet: while some DJs were playing more contemporary sounds there was also a reliance on boogie tracks that fulfilled more specialist tastes in the clubs but on air made it sounded dated compared to its competitors.

Kiss causes a traffic jam

Kiss' original location came to an end on 2 December. Having decided it was too dangerous to climb over the roof, the DTI got the local fire brigade to help them remove the transmitter and aerial. This took some time, causing a large rush-hour traffic jam back along the A2. The owner of the shop was threatened with prosecution and Kiss decided to move their studio as well. They returned a couple of days later with the transmitter on a tower block and the studio in Gordon's front room. For the next couple of weeks Kiss tried to keep up a full seven-day schedule, but the raids continued. Low on financial resources they left the air for two months. It didn't help when Gordon and his wife Kim were interviewed by social services worried about the stream of men turning up at their Walthamstow flat.

On 22 March 1986 Kiss FM returned to the airwaves, moving almost immediately to a new frequency of 95.3 and now operating weekends only. Several new names joined: Norman's brother Joey Jay with roots reggae, Meltdown's Jonathan More (who Gordon met in his other job driving a minicab), Max LX's DJing partner Dave VJ who had been away before, future rapper Derek Boland, Colin Dale, Paul Oakenfold and Danny Rampling. George Power dropped out of regular shows at this time, as London Greek Radio came back on the air, though he still guested occasionally. Kiss was now becoming more representative of the sound of London's clubland.

Through 1986 they became an established presence on London's airwaves, with a healthy line-up of advertisers and before long Kiss-sponsored gigs. They had now moved to a permanent transmitter site at Crystal Palace, but were still hit by regular raids. At one time the DTI seemed to be particularly fond of taking them off during Gordon's show – but Kiss almost always bounced back the next week. On the August Bank Holiday they put out their first outside broadcast, with a carnival party at Bentley's Nightclub in Canning Town. In September BBC Essex began test transmissions on their 95.3 frequency, so Kiss were forced back to the less clear 94 FM. Their first birthday in October was celebrated with a party and a special show with several DJs in the studios talking about the first year and what Kiss meant to them – unfortunately curtailed by the DTI taking away the rig.

Over the Christmas period Kiss FM planned to be on the air every day, though because of raids they didn't quite manage this. More new DJs arrived at the station at this time. Trevor Nelson from the Madhatter sound system had joined in the autumn after being spotted at a party by Tosca. He was followed by Steve Jackson, whose recent show on TKO had been very popular, and Tim Westwood, who had found himself off air for the first time after the failure of Derek Boland's new station, WBLS. As house music imports began to appear in the racks of London's dance music shops, the new sound grew in DJs' sets, particularly those of Steve Jackson, Colin Dale and Colin Faver.

KISS 94 FM
RADICAL RADIO

BASE
EVERY SATURDAY
AT
THE H Q 33 WEST YARD
CAMDEN LOCK
10.30PM TILL 3.00AM

5 £££££

HARD NOISE BIG PLASTIC

Gordon takes control

Although Kiss was increasingly popular with young London clubbers, it initially was not such a success financially. There was expensive rent to pay on their transmitter site and raids had been much heavier than expected. By now Pyers Easton and former Caroline engineer Andy Howard were running a successful business supplying broadcast equipment to stations across Europe and he wanted to concentrate on that rather than returning to climbing tower blocks in the middle of the night.

George Power was busy with London Greek Radio and Tosca had different ideas about the direction of the station.

A plan to make DJs pay more for doing shows on the station led to rumours of people leaving to form a new station, though in the end only Tosca went. He later explained "It was a mixture of my own arrogance and jealousy from others that saw me depart the station."[128] Gordon Mac bought out his previous partners and Martin Spencer and Lawrie Hallet from Alice's Restaurant's replaced Pyers on engineering duties.

House and rare groove

Through 1987 the success of the station built and built. The DJ roster on the station further expanded, so they were now going on air from Friday night and then by the autumn all day Friday too. Tim Westwood left for Capital Radio, with his former colleague at WBLS Jay Strongman taking over his Sunday lunchtime slot. There was roots reggae from Manasseh, and for several months the station came from a studio in Nick Manasseh's 23rd floor flat on the Commercial Road. Later they switched the studio to Trevor Nelson's flat, forcing him and his partner to sleep on the lounge floor at weekends.

House and then acid house began to dominate the younger DJs' shows, then after a summer visit to Ibiza Danny Rampling was the first on UK radio to go Balearic (his co-travellers Paul Oakenfold and Nicky Holloway had left Kiss some time back). Meanwhile, the soul DJs had now gone back further than the boogie they were playing when Kiss first came on air to seventies funk – rebranded as Rare Groove. Kiss and DJs like Norman Jay and Trevor Nelson were to play a major part in rare groove's success, though Gordon Mac later described it as "a monster that got out of our control."

Get on the Goodfoot

That autumn Goodfoot Promotions Ltd was formed as the legal wing of Kiss FM. Gordon sold shares to a number of DJs to help finance the station. Joey Jay, Trevor Nelson, Dean Savonne, DJ Tee Harris, Norman Jay, DJ Selwyn and Jonathan More took him up on his offer. Soon the station had a small full-time office in Greenland St, Camden Town, arranging club promotions like The Base in nearby Camden Lock and dealing with advertising. It was also home to a separate record label, Graphic Records, run by Gordon and Heddi Greenwood, which

Gordon Mac in a 1986 Kiss-FM studio. Photo by Pyers Easton.

put out compilations of old soul and boogie. Hooking up with promoter Guy Wingate's Ellerdale Productions they began events at The Wag club and other West-End venues. The Wag, where Steve Jackson was a resident, was also the location of the station's public second birthday party.

As usual over Christmas they moved to 24 hour broadcasting, with DJs doubling up on shows to mix up the music and make it more entertaining. These broadcasts also marked the start of The Word, a fifteen minute show covering music news, gossip, events and fashion. Although often reliant on what was in the music press that week, it also carried some more interesting original reporting and interviews. The Word was put together by Tony Farsides (aka 'Fast-ideas') with Lisa I'Anson. The rest of Kiss' output, however, remained resolutely male.

London's radical radio

1988 saw Kiss FM at its strongest, with a line-up that was the envy of other stations. Two more DJs from the short-lived WBLS had joined: Family Funktion's Judge Jules and Soul II Soul's Jazzy B. Matt Black began his eclectic late-night Mastermix Dance Party (the name another lift from NYC's Kiss FM), tempting musicians like techno godfather Juan Atkins into the Kiss studio. There was the first jazz show with Patrick Forge (ex Solar and now running the Sunday afternoon sessions at Dingwalls with Gilles Peterson), garage with the Zoo Experience's Bobby and Steve and even a short-lived attempt at a bhangra show.

Having been closed down at HQ for not having a dancing licence, The Base turned into Second Base at Dingwall's, a hugely popular event that bankrolled the station's activities through the year. Kiss FM merchandise began appearing in record shops and the lips logo stickers became a regular sight on the back of cars. Gordon Mac claimed they were getting up to 500 letters from listeners every week and Kiss came second in a poll of radio stations run by the Evening Standard. A later piece of market research in support of their licence application found 34% of 15 to 24 year olds had listened to the station while it was a pirate.

Lenny Henry, who not long before had been appearing in a sitcom as pirate DJ Delbert Wilkins, took on an honorary role as 'President' of Kiss FM and appeared in the press supporting the station. For their third birthday they organised three separate parties, a warehouse-style event at The Arch in South London with the station's house DJs, a special Second Base at Dingwall's and at the Hammersmith Palais three live acid jazz bands.

Quit while you're ahead

Amid this success, time was running out for the unlicensed station. In November it was announced that the IBA would be licensing a new series of 'incremental' stations. However, to be considered any pirates would need to be off the air when they applied. Anyone caught after 1st January 1989 would be banned from working in legal radio for five years.

Meanwhile there had been large raids on the offices of London Greek Radio and Faze1 FM as the DTI's Radio Investigation Service sought financial evidence of the stations' operations. These had resulted in massive fines when the cases came to court. It seemed very likely that Kiss was to be next. Goodfoot Promotions was by now operating openly from bigger premises in Finsbury Park's Blackstock Mews, while their studio was a couple of miles away in the back of Soul II Soul's shop in Camden and rather obvious to all its neighbours, despite DJs being banned from using record bags.

The Kiss FM team in 1988. Photo courtesy of Kiss 94 FM.

That December, Gordon Mac announced that he and the other shareholders had decided Kiss would close down to apply for a licence at the end of the year. For the last few weeks they broadcast 24 hours a day, with DJs playing their favourites and reminiscing about their time on the station. On New Year's Eve 1988 the final programme went out, with DJs saying goodbye in the studio and an outside broadcast at Dingwall's. After a final countdown Kiss FM disappeared as an unlicensed station.

Kiss 100 FM

Kiss was not successful in its first application, narrowly losing to Jazz FM. When a second set of licences were offered they applied again and this time won. Gordon Mac told the press "As a legal station, the door is open for us to do so much more. The listener will get a better service and for the first time London will get a genuine dance music radio station."[129] Kiss returned to the air on 1 September 1990.

Trevor Nelson, the DJ's representative on the station's board, admits the difficulty in adapting to the new broadcast environment: "Everything changed when Kiss went legal and we weren't ready for the market forces as really we were still pirate boys on a legal station. We made a lot of mistakes but what saved us was the wealth of new music."[130] In April 1992, EMAP bought out the remaining institutional shareholders in the station, taking over the remaining 6% still owned by Gordon Mac and the DJs in August. By June 1993 Kiss was giving its owner a profit of £400,000 a year on its £4 million turnover, though to achieve such profitability its format had changed out of all recognition from the pirate days.

· · · · · · · · · · · · · · · · ·

In 2011 Gordon Mac launched a new Internet radio station, mi-soul.com, featuring several of the original pirate Kiss FM DJs – including his co-founder Tosca.

K-Jazz
London's original jazz music station, 1985-1988

Early in 1985 a group of mostly Solar Radio DJs under the leadership of Gilles Peterson decided it was time to start their own specialist jazz station, K-Jazz. Gilles explained his raison d'etre: "There is nowhere to hear the great jazz classics that get people hooked on this music."[131]

Programmes on K-Jazz went out on Sundays between 10am and 8pm on 94.2 FM, rather than the late night slots to which jazz was often relegated. Initial DJs were Chris Bangs, Jez Nelson, Baz Fe Jazz and Paul Murphy, who had been a major influence on Gilles' sound. K-Jazz only had a 25 watt transmitter so they did not get out too far from their South-West London base and were regularly swamped by other stations.

In the autumn of 1985 Chris Philips approached the team with the idea of the station sharing time with Radio Activity and some other stations as part of a collective called the London Alternative Broadcasting Network. These were to be high power transmissions, reaching the whole of London from a transmitter located on Crystal Palace's famous pirate row. A first broadcast went out on 89.9 FM on 6 October, but they were taken off the air that evening.

According to Gilles, "LWR was pretty much the monopoly station in south London. We got busted, and we quickly ran up to our site in Crystal Palace only to be confronted by some bad boys. It wasn't the Old Bill, it was another pirate station. In other words, LWR."[132] It was two weeks before they returned, now on a new frequency of 88.6. Shows were presented by Kevin Beadle, Gilles Peterson, Chris Philips, Baz Fe Jazz and Tomek. They managed a few broadcasts through until mid-November, when the transmitter sharing idea collapsed. Chris Philips returned the weekend after with a new station, Starpoint FM, where Jez Nelson and Tomek also found a home.

Some of the other people associated with K-Jazz attempted a return to the air-waves in 1988, still on 94.2 but minus Gilles Peterson who was now on the BBC. This lasted just a few minutes before they were taken off air by another station. They then shared time for a few weeks with Starpoint Radio before giving up.

Starpoint FM
The revolution in (anti-)radio, 1985-1990

Chris Philips and Ben West worked together at a TV hire company and despite differences in musical tastes – Chris was a jazzhead while Ben preferred Italian pop – both shared an interest in starting a pirate station. They acquired a transmitter and on 5 October 1985 Ben West's Radio Activity took to the air on 89.9 FM and then the next day Chris Philips joined K-Jazz with Gilles Peterson and the rest of its DJs.

London Alternative Broadcasting network

The initial plan was for several stations to share the same transmitter as part of a collective called the London Alternative Broadcasting Network; others included Thames Music Radio from Steve Bishop and Tim Roberts (who brought more pirate experience from earlier West London stations) and Liberty FM (who never actually made it on air). Unfortunately they had their transmitter stolen on their first weekend on air, returning two weeks later on a better frequency of 88.6 FM. However, the collective quickly fell apart and so on 1 December 1985 Starpoint FM was born in its place.

The format for the first few weeks was a complete mix: Tom Ingram playing rock 'n' roll, Radio Caroline's Neil Francis playing sixties R&B, K-Jazz's Tomek with Salsa, plus reggae, gospel, jazz, hip-hop and top forty shows. Several names from the past appeared, including Skyline's Pat French and Ray Thomson, Jackie's Jerry King and Solar's Nicky Lawrence. John Dawson also jumped ship from LWR, helping out Ben West on the engineering side and presenting a soft soul show. Another early recruit was DJC (Carl Webster) who was to play a growing role in keeping the station on air, before long taking over from Ben West in running the station with Chris Philips.

A change in format

Broadcasting on a clear frequency from above a shop on Westow Hill, Crystal Palace with a high-power transmitter and a tall aerial stack, Starpoint was getting out across the whole of London and much of the surrounding Home Counties. Each time they opened a phone line for requests they would be inundated with calls. However, it was becoming clearer that such a diverse format

Chris Philips of Starpoint Radio in 1988.

wasn't really working. As they went into the spring of 1986 they began to change, dropping some of the specialist shows in favour of a tighter soul and jazz format from a core of committed presenters.

In May of 1986 they had a close escape when one Sunday morning the DTI turned up at their studio location, but with a warrant for a different address. They were refused access and the studio was quickly moved to an alternate location, restarting programmes in the evening. However, this marked the beginning of greater attention from the authorities. Two weeks later the DTI turned up at their main transmitter site and removed their aerial mast with a massive crane. They still managed to return the following week, though on reduced power.

The challenge of seven day broadcasting

At the start of July they made the move to seven-day broadcasting, with DJC, Chris Philips and Mark Mason presenting the daytime shows. However, this only lasted a few weeks. The DTI had begun more regularly tracing the links that connected stations' studios to their transmitters and were now also using private investigators to try and identify studio locations and key personnel. Chris Philips was caught in a studio raid, later fined £450 plus £100 costs, and from August Starpoint moved to continuous music tapes before disappearing from the air.

It wasn't until October that regular programmes were re-established, still broadcasting seven days a week but now with shows recorded on tape. DJC would get up at 3am to record the breakfast show, before taking the tapes over to the transmitter site for broadcast. According to Mix Master Mac, "I think when we hit 7 days it was such a big step, and maybe we weren't really ready for it. I don't think we realised what it entailed. Well, now we do. It's hard work, but then again, now we've started it can only get better."[133]

The problems from the authorities resulted in some DJs deciding it was too risky to continue, while others were convinced to move to TKO. DJC, Dave Sherry, Chris Philips, Mix Master Mac and DJ Dorsky now did weekday daytime shows while a number of names new to radio were added at the weekend. Over the winter they went through a sustained period of raids. One transmitter lasted just 55 minutes, another 65 minutes and one DJ was caught changing the tapes. However, in the spring they returned to live broadcasting with more new DJs, only to disappear in the summer of '87 as the raids intensified once more. Through the rest of the year they would appear for a week or a day only to disappear again.

It took until the summer of 1988 before Starpoint was a permanent feature on the airwaves once more, with a new weekends-only schedule, a new frequency of 94.3 and a change in style – what Chris Philips now describes as anti-radio. Shows from DJ Willber (Willber Willberforce, who originally broadcast as DJ Jazz), Chris Philips, Jez Nelson and Rob Galliano (Rob Gallagher) were built around a core of acid jazz – harder, danceable jazz mixed in with rap and funk – and presented with a big dash of dry humour in defiant opposition to what was on the rest of the dial, poking fun at more po-faced DJs with their endlessly-recycled clichés. It was often rough round the edges but at times brilliant, smart radio the likes of which you couldn't find on any other station.

From Crystal Palace to Sky Digital

Starpoint closed down briefly at the end of 1988 to see what happened, with Chris Philips and some of the other DJs leaving. Carl Webster brought back the station in the spring and continued running Starpoint on his own through to 1990 with a mostly new team. Just Paul Phillips is believed to have remained from the earlier days. From March 1990 they even went back to seven day programming, although raids did not let up and they were off the air for several weeks before a return in July. The station was also hit by thefts of transmitters, apparently involving stations that had moved onto nearby frequencies.

The final broadcast on 93.2 went out just after Starpoint's fifth birthday, in October 1990, with a party at Crazy Larry's in Chelsea. Carl said his last goodbye and the station closed with You Can Do It by Dino Terrell before disappearing into the static.

• • • • • • • • • • • • • • • •

A year later Starpoint returned with a Restricted Service Licence and Carl Webster then began working with Solar Radio on the Southport Soul Weekender special event stations before joining the management of Solar's satellite service. In 2005 he set out on his own and relaunched Starpoint on Sky Digital and the Internet, where it continues broadcasting today at starpointradio.com. Chris Philips joined Jazz FM and then later spent fifteen years at Kiss FM. Willber Willberforce joined Kiss FM as a producer, before moving to Radio One and becoming launch programme editor of its black music service 1Xtra. Jez Nelson was an early presenter on Jazz FM then launched Somethin' Else Productions, who became a leading supplier of independent programming to the BBC. He now presents the jazz show on Radio 3.

TKO

Son of Solar, 1985-1988

TKO was put together by former Solar Radio DJ Louie St Clair with help from Paul Buick and CJ Carlos after Solar decided to leave the air to apply for one of the community radio licences.

There was some cynicism that a soul station would be able to win a licence and that if it did then anyway not everyone would be able to broadcast that wanted to. Having got used to the publicity their pirate shows generated, DJs also worried about attendances dropping at their clubs. Solar's Tony Monson was upset that the new pirate might jeopardise their chances of a licence and made it clear in the music press that nobody appearing on TKO could be a part of a legal station. After supplying the initial 90 watt transmitter, engineer Keith Renton pulled out of doing any further work.

TKO first appeared on 11 November 1985 with test transmissions, which continued until the first live show from CJ Carlos on Sunday 1 December. In its early days much of the time was spent playing continuous music and it was also off the air for substantial periods. A lack of technical skills also led to other issues, with TKO and neighbouring Fame FM finding the signals from each other's studios interfering with each other for several days.

The following May they had their transmitter mast removed by the DTI and as they began assembling a new one DTI investigator John Garlic appeared in the street below to ask them what they were doing and suggesting that maybe they should stop. Studios were a problem too: on one broadcast Alastair Wright described how they were broadcasting from "a kitchen somewhere in London" and told his listeners "I've just sat the record deck on my lap and it's much better like that!"

It took until the autumn of 1986 for the station to properly come together. Nigel B took over as programme controller, organising the DJ roster and recruiting new talent. More quality DJs joined and TKO added a number of excellent specialist music shows including Dominique playing salsa, Steve Jackson's house show, Danny Mac and Sir Lloyd's reggae revival selection, Aitch with jazz and Ian Laird's African and world music show. In January of 1987 they even tempted former Horizon Radio boss Chris Stewart back on the air, though his shows appeared to be on tape. Other presenters included Jude James, Patrick Meads, Lyndon T, Mark Sebastian, Tony Norris, Ray Bradshaw, Tony Bevins and Nick Chemist.

TKO's transmitter site at Westow Hill in 1986. Photo by Pyers Easton.

By summer 1988 the station seemed to be going through a difficult time again. Transmissions were scaled back to weekends only and a number of DJs had left. Musically they also shifted to playing mostly reggae and lovers rock rather than the wider range of black music they had carried previously. TKO closed in September 1988. There were some broadcasts later as Atlantic Radio with the same team of presenters as at the end of TKO but that station did not last long.

Radio Badger

Two hours of pop music to West London every Sunday evening on 92 FM. They later adopted more of a dance music format and by 1987 were on the air every evening. The station is believed to have closed in 1988.

Bert's Hot Dog Stand

A one-off spoof broadcast of Alice's Restaurant on 92.6 FM from Radio Free London's Steve Ego and Andy Allman at Christmas 1985 with rock music and sketches from the station's kitchen.

Radio Capricorn

Broadcasting to the Hoddesden / East Hertford area on 90.3 FM – although early on their transmitter had a tendency to drift badly. Programmes were mostly chart pop presented by Gary Osbourne, Dave Brooks and Chris Turner.

Radio Contact

A dance music station broadcasting on Monday nights from South West London on 102.9 FM. Presenters included Les Adams with his mastermixes.

D.A.D.

Britain's first Asian soul station, D.A.D. – it stood for Davinder, Amir and David – began broadcasts in the winter of 1985. The station later returned as Trax FM following a raid.

Epsilon Radio

Broadcasting on 103.2 FM on Fridays from 9pm-3am with what is described as a magazine programme.

Radio Fulham

Broadcasting soul music weekends on 92.1 in South London.

Radio Galaxy

Broadcasting from Chelmsford between 1985 and 1988 with pop, dance and rock. Originally operating live from the house of one of the DJs, it moved to a lock-up garage after its first raid. They complained in the press that the DTI had damaged their roof when they took down the aerial from the chimney.

HMR

Harlow's Heavy Metal Radio operated for two years on 94.2 FM, delivering four hours of hard rock and heavy metal every Wednesday night from a 20W transmitter. The station's Barry Morgan later went on to do shows on RFM and Radio Jennifer.

Radio Infinity

A short-lived soul and jazz funk station broadcasting on 92.4 FM for four hours every Sunday afternoon.

Inner City Radio

Operating from South Essex, Inner City Radio was run by veteran DJ Mark Roman with engineering by Keith Stafford. It took to the air on 8 December 1985. The station was reminiscent of JFM in its heyday – where both had previously worked – with a classic soul sound presented by a group of professional DJs. Other presenters included Darren Fogle, Colin Edwards and Nick Jones. Initially broadcasting on 103.5, ICR later moved to 105.6. The station continued into the nineties.

London Town

Although one of the smaller soul stations, for a couple of years London Town broadcast regularly every Sunday night from 5-7pm with taped shows on 90.2 FM from the Watford area.

North West Radio

Broadcasting Sunday evenings in the winter of 1985 to North West London on 104.5 FM.

Radio Nova

Put together by Paul McKenna and Gary King, Radio Nova broadcast from above an estate agents in Bush Hill Park in Enfield. Like its founders, the other presenters were mostly drawn from Radio Topshop and included Andrew Hewkin and Patrick Lambe. The jingles came from Chris Carey's Dublin station of the same name. It lasted a month before it was raided and did not return to the air. Paul, Gary and Andrew all went on to join Hertfordshire ILR station Chiltern Radio.

Renegade Radio
Founded by former Alice's Restaurant DJ Paul Chamberlain, who wanted to have a station that had more of a hard rock / southern rock spin, Renegade Radio began transmissions in early 1985. The station broadcast on the East London / Essex borders every Sunday on 1404 AM with an hour from Paul and an hour from Dominic Forbes. Raided in October 1985, the station was off the air until a brief return in the summer of 1986.

Santa Star
A Christmas station from the Imagine / Night Star people on 92 FM.

Thames Music Radio
Originally planned as a part of the London Alternative Broadcasting Network, Thames Music Radio put out just one broadcast on 88.6 FM before the plans were abandoned and Starpoint Radio took to the air. Presenters were Steve Bishop, Tim Roberts, Andy Johns and Bizarre Bill.

Three Boroughs Radio
With a name that aped the BBC local station Three Counties Radio, 3BR began broadcasting in August of 1985 to Hillingdon, Harrow and Brent. The transmitters and the team all came from Radio Floss and they even considered resurrecting the name, but Andy Richards felt having had an official closedown it would be better for them to choose something else. Presenters included Tim 'Ubiquitous' Allen, Bob Williams, Dave Scott and Keith Murray. Transmissions were on Sundays from 10am to 4pm on first 1350 and

then 1125 AM. They continued until June 1986 when two of the presenters, including Tim Allen, were caught in a raid. Several of the DJs subsequently joined neighbours Radio Gemma.

Transatlantic Radio
A black music station broadcasting from East London on 102.8 FM. Presenters included Barrister George, Asher G and Michael J.

Radio Tree
Radio Tree was an entertaining roots reggae station that broadcast from a Brixton tower block with two-hour taped shows on 106 FM in late 1985 and early 1986. To quote station manager Bonnie Prince Charlie, "I rap / toast inna reggae style, Mac MacGregor, a red-dread-locked Scots Rasta, spins the discs and Bernadette makes tea and gives Afro vibes inna Caribbean black-gal style!"

Twilight Radio
One of the first black community stations, Twilight began broadcasting in November 1985 on 94.2 FM from South East London. Initially transmissions were on Saturday and Sunday afternoons only with a soul show followed by a reggae show. Gradually through 1986 the hours were extended and by early 1987 the station was operating a full seven-day schedule. Presenters included Sean Hatch, Pete Martin, Paul J, Del Brisco, Chris Nat, Hot Rod and Tony Andrews. DJs from the station joined Sky Radio before returning in 1989 as Twilight.

Voice of Cyprus
Broadcasting on 1611 AM to North London on Saturdays. This may have become Voice of London Turkish Radio.

Voice of London Turkish Radio
A rare medium wave station, broadcasting for two years – though not continuously – on 1611 AM to North London.

1986

The axing of the community radio experiment

The deadline for applicants to the community radio experiment had passed at the end of October 1985. Early in 1986 the panel to decide the winners met and submitted their recommendations to the Home Office. Now there was an ominous silence.

The previous September Leon Brittan had resigned his job at the Home Office in the wake of the Westland Helicopters affair. In his place as Home Secretary was Douglas Hurd, who came from a more traditional conservatism than the libertarian Brittan and had less of a personal interest in the project. It would take him time to get up to speed on matters in his new department. There were other difficulties with the experiment too, with the practical details turning out to be not quite so simple.

The original backers in the Home Office wanted very little regulation at all over how the new stations were to operate. It was the marketplace that would supply the balance: stations were to be given a licence and left to get on with it. With no regulatory body controlling what was broadcast, the only sanction Ministers would have against inappropriate material was to remove the licence. There was additional concern that this would be the first time that the government was directly licensing media companies, rather than working at arms-length through an independent regulator. This could open the stations up to political meddling, as had happened in other countries that had licensed stations in such a direct way. Technical standards for the new stations had been published, but turned out to be so onerous that it was unlikely even the BBC or IBA would be able to meet them. Meanwhile, the IBA and AIRC continued lobbying hard for the abolition of the experiment.

Leaks suggested that the panel had chosen groups more in tune with the Community Radio Association's view of community broadcasting, with a significant number of stations for minorities, such as the multi-ethnic Spectrum Radio. The first public hints of what was going on behind the scenes came in May when the Mail on Sunday reported "The Government is radically altering plans for experimental 'community' radio because of fears that channels may become propaganda stations for extremists."[134] The chairman of the panel, Stephen O'Brien responded that all the panel's choices would have run stations in a responsible way but, in reference to the recent riots, "Then there was Handsworth, Brixton and Tottenham and the ramifications became apparent."[135]

On the last day of June the government finally admitted that the experiment was to be indefinitely postponed. Douglas Hurd announced "various difficulties arose and anxieties were expressed about its exact form."[136] The Sunday Times reported that the axing was prompted by Norman Tebbit, who was "concerned that some ethnic-run stations, and some that had been funded by the Greater London Council before its abolition, might be undesirable."[137] Although Douglas Hurd was reported to have been in favour of the experiment continuing, Conservative Party Chairman Norman Tebbit – with an eye on the following year's general election – overruled his decision. The experiment wasn't going to deliver the small business stations like Radio Jackie that he and others on the right had championed.

In response to the announcement in the House of Commons, Clement Freud, the Liberal spokesman on broadcasting, said "Could it be that Mrs Thatcher is afraid of the voices of ordinary citizens, that it is all right for the Government to allow Mr Murdoch to take over the Times, but too dangerous to allow 21 community radio stations to experiment."[138] John Cartright from the SDP described it as a green light for pirates, saying it would now prove politically impossible to take action against them. While many from the community radio lobby were content to blame the Thatcher government, some of the former pirates pinned the blame on the involvement of the Community Radio Association.

The technology race

Since the start of the year unlicensed stations in London had been hit hard. The smaller numbers meant much more attention was paid to the operators that were still on air and there was also a rash of studio raids.

While the RIS had been able to trace studio links since as far back as 1981 this was not always an easy process. Links were directional, transmitted in a relatively narrow beam on low power between the studio and the broadcast transmitter site. There was also a lack of motivation by the RIS officers to do this extra work. Back in 1983 JFM boss Brian Anthony explained "I don't think really they're interested in looking for the studio. All they're really sent out to do is to get us off the air and that's what they do."[139]

While VHF Band III links had been the most common at the start of the decade, UHF links were now more widespread and these higher frequencies made it slightly harder to find the source. By 1986 engineer Pyers Easton had moved Kiss

FM and London Greek Radio to microwave links, which the RIS lacked the technology to trace and which used such a narrow beam that it was almost impossible even if they had (this could also make them a pain to align). Over time microwave kit became more widespread and affordable, adapting cheaper components from consumer satellite TV. Thanks to this technology Kiss FM never suffered a single studio raid in all their time as a pirate.

On top of these basic transmission methods additional techniques were incorporated. Some stations used one or more relays for their links, so the signal from the studio would bounce between different locations before arriving at the main transmitter. This made it easier to tell when RIS staff were on their tail and also meant that cheaper gear could be used for the final hop. The main transmitter that listeners tuned into was the one most likely to be taken away in a raid so its cost needed to be kept to a minimum. When microwave gear was so pricy it made sense that the broadcast transmitter should relay a UHF signal instead.

Also used were mains links, overlaying an audio signal on the electricity cables in a building, which could be handy to get audio from a studio in a tower block flat up to a link transmitter on the roof. There was some experimentation with infra-red links, although these had a very short distance and were prone to obstructions. The more money a station had to throw at the problem then the more the technical risks of pirate broadcasting could be mitigated. What they couldn't do anything about was the human aspect. According to Starpoint's Chris Philips "It was normally a lack of studio security that gave us up, rather than the technology." The RIS's David Mason was more sanguine: "They change their technologies, we change our technologies, they hide them, we find them, whatever..."[140]

In 1986 things changed as the RIS began putting more effort into raiding studios and brought in new gear that made it simpler for them to trace the VHF and UHF links. Alongside this they began using private detectives to follow engineers and DJs that they knew to be involved – their own officers were too well known by now. Almost overnight station studios began being regularly busted. In just a few weeks LWR, TKO, Starpoint and others were forced to give up live broadcasting and revert to taped programmes like the medium wave pirates of old. Unfortunately this then put them at the equally-old risk of being caught changing the tapes.

Raids, tactics and priorities

The first step for the officers in raiding a studio was to quietly find the location without tipping off the station that they'd done so. If they couldn't follow a DJ or engineer to the studio then they would need to begin at the main transmission site and follow the links back. Once they were certain they had the right building they would go to a magistrate to get a warrant allowing them to enter and search the premises before calling in the local police to accompany them on the raid.

Getting the evidence to show that the people inside were involved in illegal broadcasting was crucial. Prior to going in to raid a studio, the officers would log the music being played so that it could be matched with records seized in the studio. Next they would head for the premises with the police, showing the warrant to whoever answered the door or occasionally using force to enter the building. Once at the studio, the equipment would be switched off and an investigator back in the vehicle would record that this had put an end to the transmissions. Photos would be taken as evidence and those present would be asked to identify themselves before being cautioned. Anyone failing to do so or causing a problem with the process would be arrested by the police.

While those caught didn't have to say anything further, the investigators would still ask questions, making sure they had a rock-solid case should anyone decide to plead not guilty. They also hoped to gain intelligence that might be useful in future action against the station: the RIS had a database on many of the people involved, so when cases did come to court they could demonstrate individuals' long-term involvement and secure greater penalties. Thinking they were having only a casual conversation after the notebooks had been put away, more than a few DJs let slip information that was later used in court.

Finally the equipment, records, notices on the wall and anything else relevant in the building would be itemised and carried through to the vehicle waiting outside. Although in 1987 it was ruled by the Law Lords that records were not part of the broadcasting apparatus, they could still be taken as evidence for the case even if they had to be returned after. Alone at last, the former broadcasters would finally be left in an empty room to contemplate the impending magistrates' court summons dropping through the letterbox at home.

As well as raiding studios, action was also taken against the permanent transmitter sites on top of buildings at Crystal Palace and elsewhere. In May the RIS hired a crane to take down the high aerial masts that the big stations used. TKO

DJ Tony Norris had a close escape: "I was getting a coffee just before my breakfast show and watched the aerial of Kiss come down in front of my eyes. Ours was opposite and quickly followed. I went round to the studio and shut all the power and lights off, sat there for a bit and just left with the studio intact. Very lucky, as when I came round the corner Mr Eric Gotts was stood there no more than twenty feet away."[141]

The RIS also began putting pressure on the owners of the premises from which the stations operated, using the new powers in the 1984 Telecoms Act against providing support for unlicensed services. London Greek Radio broadcast above a Greek delicatessen, the owner of which was successfully prosecuted and fined for unlicensed broadcasting despite claiming no knowledge of what was happening on his roof.

RIS officials took to breaking in to premises to remove transmitters rather than waiting until landlords or shop managers were around to give them access. Later in the decade local councils were pressured to take action against pirates' landlords for not having planning permission for the tall aerial masts. These combined tactics eventually made using rented sites impossible and by the end

1986 transmitter sites for Kiss FM (left) and TKO (right) on Westow Hill. Photo by Pyers Easton.

of 1987 almost everyone was forced back to tower blocks. When raiding those no warrant was needed from a magistrate, making the investigators' job much speedier and a station's operation more precarious. A further strengthening of laws in 1990 ruled out rented transmitter sites forever.

O ver the years, those involved with pirate radio have tried to figure out why it was that some stations were subjected to heavy treatment while others seemingly escaped lightly. Looking back it's still hard to understand the authorities' priorities for raids, even if it is clearer quite how chronically outnumbered the investigators actually were at times.

Transmitters causing interference always went to the top of the list to be raided, though with unattended gear their owners often didn't find out why and would return with the same problem. Broadcasting seven days a week obviously put you at greater risk than the part-time stations. Pirates that had been previously operated for the love of it noted that they attracted more attention after engaging in commercial activities, like putting on regular gigs to raise funds to keep them on air. Despite this, the RIS insisted "They could be broadcasting a version of Gardeners' Question Time for all we care. It's the fact they cause interference that's the problem."[142]

Anecdotal evidence suggested stations involved in politics were more likely to be raided and most broadcasters self-censored as a result. Some pirates went as far as trying to take others off the air whom they felt were bringing unlicensed radio into disrepute. Members of one London rock station were alleged to have gone on a trip to the Midlands to shut down far-right shortwave station Radio Enoch. At the other end of the political spectrum, Our Radio reported more problems from fellow stations that disliked their programming than with the authorities – at least until they aired an interview with Sinn Fein's Danny Morrison when they were suddenly the focus of attention.

Our Radio make clear their stance.

Certain unlicensed stations with political content did appear on politicians' radars – notably Radio Concord and Sheffield Peace Radio – and they were heavily targeted compared to other stations on the air at the same time. DBC and Radio Zodiac also linked raids to specific pieces of political programming that they had carried. The mix of populist music with politics was perhaps the most alarming to the authorities. Douglas Hurd, however, insisted in an interview that he was equally concerned by a station like Jackie playing pop music and one like Radio Arthur supporting striking miners, declaring "Illegality is illegality"[143].

There were rumours that the Greek and Turkish stations were heavily targeted because there were concerns that their political stances might be a destabilising influence on their communities. However, with the major pirate stations taking the best frequencies, the smaller Greek and Turkish operators were often found close to licensed services, so the RIS was regularly under pressure from BBC and ILR stations to take action. The RIS reported raiding Greek Community Radio 59 times in 1987 – three times more than the next most-raided, RJR – and interference from a Greek station on 95.5 FM to Capital Radio was even raised in Parliament on one occasion.

Then there might also have been some personal preferences. The older officers admitted to a liking for oldies from the sixties, so those stations were more likely to be left until the end of the day out raiding. Whatever the programming, they usually got round to everyone in the end.

| | Times raided | | | |
Station	1988	1987	1986	1985
Britannia Radio	3	—	—	—
City Radio	2	4	—	—
Classic Radio	4	—	—	—
Faze One	7	14	—	—
Fresh	6	4	—	—
GCR	20	59	2	—
Girls FM	1	3	—	—
Gremlins	1	—	—	—
Grooves FM	1	—	—	—
Hits FM	1	—	1	—
Ice House Radio	2	—	—	—
Kiss FM	3	18	11	11
London 88	7	—	—	—
London Irish Community Radio	1	—	—	—
LWR	15	15	14	14
NMR	1	1	—	—
Passion	2	2	—	—
Playback	4	1	—	—
PRS	3	—	—	—
Raiders FM	2	1	—	—
Ramjam	1	—	—	—
RJR	1	20	—	—
Rock to Rock	4	3	1	—
Roots FM	1	—	1	—
Sangam Radio	9	1	—	—
Sina Radio	11	7	3	4
Sky Radio	7	4	—	—
Solar	3	13	2	12
Starpoint	3	5	10	. .
Traffic Jam	2	1	—	...
Time FM	4	4	2	—
TKO	8	8	11	1
WNK	1	4	—	—

A further eight unidentified stations have been raided on 27 occasions so far during 1988.

Figures given by the RIS in July 1988 for the number of raids on stations in London.

Protest stations

With the collapse in the community radio experiment there was considerable upset from those who had put great effort into their applications. A protest group ANCOR – Action Now for Community Radio – hijacked Capital Radio's airwaves in North London to protest the decision, gaining widespread media coverage for their actions. However, it brought them condemnation from other pirates, especially after they were all raided in response. One of the applicant groups broadcast briefly as the Hackney Broadcasting Authority, but unfortunately chose the same frequency as the much higher-powered Kiss FM so not many people heard them. Also on air in a separate protest was Radio Wapping, who interrupted LBC to protest the sacking of print workers in the News International dispute.

There was not, however, a big rush to the unlicensed airwaves even if the government's turnaround had made it seem more acceptable. London Greek Radio had quietly returned earlier in the year when it became clear a licence was not going to be forthcoming. In October one of the applicant groups, Community Development Radio, launched for what they specified was a one year trial only. Many of the earlier generation, however, realised the conditions for unlicensed broadcasting were now very different and had moved on in their lives: for them, jobs and families made it more problematic to go back on the air illegally. Instead the biggest wave of new broadcasters were those who felt most excluded from the legitimate radio system.

Radio for the Afro Caribbean community

In 1984 DBC had joined to the airwaves of West London as a seven day station. When several of the DJs decided they didn't want to continue, it was relaunched as JBC from the back of Challenger's Harlesden TV repair shop. Named after the Jamaican state broadcaster, JBC targeted a different audience from the stations that came from a clubbing background, more attuned to the musical tastes of the wider Afro Caribbean community. While programming was primarily music, JBC took its community involvement seriously. Over time it added more speech programming, with phone-ins on local topics, religious and kids shows as well as shows for other ethnic communities in its broadcasting area.

Although JBC was a little different to the rest, it was soon followed onto the airwaves by other black community stations. All of them tapped into the city's pre-existing ecosystem based around lovers' rock and reggae, which felt discriminated against and was desperate for radio exposure. In the early seventies while roots reggae was on top in Jamaica, a separate scene had developed in London. Roots, with its heavier sound and lyrics about sufferation, was picked up by mainstream British record companies eager to capitalise on the success of Bob Marley and marketed by them to a mostly student audience of male rock fans. Lovers' rock was still reggae but it was constructed with the song structure of soul and spoke to the second generation of Afro Caribbean immigrants, young women especially: more aspirational, more concerned with the everyday aspects of life like love and heartbreak.

Cut off from the rest of the music industry, lovers' rock had developed its own stars and producers, its own labels and distribution network, its own sound systems and its own dances and clubs. Although from the eighties dancehall from Jamaica began making inroads into the younger generation's affections, lovers' rock remained the core staple of London's Afro Caribbean pirates, not especially changed since its seventies heyday.

Rock 2 Rock from New Cross launched in April followed RJR from Tottenham in December. By 1990 all the areas of London with a significant black community had their own stations, with splits and copycat operations often giving listeners a choice of several alternatives in each area, each with a subtly different blend of music. A survey in 1988 showed that half of those from an Afro Caribbean background listened to the pirates each week in London.

The commitment to community involvement, rather than just to playing music or making money, varied significantly between stations. Some put an effort into carrying information and news items that might be of interest to their listeners but others had a rather tokenistic listing of helplines that could have been found by anyone with a telephone directory. Religious programmes played a part on many stations, whether it was a Sunday morning show playing gospel or inviting evangelical ministers to preach on air or take part in phone-ins.

It was now the lack of frequencies that became the primary impediment to broadcasting: new technology made it safe for these stations to operate, local ads and station events quickly covered any costs and there were always more than enough volunteers willing to break the broadcasting laws. In 1987 Tottenham's Broadwater Farm, home to RJR and WNK, had an unemployment rate of 43%, three times higher than the London average.

On The Air

Action For Choice on the Air
Campaigning for media freedom, 1986

AFCA began broadcasting half hour scratch tapes at random times from random locations in North London in the autumn of 1986 on 96.5 FM. Programmes were on the theme of the control of the media, with cut-ups of radio and TV news, speeches, ads and other found material mixed in with material by the group itself.

Action Now For Community Radio
Protesting for community radio, 1987

ANCOR interrupted the programmes of Capital Radio's 95.8 frequency across North London in July 1986 with taped messages demanding the government reconsider the axing of its community radio plans. The perpetrators had previous involvement in unlicensed community radio stations from North London. ANCOR's activities got them and their message in the press but provoked a backlash from the DTI that resulted in heavy raids on a number of other pirate stations.

There were later plans for a station to broadcast under the name Platform 88 and the station announced it had thirty hours of material ready to go out but these were never realised.

The Clockwork Wireless Broadcasting Company
Thamesiders return, 1986-1987

Three years on since the close of Thameside Radio, Dave Birdman had a head full of programme ideas and nowhere to realise them. Having got hold of a transmitter he put out a first broadcast on Boxing Day: "I recognise that no one else is going to employ me so I have to buy my own radio station to put my own voice out. It's tragic really."[144] Unfortunately the transmitter turned out to cause big interference problems nearby so he didn't repeat the experiment, though the people who did pick it up were excited by what they heard.

Early in the new year, a group of former Thameside members got together to consider doing a one-off broadcast to celebrate the station's tenth anniversary.

When it became clear that there was an appetite for a proper radio station, Clockwork Wireless was reborn. Broadcasts were at the traditional 7pm on a Sunday, with a first hour presented by Terry Anderson and a second hour by Dave Birdman. Aleks Wright and Buzby Berkley did a news slot focussing mostly on music while Hilly Downes did celebrity gossip.

Like Thameside's later days, engineering for the station was done by Ian Stewart, who built a 90 watt transmitter. The first broadcasts were from a wood at Old Redding near Harrow with an aerial array camouflaged in a tree and the transmitter buried in a ventilated box. When these turned out not to give the coverage they wanted a switch was made to a tower block in Shepherd's Bush. By chance Aleks found a cabinet that matched one on the block holding equipment for a private mobile service, so this was installed alongside to house their gear. Unfortunately the transmitter – now boosted to 175 watts – had heat problems which took a few weeks to resolve. Programmes were played over a Band IV VHF link from an auto-reverse cassette player, which gave them a bit more security than running tapes from the top of a tower block. By now the team had jobs that they couldn't jeopardise by being prosecuted for illegal broadcasting.

Creative radio

The shows were recorded on a Sunday afternoon to ensure they remained topical. Terry's developed his style from Uptown Radio, covering stories that were in the media that week mixed in with more offbeat items: "The comedy is quite difficult, when you have to come up with the whole show virtually by yourself." The different segments of the show were broken up by records: "At the moment I like quite a lot of the bands that turn up in the independent charts but don't find their way into the Top Forty. I think that there is a need for exposure of those bands because they're caught between two stools. They don't make it to Radio One / Capital Radio daytime type programming and they're not weird enough for John Peel."

Dave Birdman's show was less laid back in presentation style. A big part of it was given over to the Do It Yourself segment with guides on home surgery for beginners or how to make it in today's music business – that particular guide followed a sheep called Eric seeking fame. According to Dave, "You could say that it was thought provoking – or you could say that it was totally lunatic. That's how I think of it, just lunacy." These wonderfully scripted and edited sketches mixed in with daft sound effects and related tracks were unlike anything else on the radio at the time, legal or illegal.

The last transmission from Clockwork Wireless went out on 22 November. Each week they hid a bag containing an auto-reverse cassette recorder, stereo encoder and the link transmitter in bushes in a nearby park, which would be retrieved at the end of the broadcast when they were sure it was safe. Unfortunately the previous week some kids had found the bag and started to mess with its contents. As Dave stepped in to try and dissuade them, a nearby resident called in the police and he and Buzby were forced to make a quick escape. Clockwork returned as usual the following week, but that was the final broadcast to go out.

Although Clockwork Wireless produced some fantastically creative radio, in the more crowded wavebands of the late eighties it was hard for them to make an impact. Listeners were now sadly less likely to stumble upon stations broadcasting only a couple of hours each week, no matter how special they were.

The Clockwork Wireless transmitter. Photo by Ian Stewart.

Community Development Radio
Black access radio, 1986-1988

CDR began operations on 88.6 FM on 19 October 1986. The station was closely allied with the National Federation of Self-Help Groups and the Black Oral History Archives and broadcast one of the widest range of programmes of all the unlicensed stations in London.

Community   Development   Radio   Symbol of Truth

Initial help to get CDR on air came from Steve Bishop and Tim Roberts who had left Starpoint not long after it started – which may explain why CDR opted to use Starpoint's frequency during a break in broadcasting following a raid. At its launch, CDR was on the air at 4pm each day with a music show. Every evening there was a more community-oriented programme at 8pm and then back to music shows for the rest of the night. The station was unusual in preferring programmes to have sponsors rather than carrying advertising, which made a welcome change from the lengthy ad breaks on other broadcasters.

From its initial shows primarily aimed at a black audience they expanded with programmes for a wide range of London's minority ethnic groups as well as weekly programmes for senior citizens, women, students, and gay and lesbian people. The music format remained primarily black music, though it covered everything from the usual soul and reggae through to African beat and zouk. Phone-ins played a part of many live shows and brought to the air many voices that you would not hear on their legal equivalents.

Religion also featured strongly on the CDR, with weekly programmes covering the major faiths. These sometimes attracted controversy. On two occasions the station aired speeches by Louis Farrakhan, leader of African American group the Nation of Islam, in which he attacked Jewish people. The Board of Deputies of British Jews issued a statement describing these as "an insult to the Jewish people", adding "Black people, with whom we have very god relations on the whole, should be the very last to broadcast such bigoted material." CDR responded that the programmes were part of its community education programme and it would consider giving a right to reply. It stressed that "no way would we broadcast racist material."[145]

CDR was initially planned as a twelve month experiment, though in the end it continued broadcasting until January 1988. Throughout this time it was involved in regular lobbying of the IBA, Home Office and politicians in support of a licence. It put together a detailed application for the South London licence in 1989's incremental radio scheme, losing out to Choice FM.

Radio Duck
All feathers radio, 1979-1989

Radio Duck originally began transmissions from Tim Allen's bedroom in 1979, with its very low power broadcasts continuing until 1981. It relaunched on 17 August 1986 with the pop and oldies presenters from previous North West London station Radio Gemma. Initially broadcasting for four hours every Sunday evening, they later added Wednesday night shows as well. DJs were Tim Allen, Stuart Price, John Silver and Mike Peters. Shows were high energy affairs, packed with uptempo oldies and jingles spliced together from old sixties offshore packages and resung by Tim Allen. While usually on tape, there were also live broadcasts on Christmas Eve and New Year's Eve. This version of the station lasted for around a year, though there was a brief return in the summer of 1989.

• • • • • • • • • • • • • • • •

Many years later Duck returned as an Internet radio station at radioduck.net. After a stint on Radio Caroline, Tim Allen went to HMV's in-store radio while also doing occasional broadcasts as Middlesex Music Radio before going legal on Bedfordshire ILR station Chiltern Radio. He currently works at Wave 105 in Hampshire.

Hackney Broadcasting Authority
A community radio group goes pirate, 1986

HBA put out a broadcast on Saturday 4 October 1986 to coincide with the Community Radio Association's day of action in support of community radio. The station put out a press release that announced "There's no option. It's either sit around for another three years and hope for community radio or start to do something about it."

Amongst HBA's output were programmes on arranged marriages in the Turkish community, women's safety on housing estates, a history of Latin-American culture and a telephone link-up with community station WEFT in Illinois, USA. Unfortunately their 94 FM frequency was the same as Kiss FM who were using rather greater power so not many people were actually able to pick up the station. They announced plans to move to a new channel for regular transmissions but it is unclear if these ever took place. It was reported that having actually tried unlicensed broadcasting they became unsure whether it was really the way they should go.

Joy Radio
Soul from South East London, 1986-1995

Broadcasting from a Crystal Palace tower block, Joy Radio launched its weekend soul music service in 1986. As the bigger soul stations left the air it found increasing success and from 1991 moved to a seven day operation.

Joy played a mix of classic soul, R&B, rare groove and reggae. The original DJ team included reggae and lovers' rock specialist Darren R, engineer Noel

Joy Radio's Steve Collins. Photo courtesy of Steve Collins.

Humphrey and station owner Micky Toskin. Over time they were joined by Mike Howard, Clive Brady, Ian Eastwood, Dave Black, Steve Collins and Ray Bradshaw. Early on the station regularly moved studios between different friends' flats and lock-up garages. After Noel devised a more secure double microwave link system they took up permanent residence in a ground-floor flat in Anerley, a suitably-safe distance south of their main broadcast site.

According to DJ Steve Collins, "The double link kept the DTI off the station's back for quite a long period. The main transmitter location proved to be one of the best positions in London, giving an excellent broadcast coverage which reached all areas of the capital and deep into the Home Counties, with an impressively strong signal, without the need for an over-powerful rig."[146]

Joy Radio finally closed in 1995 due to a combination of its staff moving on to other things and an increasing loss of transmitters to the DTI and other stations. Many of its presenters remained involved with radio and music.

Network 21

TV on the radio, 1986-1988

Having attracted attention with their experimental pirate TV station, Network 21 turned their attention to radio. On the air on Friday and Saturday nights from 8pm to 5am, Network 21 carried a mix of left-field arts coverage with alter-

native and dance music. Reception on 89.5 FM was mostly limited to the south and central parts of London but the station's PR agency ensured it got press coverage greatly beyond its size.

Network 21 wasn't the first pirate TV broadcaster, with Thameside TV and Channel 36 putting out earlier transmissions, but it was the first – and only one – to manage regular programmes. Between April and September 1986 it broadcast a half hour of shows at midnight every

Friday on TV channel 21 from a site at Crystal Palace. Although these got out reasonably well to the centre of London, unlike radio listeners television viewers had no reason to tune around, making it hard for anyone to stumble upon their broadcasts. Programmes

"showed slices of London's artistic buzzing underground life as well as casual glimpses of everyday life, something which the normal television stations never showed ... We were also free to choose program content and style according to our own mood, without having to worry about ratings, advertisers or good taste standards."[147] They can now all be viewed at network21tv.co.uk.

The radio station came on air on 7 November 1986, a month after the last TV broadcast, and was less enigmatic in style. The first 3 hours on Friday were given over to The Magazine, a mixture of news, listings for cinema, concerts and theatre, interviews and new record releases. On Saturdays at the same time they had guest DJs with names like Gaz Mayall, Josh Ritchie, Jon Savage, Laibach, Daniel Miller and Kiss' Jonathan More. Other shows included the Mongolian Hip Hop show with Mix Master Morris, World Service with non-UK releases, The Bleach Boys with forties and fifties oldies and Sophie with new releases.

Network 21's radio service filled a gap in London for a much-needed smart, alternative station. It vanished from the airwaves in 1988.

RFM

The last rock giant, 1986-1990

The idea for Rock FM took shape in a pub as Dave Fuller explained CB radio to co-founder Claire Mansfield and described how it was possible to convert a CB rig to a normal VHF transmitter. It turned out that it wasn't, but they were now set on the idea of a station anyway and on 14 August 1986 RFM took to the air using a transmitter bought from Radio Infinity. While they had some knowledge

Claire Mansfield in their early studio. Photo courtesy of Dave Fuller and Claire Mansfield.

of how other unlicensed stations operated, they learned most of the fundamentals of putting together a show and how to transmit from getting out and doing it. The early broadcasts, which featured joint shows from Claire and Dave, were consequently rather rough and ready in presentation style and with occasional technical problems. They were, however, one of the few places that you could now hear contemporary rock music.

Gradually RFM started to come together and became a regular Sunday night fixture with six hours of programmes on 90 FM. Dave opened broadcasts with a show playing softer rock, Claire followed with contemporary rock and metal and then Dana Jay closed with two hours of indie. At this time shows were still on tape, necessitating dangerous trips to the top of a North London tower block. That winter Claire had a close escape when climbing down an ice-covered sloping roof. Starting to slip she thought she was going to go over the edge of the twenty-story block but luckily managed to hold on. They did some live gigs in conjunction with Colin Ward's rock roadshow, which featured in broadcasts. At Christmas they did a spoof live transmission supposedly coming from a pub, only for a number of people to actually turn up there, much to their embarrassment.

RFM were soon approached by people from earlier rock stations wanting to do shows. One night while installing the transmitter in Highbury they were accosted by Phil Thomas, formerly of the Alice's Restaurant site crew and rig builder for several stations. With his help they began live all-Sunday broadcasting. According to Clare, most presenters "simply turned up and introduced themselves at our infamous weekly Monday night meetings in the notorious bikers' (back) bar at the Moss Hall Tavern, North Finchley. On reflection it was probably because of the extremely relaxed atmosphere within the group and the copious amounts of free beer offered to them."[148]

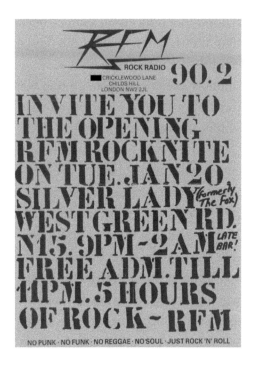

Joining the station came Arthur Burton (RFL's Andy Allman), Imagine's Steve Martin, Amanda's John Shakespeare, The Marquee Club's Monty Zero, Wolf and Mark Rogers. However, the younger Claire and Dave wanted a station that reflected the contemporary rock scene while the older DJs had tastes that lay more with a classic rock sound. This resulted in Claire and Dave leaving in October 1987 to form first DFCM and then Radio Jennifer, with Claire and Dana also doing shows on Raiders FM.

RFM continued its all-day Sunday broadcasts, now on 94.3 FM, adding more veteran DJs including Hugo Lee Jay, Christopher England and Bear Freeman, who reprised his Breakfast with Bear show from Alice's Restaurant. Several different studios were used for a single broadcast, linking to a mid-point relay that took the signal to the final VHF transmitter, usually in North East London. There wasn't any advertising, with the station funded instead by DJ subscriptions.

With the possibility of licences, RFM decided to abandon unlicensed broadcasting, although not all the DJs approved of the decision. The final broadcast as a pirate station went out on 25 March 1990.

* * * * * * * * * * * * * * * * *

Later in 1990, RFM did two broadcasts at bikers' rallies with Restricted Service Licence stations. They complained that one was spoiled by interference from pirates, which the RIS gave them no help in clearing. The plans for a full-time licence were not taken forward and the group fell apart due to musical differences. With some of the other DJs Bear was involved in Rock 106, an unlicensed station that launched in 1992. Arthur Burton has since presented shows on Southampton's Skyline Radio and several Internet radio stations. Claire Mansfield is now programme controller at Internet station Raiders FM. Dave Fuller presents a rock show on Sittingbourne FM with Claire as an occasional guest.

RJR

Black radio from Tottenham, 1986-1992

Like the earlier JBC, RJR took its name from a Jamaican station and began broadcasting from Tottenham in December 1986. It was aimed at a local Afro Caribbean audience across all ages, playing predominantly reggae, lovers' rock and a little soul. It also carried some community news and listings and for a while there was a church service every Sunday morning.

In March 1987 the Sunday Express accused RJR of helping to start the October 1985 riot at Broadwater Farm, despite the station not coming into existence for another year. DJs from RJR were dismayed at having to defend what they viewed as a family-oriented operation: "RJR is not politically motivated ... we are here to serve and entertain the community. We are DJs who want to play music we love and enjoy ourselves at the same time. I can't believe they think that's dangerous. RJR being on the air is helping the youth in so many ways. It's almost the only free entertainment left. The society is much happier and calmer."[148]

The station was successful in picking up local advertisers and DJs contributed a percentage of their earnings from gigs, although they insisted "RJR is not in this for the money, although the raids make finances tight." In its first eight months the station was hit fifteen times. Presenters included Chancellor D, Joe Douglas, Howie T, Robin B and future Station FM boss DJ Keithley.

In the autumn of 1987 co-founder Joe Douglas left to start WNK and a split not long after resulted in the short-lived City Radio. The original RJR is believed to have left the airwaves in 1992, though the name has since been used for another station operating in the same area.

Rock 2 Rock

Black radio from Lewisham, 1986-1990

Rock 2 Rock launched in April 1986, initially broadcasting on Sundays only on 90.2 FM from a set of tower blocks in New Cross. DJs on the station were almost all from the local area, many having met through local reggae shop Sound City Records. Rock 2 Rock played a mix of soul and reggae along with ads for local businesses and also put out some community information. By 1987 they were operating seven days a week, with a team of twenty DJs playing an expanded range of music aimed primarily at the local Afro Caribbean community.

Rock 2 Rock was hit quite heavily in raids, especially after an occasion when they caused interference to the Heathrow aircraft landing system. In one January 1988 raid the police were reported to have sealed off roads around their broadcasting site. After the harsh new broadcasting laws took effect in 1990 Rock 2 Rock decided the risk of continuing was too great and voluntarily closed down. DJ Mistri moved to North London's newly-licensed WNK, Angie Dee got a job on Kiss, while many of the others started a group called First Love Radio to campaign for a radio licence for South East London.

After several successful Restricted Service Licence stations operating for a month at a time, the group won a local licence in conjunction with broadcasting group UKRD. However, the station that came on air in 1999 was very different to Rock 2 Rock, with the black music it played seemingly only to satisfy the licence conditions. After changes of name to Fusion and then South London Radio, several changes in ownership and a further watering-down of the format it finally left the air in 2009. In their annual report, final owner Sunrise Radio blamed competition from unlicensed operators for the failure of the station.

Radio Wapping
Print worker protests, 1986

In January 1986, workers at News International, publishers of the Sun and the Times, went on strike after negotiations over new contract terms broke down. News International had built a new printing plant in Wapping, which they had said was for a new evening paper, but instead they switched production of the Sun and Times there using staff who weren't members of the print unions. The resulting dispute turned ugly, with large demonstrations outside the Wapping plant resulting in hundreds of arrests.

Into this situation came Radio Wapping. On 27 April it began broadcasts in East London using a mobile transmitter on the air for no more than half an hour at a time on the same 97.3 frequency as LBC. Holes in LBC's coverage in the area helped the pirate's broadcasts get through to listeners. It reappeared on several subsequent occasions, alongside LBC rather than on top of it. Technical assistance in getting the station on air came from former Our Radio anarchists while programmes were reportedly recorded in the studio of one of the community radio experiment applicants.

WBLS

Competition for Kiss, 1986-1987

In the autumn of 1986, Derek Boland quietly left Kiss FM to start his own station. It was to be named WBLS, after the main competitor in New York to Kiss. Rather than poaching staff from Kiss, he instead assembled an impressive line-up of DJs from many of the top West-End clubs and warehouse parties: Jay Strongman, Soul II Soul's Jazzy B and Aitch B, Barry Sharpe, Dave Dorrell, Family Funktion's Judge Jules and many more. Tim Westwood also jumped ship from LWR. Transmission equipment was sourced from Kiss engineer Pyers Easton's company, a studio constructed and everything put in place for the live launch party at the fashionable Limelight nightclub in Shaftesbury Avenue on November 6th.

However, before WBLS could come on air their studio was trashed. The station's Gary Neal revealed "We lost our decks, mixer, etc and also our transmitting part of our microwave link, which forced us to use inferior equipment. We are still confused as to who and why our first studio was smashed up as nothing was stolen. We expect it was another station and not the DTI."[150]

Concerned about this major new competition, Kiss asked Pyers not to provide them with any further equipment. Not long after, someone associated with WBLS threatened Pyers' business partner Andy Howard and a colleague and robbed them of a transmitter. WBLS managed a few broadcasts through until 1987, though with a poor signal on 88.5 that was masked in most of London by its much stronger neighbour Community Development Radio on 88.6. Derek Boland eventually decided he'd sunk enough money into the project and called it quits.

While it might not have made much impact on London, the style of music and the way that WBLS was marketed did appear to influence the future direction of Kiss FM and several of WBLS's DJs later joined Kiss.

Radio Activity

No connection with the earlier station, Activity began broadcasting in November 1986 with shows every evening in the week and all day at the weekend. Activity came from South East London with a team of 16 DJs playing soul, hip hop, reggae and other dance music on 89.5 FM. For some of the time the same group broadcast as TCR. Presenters included Mark Atkins, Trevor Dawson, Paul Taylor, Gary Fuller and Tosca.

Black Invicta

A low-power station that appeared briefly in the summer of 1986, describing itself as "The Voice of the Black Revolution".

BWL

A one-off broadcast in October 1986 on 105 FM that seemed to be mainly to take swipes at LWR.

Chic FM / Media Sounds Broadcasting

Sharing time on 92.9 FM every Monday evening from November 1986, though both had identical soul formats.

Community Radio Canvey

A small station broadcasting solely to Canvey Island on 93 FM with a mix of pop music and local information. On 17 May 1987 the station was raided at its studios with six RIS investigators and four police cars in attendance.

Radio Confidence

A reggae station that appeared in South West London on 92.7 FM in the summer of 1986 and continued to operate through to the following year. Broadcasts were on late Friday night into early Sunday morning with mostly music and little chat. At times they consisted of the same record being played repeatedly.

Radio Confusion

A low power soul, jazz and fusion station that broadcast for a few months in the summer of 1986 from South West London.

Direct Line Radio

DLR broadcast intermittently from the spring of 1986, though didn't usually manage to get out further than South London. Started by 'Dancing' Danny T (Dan Mills, who went on to join the BBC) and Nick Day (Nick Piggott, later of Global Radio), programmes were a mix of different styles though tended towards the pop and dance of the day. What they lacked in resources they made up for with youthful enthusiasm. Presenters included Danny T, Timbo, James Lawson, Tim Crushell, Def Jeff, Ben & Bill, Marconi, DJ Cyclone, The Godfather, Original T, Steve James, Paul Cook and The Soul Doctor.

Electron Radio

A low power soul station that began broadcasting to South West London in February of 1986. Programmes were four hours on a Sunday evening on 105.3, though these did not last too long.

Emperor Radio

A small soul station from the Streatham area broadcasting in early 1986 on 102.8 FM. Founder Scully went on to join LWR, where he also helped behind the scenes.

Radio Expansion

A soft rock and 'quality' pop music station that made use of London Greek Radio's transmitter after it had closed down for the night on Friday and Saturday nights. Presenters were Peter Wally (Pyers Easton – LGR's engineer), Mike Fish (known as Mike Andrews on RFM) and Steve Davies. The station later renamed itself Quality Music Radio but closed in the summer when other activities took precedence.

Radio Funk

A small soul station from the East End which attempted a seven day week schedule early in 1986 before apparently giving up not long after.

Radio Galaxy

A pop station that broadcast for a few months from South East London on 104 FM every Friday night. The presenters were very inexperienced making the early programmes somewhat painful to listen to.

Genesis Radio

A black music station from South London that took to the air in August. Initially only at weekends they planned seven day operation but were raided not long after and did not return. There was a later station with the same name and a similar format that began operation in the nineties.

JWT

A black music station that began broadcasting in July with seven day a week programmes on 104.3 FM.

Radio Liberty

A short-lived FM station that included some of the DJs that had previously been involved with Cityside Radio and Radio Memphis.

Radio Lion

A pop station broadcasting to Harlow every Sunday evening on 90.2 FM.

Radio Lumberjack

A low-power station broadcasting to the Bromley area on 92.5 FM from the spring of 1986 with a mix of different music styles interspersed with comedy bits. The station continued through until 1988 and was reportedly run by someone who worked at the Radio Investigation Service. This apparently enabled them to conveniently lose any information about the station so it was never subject to raids.

Lynx FM

A soul music station that launched in September.

Night Star

A return to the airwaves for Imagine's Steve Martin, Pete Simmons and Mark Jones in the winter of 1986. Broadcasts were on Saturday nights on 93.1 FM with a classic rock format.

People's Choice

Broadcasting soul to the South London / North Surrey borders, People's Choice began transmissions in April 1986 on 103.5 FM. The station was associated with the roadshow of the same name and DJs included "The General" Lee Doyle, ex JFM. Several DJs went on to work on LWR including Lee, Paul Simpson and founder Steve Harris. PCR broadcast from a very high location giving them excellent coverage even out into Hertfordshire despite using only 50W power. Initially broadcasting Saturdays only, they tried a seven day operation in the winter of 1986 but this did not last. After spending much of 1987 off the air PCR made a brief return in the summer of 1988.

Quest FM

A soul music station that broadcast at weekends on 90 FM from South West London. Quest launched in early 1986 but issues with their transmitter supplier resulted in a long gap until a return in the winter of that year. The station was raided regularly, though on one occasion the DTI turned up at what they thought was their transmitter site complete with a warrant only to find they had moved. There was also a lucky escape when a lightning discharge hit an aerial being held at the time by DJ Gary M.

Reach FM

A soul music station that broadcast on 94.2 FM for a few months in the summer of 1986.

Radio Reflection

On the air briefly in the summer of 1986 from North London on 94.4 FM. Described at the time as broadcasting black music interspersed with black political speeches.

Rock 1413

Rock 1413 managed a few broadcasts in the summer of 1986. They were linked to Electron Radio.

Spectrum Radio

No connection with the community broadcaster, Spectrum was a low-power station operating in the Epsom area in the summer of 1986 with a pop format on 90.1 FM.

Radio Star

A jazz funk station broadcasting on low power to North London in early 1986.

Studio FM

Initially known as Studio One, this was a dance music station that began in the spring of 1986 with a young team of DJs. Early DJs included Chris Phillips (not the Starpoint one) and Tony Humphries (not that one either). The station continued regular transmissions until 1988 on 92.9 FM. Several studio raids in late 1986 and early in 1987 resulted in time off the air. At one of these raids they reported that the DTI had turned up with what seemed like "half of North London's police force." For a while after this they ran taped shows with weekly outside broadcasts from Hackney's Mankind Club. The music format was initially soul, electro and hip hop but by 1988 they were spinning more house and rave.

Trax FM

Originally called D.A.D., Trax broadcast for much of 1986 from North West London on 103.3 FM with a team of nine DJs, sometimes weekends only but also at times for seven days a week. The studio was apparently in a caravan. It is now an Internet station at traxfm.org.

Turkish Community Radio

One of several Turkish stations that broadcast to the North London area in the mid-eighties.

United Kingdom Good Music

Named after the sixties offshore station, broadcasting for three hours on a Tuesday evening on 90.2 FM with jazz and blues.

Victory FM

Another South East London station from people associated with Radio Free London which broadcast intermittently in the late eighties.

Radio Vicky

An offshoot of Radio Gemini, broadcasting in South London with pop music from the fifties to the present day on 105.6 in the summer of 1986. Presenters included Marty D, Terry and Spotty G.

WONE

Briefly on the air in the winter of 1986 with taped soul music shows every weekend on 94.5 FM to the Romford area. There were reports that the station interfered with the police communications and after the DTI were called in they recovered an aerial strapped to a tree, a tape deck buried underground and car batteries hidden in the undergrowth.

1987

Payola and powerplays

With the recession now long gone, London's economy was heading for boom time – and so were its pirates. The number of stations was again climbing towards the level at which they would overwhelm the authorities' ability to deal with them, while microwave link technology was making illegal broadcasting safer. The previous year's activities by the Radio Investigation Service – hiring cranes to remove aerial masts, employing private investigators to follow station staff and investing in new tracking technology – had been expensive. The early months of 1987, before the start of the government's new financial year, saw a drop in activity against unlicensed stations, which made some suspect the RIS was short of money. Now they turned to the media to try and win more sympathy for their work and help build their case for a bigger budget.

First in June was an expose in the Evening Standard of payola on the London pirates. Paying radio stations to play records had a history in the UK going back to Radio Luxembourg, where the only way an artist could get significant play of their new record was to be on a major label that was paying for the promotion. On the sixties' offshore stations it became common practice, though presenters would sometimes rebel and refuse to play paid singles because of their often inferior quality – especially after one independent label invested in the debt-ridden Caroline and flooded it with their releases.

Once the 1967 Marine Offences Act made it illegal for British companies to advertise on an offshore station, pay-for-play became a key source of income for Radio Caroline and later Laser 558. A 1980 brochure to attract investors prior to Caroline's relaunch quotes £1,000 per week for an album package of six plays per day and £100 per week for a singles package of four plays per day. Although Radio One and Capital Radio did not have the overt payola of the pirates, record pluggers still made sure presenters and producers were taken care of exceedingly well, with access to stars, lavish hospitality and – if the stories are to be believed – the occasional bag of cocaine left behind with the new releases. Occasionally this kind of activity got out of hand: in 1973 there was a police investigation into payola at Radio One following a sting by the News of the World, which resulted in nine arrests.

The Musicians' Union and the copyright licensing agencies publicly bemoaned the pirates' failure to pay copyright fees. Earlier in the decade some had actually tried to pay: Radio Jackie boss Tony Collis insisted they had "tried writing on numerous occasions to the performing rights bodies. We have in fact sent them a cheque which they have returned."[151] In private, however, record companies across the board were regularly supplying pirates with free records and pluggers were on the phone pushing for airplay. Seeing an opportunity, several stations introduced a pay-for-play package, with LWR boss Zak claiming the credit for its 1980s reinvention as the 'powerplay'. At the top of every hour, either before or after the adverts, the presenter ran the powerplay record – it wasn't explicitly labelled as advertising but more savvy listeners soon caught on that it was.

The Evening Standard investigation revealed that LWR charged £500 per week for eight plays a day on its daytime shows. Its spokesman said "The only way to guarantee play on the station is to pay for it. Everyone knows pirate stations charge for playing some records. We think we're providing a service for new talent." The less popular TKO charged £300 per week with twelve plays a day, telling the Standard "The major record labels certainly use our service and it's often the only way new records receive any play." The weekend-only Kiss FM charged £100 for one play every two hours during its broadcast, saying "The major record labels prefer this method rather than straight advertisements."[152]

Record industry trade body the BPI tried to pour cold water on the allegations, responding "It's a new one on us and sounds highly unlikely. It would be illegal anyway and I don't think our members would get involved in anything like that."[153] In practice the vast majority of powerplay records were from independents, particularly the specialist reggae distributors. Pirates sought to give the system legitimacy by pushing its rarer use for tracks on major labels, though such plays were more likely bought by artist management rather than the labels themselves.

There were two or three powerplay tracks that unexpectedly reached the Top Forty chart around this time, but it's difficult to quantify how much impact the practice really had on mainstream music and the top forty. TKO claimed "We reckon we helped Judy Boucher's hit, Can't Be With You Tonight, on its way to number one", but the BPI poured cold water on the idea that later hit House Arrest by Krush Groove had anything to do with the powerplays bought by the band's manager. Kiss quietly dropped the scheme in reaction to the negative publicity it had generated.

Smearing the pirates

The second press attack on the pirates came coincidentally just a month later. Journalists from the Times and Daily Telegraph were briefed by government officials about a growth in violence against radio investigators from the Department of Trade and Industry and the story was soon picked up by the rest of the media. DTI Minister John Butcher (whose postgraduate research was on guerrilla warfare) attempted to connect several independent incidents with a booklet called Radio Is My Bomb. Written by the Hurricane group of anarchists who had been involved in Our Radio, this included one section advocating violence against both police and Radio Investigation Service officers.

The press reports listed four incidents in London:

- Four staff were ambushed in their car on the Edgware Road on the way back from monitoring duties. A gang in two cars blocked them in and the officers were dragged from their car and beaten with baseball bats.
- An officer climbing a ladder at a South London tower block had the ladder kicked from under him, though someone else broke his fall.
- Staff had been chased by gangs while carrying out their work. In one incident officers monitoring taxi communications had to run a red light to escape from what they perceived were a series of attempts to run them off the road. After the officers took refuge in Gypsy Hill police station their pursuers followed them in and started a stand-up row with the RIS officers, alleging they had 'harassed' an associate. The police took no action but suggested the pursuers should bring in the alleged injured party as a witness.
- A British Gas communications engineer was told over the phone that he would be 'done over outside' after an argument over interference to British Gas communications from an unlicensed station.

It was also alleged that staff at the RIS had received menacing phone calls from pirate operators, which had included threats against their families.

Stations were quick to refute the allegations that the violence was widespread. Solar's Tony Monson said "Longer running stations like ourselves, Kiss FM, TKO and LWR are run by responsible people with one eye firmly fixed on future community radio licences. We certainly wouldn't jeopardise our potential in this way."[154] An LWR spokesman added "The accusations are absolutely ridiculous. We have never used violence, and have no intention of using violence, against any government official. To claim that pirate radio stations are doing this is just an excuse to attack us."[155]

There was also little support for the minister from the Institution of Professional Civil Servants, which represented RIS staff. Peter Downton, the Union's Assistant Secretary was quoted saying "We want to know why he is raising these old-hat cases at this particular juncture. What we are concerned about is not just attacks but the gradual run-down of the service. The government has told us it wants staff cuts of between thirty and fifty in the next two to three years."[156] The Telegraph was suspicious about the timing of the story, with an editorial saying "There is something not quite right about sudden revelations from the DTI that their radio engineers are being terrorised by certain pirates, aided and abetted by anarchist groups ... Were there to be a licensing system, even a strictly limited one, action against those outside it might command more of the public support which is now being sought against the thugs."[157]

By presenting these incidents as an anarchist plot, which was quickly debunked when it turned out that no operating pirates had actually seen the booklet in question, it not only lost any sympathy the DTI expected from the public but it also devalued the individual incidents. The portrayal of the stations as anarchist vigilantes was too far removed from the presenters that people knew on the radio or met in the clubs. It didn't help that pirates could in turn point at violence from RIS officers, such as the assault on Radio Jackie's Mike Barrington and the unnecessary destruction of property in more recent raids on Jackie and Border Radio – neither of which were anyone's image of anarchist troublemakers.

CONFRONTATION

A good trick if you can get away with it. The DTI and police (they normally only bring a few) are wide open to attack (the mouse becomes the cat!) when coming to get you. The problem is that in future you'll have to change your station name, frequency, even your radio voice and they'll always be on your trail. The good thing is that if pirates start attacking them they have to bring many more police with them, and can only do it when spare police are available. Also they are always looking over their shoulders, and have to be more careful with their surveillance work.

One easy way to hit back, on tower blocks, is to trap them in the lifts. The lookout signals up when they're in and you throw the main power switches in the lift room. (Careful you don't trap residents as well). Then you take your gear down the the stairs, beating up any of them you meet on the

way, and make off. Their cars are also vulnerable, usually they're parked unguarded around the corner. If you're going to attack them directly make sure you're well masked and tooled up and have enough skill and numbers to get past them. Go straight for the police officers and disable them before they can make their 'officer in distress' call (take or smash their radios, or have someone jamming their frequencies).

Other direct ways of hitting back are, attacking the DTI at their bases, attacking their vehicles at their depot, obtaining home addresses/phone numbers of chief officers and harassing them, etc.etc..

Remember, they have the entire state apparatus backing them up, any form of direct attack should therefore be anonymous and never spoken of or boasted about later.   or before hahahahahahah:

The section of the Radio Is My Bomb booklet that sparked the outrage.

Most stations realised that attacking RIS investigators and building up resentment from them would only lead to troubles down the line. What was undeniable, however, was that the growing influx of money into pirate radio was changing the environment in which it operated. There were now individuals who were attracted primarily because it seemed an easy way to make a lot of cash and there were some prepared to do whatever they felt was necessary to protect their business. The big growth in cocaine as a club drug in the mid-eighties possibly didn't help in calming some situations either. From one violent incident against RIS officers in 1984, two in 1985 and three in 1986 there had been seven in the first three months of 1987.

Many DJs from this time seem to have had limited knowledge of exactly what was going on behind the scenes to keep the stations they worked for on the air. In the days of medium wave broadcasting you didn't get to do your programme unless you joined in as a member of the transmission site crew and then at the end of the broadcast there was a debrief in the pub, where listeners also often joined in. Some stations still had monthly DJ meetings but since the introduction of seven-day FM broadcasting there was generally far less camaraderie between those taking part.

Presenters would now turn up to do their show, exchange a few words with the DJs before and after, and get out quickly in case the DTI turned up. Looking back on her time on the pirates, DJ Angie Dee remembers experiencing "feelings of isolation and having to work out of some unpleasant buildings in some very unsafe places."[158] Lewis Dene concurs: "Many were as dodgy as hell: squats, abandoned flats, run-down council estates where you felt your neighbours were drug dealers, robbers and rapists! It's amazing how much we loved the music to put ourselves in these positions."[159]

Amid cost-cutting across government departments the Radio Investigation Service budget was £6.5 million for the 1987 to 1988 financial year, just £100,000 less than the previous year, while the amount spent on broadcasting enforcement grew from £600,000 to £800,000. The following year there was a massive £400,000 investment in new technology. While the media and listeners might have been unconvinced, the stories of payola and violence were certainly successful in helping the service defend its budget and gain support in Parliament for future legislation.

In an acutely-observed profile in Campaign magazine that November, Nick Higham revealed that LWR was the station responsible for chasing the officers through the streets and into the police station. It was done "for the fun of it ... but Eddie and Zak claim that they were only putting the wind up the opposition. It amuses Eddie and Zak no end, because it punctures the self-esteem of the RIS men they refer to as Bodie and Doyle."[160]

Just when everyone thought the allegations were all played out, London Weekend Television's London Programme decided to rehash the powerplay and violence stories in a January 1988 edition of the current affairs show. Presented to contributors as a sympathetic look at pirate radio and the prospects for legalisation, it turned out that the programme makers had settled on a more exciting narrative portraying LWR as the bad guys – stealing transmitters, baiting the authorities and taking money to play records – while Kiss were the good guys who deserved to be supported in their bid for a licence. In a 1992 interview Zak was still angry at LWR's treatment: "What went wrong was our popularity and our misrepresentation in the media ... A lot of it had to do with the London Programme ... They sought to destroy the whole fabric of pirate radio beginning with us because of our success."[161]

Sound systems, rare groove and making DJs cool again

Meanwhile, wider changes in music and clubbing were beginning to have an impact on pirate radio. For some time DJs had, frankly, not generally been seen as cool. The radio DJ was epitomised by Mike Read or Steve Wright, spouting inanities and caring more for their egos than the music they played. John Peel described going to Dave Lee Travis' house for a party and discovering that he did not possess a single record. Asking him about this, DLT replied, "Oh no, it's too much trouble and the dust ... Anything I really like I've copied on tape. I've got quite a lot of tapes and I play them in the car, you see."[162] Even Radio One's boss, Johnny Beerling, had realised the problem, admitting "we're in danger of letting the cult of the personality get too big and the station submerged under it."[163]

DJs were also almost without exception still male. DJ Camilla, who worked on LWR and earlier DBC, described how "All my life when I grew up I never ever heard any women DJs, never. I never heard people with accents. It was all sort of the real mundane, boring, medallion man type of DJs, you know."[164] Like their radio counterparts, club jocks were paid to be entertainers and it was their

personality rather than their technical skill that got them the gigs – and
enabled them to cross-over so easily to
radio. Soul Mafia DJs like Steve Walsh
and Chris Hill might have played the
hottest releases, but their ability to
work a crowd was what counted with
their employers.

By the mid-eighties this type of DJ
presentation was increasingly at odds
with coolness. The younger generation, brought up on New York hip-hop
DJs as role models and technique on
the decks as what counted, squirmed
in embarrassment at the traditional
British club scene. There was also,
it has to be said, some middle-class sneering at the values of the more work-
ing-class soul scene with its dress codes and sexism: "ladies free before 11pm,
smart dress please, no jeans or trainers". While clubs playing rhythm & blues had
been trendy with a broader cross-section of young people in the earlier half of the
sixties, since rock's ascendency music's tribes had often divided on class lines.

Despite the social advances that had been made in London, if you were in
a mixed group of friends – white, black, Asian – then going out to somewhere
that everyone could get into and feel comfortable at was still a problem. Even
with anti-discrimination legislation, West End clubs were often still limiting
how many black people they let in. Trevor Nelson's experience at The Wag in
Wardour Street was typical: "The first time I was ever allowed in the place was
when they phoned me up and asked me to deejay – they'd never ever let me in
as a punter."[165] Meanwhile, as Trevor put it, "The East End is house parties and
soul blues (blues parties) where a lot of white people don't really want to go."[166]
Instead, a new generation of soul sound systems became the breeding ground
for events in a more multicultural common space: the warehouse party.

London's shift away from an industrial economy meant there were now many
large disused buildings that were ideal venues for rough-and-ready parties.
Organisers sometimes paid off the owners or were given keys by friendly agents,

but more often were breaking in and relying on the large number of party-goers to ensure they couldn't be shut down. When the police did turn up there was much less likely to be a problem if they were presented with excuses ("my dad owns the building and he let me have it for my birthday party") by self-confident, white, middle-class party organisers like law student and Family Funktion DJ Judge Jules.

These new promoters went out of their way to attract a mixed crowd, targeting colleges and universities with flyers. The sound systems also became a popular accessory for fashion shows – the walls of speakers were visually fantastic – bringing their DJs into the sphere of the arty influencers. Consequently, as Jazzy B explained about the combined parties between Soul II Soul and Family Funktion: "Classes as well as races started to mix. And I believe we were the instigators: a black street crew and a white, middle-class bunch. People checked us as a form of rebelling."[167] Time has of course smoothed-over some of the realities, but there was an undoubted shift in attitudes.

Although run by a younger generation, these sound systems largely inherited the presentation of their older counterparts: music took precedence and any talk was part of the flow. In this they were a stepping stone to the beat-matching DJs and rhythmic MCs that emerged in the rave era. Where they differed from their forerunners was in the music, dropping the roots reggae or lovers' rock for a style that mixed up contemporary soul and hip-hop with the rediscovered killer cuts from the past: the rare grooves.

The major record labels in both the UK and the US spent the mid-eighties focussed on reselling baby boomers the music they'd previously bought on vinyl on a new format: CD. New music was in a slump, not only lacking investment in new artists but drifting along at the tail end of earlier scenes rather than coalescing around something radical. Club DJs began going back to an earlier time too, with Kiss FM DJs like Gordon Mac and Norman Jay playing underground black soul and disco sounds from the late seventies and earlier eighties as part of the boogie scene. As an older generation dumped their vinyl collections in second-hand shops, DJs began digging back further to seventies funk, familiar to a new generation as the sampling mainstay of contemporary rap and with a wider cross-cultural appeal. Albums that might contain just one prized track began changing hands for rapidly increasing sums while the more entrepreneurial DJs started releasing bootlegs to capitalise on the demand.

Derek Boland, who had been pushing 'good grooves' initially on his LWR show and then on Kiss, was quick to see an opportunity for bringing together the warehouse crews with the DJs from the trendier West End clubs in a station to target this new generation: WBLS. Though it wasn't to last long, hobbled by clashes with other operators, the newcomer did serve to push Kiss FM onto bigger things and after WBLS's closure Kiss was to take on both Jazzy B and Judge Jules. There was also a smaller scene focussed on the jazz counterparts to rare groove, which came to the airwaves on Gilles Peterson's K-Jazz and Chris Philips' Starpoint Radio. As that scene developed and inspired a new generation of bands it picked up its own name: acid jazz.

By 1987, the success of the warehouse parties and the cachet of the DJs involved meant they now found themselves in demand in the West End. Soul II Soul had their weekly events in Covent Garden's Africa Centre while Kiss FM promoted events at The Wag – a rare venture into the West End clubs for a pirate station. The period also saw the launch of trendier, slightly arty venues like Brixton's The Fridge, who also provided a bridge to the gay scene. Warehouse party organisers became more than willing to make this jump as illegal events were increasingly attracting the attention of less desirable elements.

With help from style magazines like The Face and i-D – possessed of the ability to package cultural phenomena for wider consumption – the reinvention of the DJ as a cool icon from an authentic, multi-cultural scene and the rehabilitation of dance music with the middle classes was underway. As house took over in 1988 and the ability to craft a beat-matched journey for your ecstasy-enhanced dancers became more important than any verbal skills, the final death-knell sounded for the old school club DJ.

Crossing over

Having for years spurned dance music as inappropriate for the radio, the legal stations now wanted a piece of the action. Radio One recruited former Invicta and JFM DJ Jeff Young to present its new Friday evening dance show while Capital Radio made Saturdays their dance night, with Pete Tong, ex LWR, followed by Chris Forbes, ex-Solar, including a live outside broadcast from a club hosted by Tim Westwood. With both stations also adding classic soul shows it was all very piratical.

Some like Time Radio DJ Smokey Joe were disappointed with the choices: "What we've noticed is a lot of the white presenters are the ones that are developing from pirate radio to local radio stations. I don't know whether it's the hindrance of the ethnic thing. I mean I have a strong Trinidadian accent and maybe that's one of the drawbacks of being a black presenter on the radio – you're not English, you're not for English radio."[168]

Capital Radio was anyway riding high. In February the company had floated on the London Stock Exchange. From the losses in its early days it was now making good money, with a profit the previous year of £1.71 million on a turnover of £18.46 million. With government levies on higher profits and IBA rental fees being slashed and new opportunities offered by deregulation, even with the prospect of greater competition the company looked an increasingly safe bet for investors.

REFLECTIONS

1, THE GREEN EDMONTON N9 7EA

TOP ATTRACTION
EVERY SAT & SUN AT REFFLECTIONS
NEVER BEFORE
TWO RADIO STATIONS D.J.'s TOGETHER

TIME RADIO
103.7 FM &
R.J.R. 90 FM

INVITE YOU TO A NITE OF JOY EVERY SAT & SUN.
PLAYING YOUR SOUNDS

DRESS TO IMPRESS – PLEASE

£5 00 AT DOOR LADIES FREE BEFORE 10 30 pm

In the year up to 9 November the Radio Investigation Service had carried out 309 raids across the country against unlicensed broadcasters, with 257 in London against 38 different stations. For the whole year 75 people were successfully prosecuted.

On The Air

Faze1 FM
Brixton's trendier black music operation, 1987-1988

Faze1 began in April 1987 with a black music format skewed towards soul, funk, hip hop and electro, as well as some early house on both Fabio's and Grooverider's shows. Fabio later explained its origins: "A guy called Mendoza, he was setting up a station. He said I want all of you local guys to come in and do a show. It was a Brixton thing, right next to a pub, a hovel, and he had a shebeen, an afterhours place, downstairs. He owned the building – he was in construction – and upstairs he had the pirate station and downstairs he had the shebeen. We used to go there, get pissed, go upstairs and play some music. A great set-up."[170] Later, downstairs at Mendoza's became the location for after-parties for several acid house nights. The station also ran its own successful events at Brixton's Fridge nightclub.

Faze1 had a rocky start, losing several transmitters in its early weeks (they said it was TKO taking them, while TKO said it was the DTI), but soon became an established presence on the airwaves. Faze1 featured many presenters who would go on to become big names so it is surprising that the station has never had more recognition. As well as future drum and bass DJs like Fabio, Grooverider and Booker T, there were shows from techno musician Dave Angel and DJs Derrick Patterson, Mark Sinclair and Desi G & Barry White. Faze1 was also one of the first pirates to allow listeners to phone through requests to the on-air DJ via a mobile phone in the studio. Transmissions came from a nearby tower block in Brixton.

Faze1 closed towards the end of 1988. In the summer the station's office had been hit by a raid. A large quantity of paperwork relating to its operation was removed and two people were subsequently successfully prosecuted. Mendoza complained "It looks like that's how they'll be working now."[171]

FAZE 1 FM 90.9

	MON	TUE	WED	THUR	FRI	SAT	SUN
7-9 AM	PAUL RICHARDS			HENRY VIII			S.T.B.
9-12 AM	BOOKER.T					DOUBLE M	GROOVE RIDER
12-2 PM	D.J. FABIO.					DESI.9 + BARRY WHITE	L.S.B
2-4 PM	ANDREW DAZZLES	COMMAND B	HEAVY DUTY	MENDOZA	CLAZZY J	WOOD HOUSE	SPUNKY G
4-6 PM	HEAVY DUTY	FUNK E.D.	CLAZZY J	FUNK E.D.	COMMAND B.		CLAZZY J
6-8 PM	L.S.B		D.J Y	JAM MASTER C	D.J. JAYNE		
8-10 PM	CRIME MASTER T	SPUNKY G	ANDREW DAZZLER	COMMAND B	G.I JOE	JAM MASTER C	MENDOZA
10-1 PM-AM	CLIVE RARE GROOVE B.	CRIME MASTER T	JAM MASTER C	PAUL RICHARDS	D.J Y	CLAZZY J	DESI.9 + BARRY WHITE
1-3 AM	GROOVE RIDER	DESI.9 + BARRY WHITE	S.J.B	CLIVE RARE GROOVE B	ESTER J	D.J L.A	VICCY P
3-5 AM	COMMAND B	ANDREW DAZZLER	COMMAND B	ANDREW DAZZLER	D.J DEAN	D.J DEAN	ISSAC J
5-7 AM	VICCY P						

Mailing Address: ■ Oval Place, London SW8
Studio No: 0860 378938   Page No: 01-367 6767   Unit 2255

Faze1's programme schedule from spring 1988.

Hits 93 FM
Nothing but non-stop hits, 1987-1990

There were two stations called Hits FM broadcasting in 1987. The first to appear operated 24 hours a day from Crystal Palace on 93 FM with a continuous two-hour loop of chart music interspersed with Bill Mitchell jingles. The station was reported to be started by one of the UK people associated with the second phase of offshore station Laser. Unhappy at the continuing problems with that project he wanted to bring the Hot Hits format to London. This is a top thirty format from the USA that plays everything from the chart regardless of genre with the top five played every hour, no recurrents (tracks that have recently left the chart) and absolutely no oldies.

Regular raids, issues in retaining technical staff and other problems meant that planned live broadcasts never took place. The station reappeared in May 1988 on 105.5, still with continuous music tapes but adding new ads for premium-rate telephone lines to support the station. Transmissions again only lasted a few weeks. There was also a brief return in February 1990.

Hits FM
Pop and oldies, 1987-1988

In late 1987 a second station with the Hits FM name began broadcasting oldies from North London. DJs included Tim Allen, Tony James, Mike Andrews, Stewart Ross and Marconi. Early on they suffered a number of misfortunes, with other stations taking their frequency, site staff caught by a caretaker and one of the team getting locked on top of a tower block. After veteran pirate DJ Garry Stevens joined it helped put them on a more stable footing. Hits FM fell apart in the spring of 1988 with Garry Stevens going on to launch Veronica Supergold, which most of the Hits FM team then subsequently joined.

Radio Interference
Anarchist radio, 1987

The first transmissions from Radio Interference were heard in March 1987. Programmes consisted of comments on current events, what's on information, personal anecdotes and alternative music. Interference also organised benefit gigs in Brixton to support the station and put out appeals for taped contributions to their programme. They also made a reasonable job of plastering stickers advertising the station all over the Northern Line.

Interference reported that they were 'visited' by police on 5 June, and were raided on 26 June when two people were arrested. Transmissions continued for a few weeks after, but stopped for a while after the court case – on air they claimed that the people caught had no connection to the station. In the autumn of 1987 they told Radio Today that they hoped to return once they had sourced a link transmitter. A lack of resources and access to modern technology seems to have been a consistent problem for London's anarchist pirates.

Occasional broadcasts have continued since under the Interference FM name in London, Brighton and Bristol. Spokesman Chris Winton told the Evening Standard in 2002, "The fact that we're illegal doesn't bother me. What's more of a crime is the way we're lied to by the corporate media with their constant onslaught of neo-liberal rubbish. Most pirate stations nowadays are motivated by greed and profit, yet the music pirates are left alone for months. We're considered dangerous, so they pull us off the air before the day is out."[169]

News Music Radio
The hits of yesterday and the news of today, 1987-1988

One of the more interesting attempts at doing something different with speech programming. NMR broadcast on 89.6 FM for five months from October '87 to February '88, shuttering when raids got too intense.

Founder Roger Ross had a background in journalism and described his station as a reaction to "a glut of purely music radio. I think people want information as well. We monitored radio news, we generated stories not covered elsewhere and used items from the specialist press. We also wrote proper radio scripts, so that news was presented in an interesting way."[172] Musically it was different to other unlicensed operators too: "It played mainly pop oldies rather than dance music, reflecting, I suppose, the fact that I and the other people involved were older than most London pirates."[173]

Programmes started in the early evening with veteran DJ Andy Walker and continued until 10am the next day. According to Roger, "I thought that would be a good way of staving off attention from the authorities, but I was soon proved wrong on that score."[174] Transmissions came from a studio in East Dulwich connected over two or three UHF links to a tower block in the Old Kent Road.

Passion Radio
Brixton's black community station, 1987-1988

Launched in December 1987, Passion Radio aimed to be a community radio station just for the Brixton area. Operating seven days a week on 90.6 FM, daytimes were predominantly reggae-based along with a large amount of local community information. Some of this was a fairly repetitive list of helpline numbers but over time they also added more information about activities happening in their local area.

Weekends included specialist jazz, soul and house shows, including the debut of Jumping Jack Frost under the name DJ Underworld. The station closed at the end of 1988 to apply for a South London licence in conjunction with the Afro Caribbean Community Association Radio Project, though it lost out to Choice FM. A number of people involved went on to launch the very similar Lightning Radio.

Raiders FM
Pop and rock all weekend, 1987-1988

After initial broadcasts from some of the team as London Town FM back in the summer, Raiders FM formally launched on 22 August. The station was run by Mike Summers, a former Jackie and Skyline DJ, and featured several jocks who had previously been on Skyline.

Mike, who had trained at the National Broadcasting School, wanted to put a station on air with a fast-moving, punchy sound presented by DJs who could build a sense of excitement in their shows. American hit radio and sixties offshore stations like Radio London served as the template for what he wanted to achieve, though Raiders was to play contemporary music rather than merely recreate the past. The early broadcasts were oriented towards both pop and adult-oriented rock, but the success of the rock shows encouraged them to move more in that direction over time. Presenters with a professional sound and good musical knowledge were sought and Mike also had a deliberate policy to put female DJs on the station, who he felt were greatly unrepresented on the airwaves. This got the station particular attention in the media, including a feature on Radio Four's Women's Hour.

Programmes came from a studio in Battersea, some on tape, with transmissions going out from a council tower block not far away. Although the station sounded great, they were initially not as lucky with their transmissions. Their first two frequencies were quickly taken over by seven-day stations and then after moving to 105.2 they were rather close to private mobile services. They also complained of being ripped off by an early transmitter supplier.

Cherry-picking from Skyline and RFM

Presenters in the early days included Steve Bishop, Ray Thomson, Tom Ingram, Sally Roach, Mike Summers, Howard Peters, Shaun Tilley, Nick Love, and John Doohan. From RFM came Claire Mansfield and Dana Jay, who broadcast alongside fellow Californian Lesley Doe. There was also Sue Wilkinson, singer of the 1980 novelty hit 'You've got to be a hustler' and Jan Kooper, who presented The Rare Rock Show. Raiders carried regular interviews with new artists including Wendy James, Danielle Dax and The Voice of the Beehive. At first they experimented with individual shows being sponsored by different businesses, but later they switched to more standard radio advertising in order to fund its operation.

Early in 1988 Raiders began to be more heavily targeted by the authorities. After one raid on their transmitter site in March there were a few weeks off air before it returned in June. A few of the early presenters dropped out at this point, replaced by new arrivals including Dave Christie, John Chapman, Dave Sherry and Nick Miller. By now they were carrying a wide range of rock programming each weekend, with indie, garage, psychedelia, metal, AOR and everything in-between. Although RFM covered a greater part of London with their transmissions, Raiders became the rock station with the more modern sound.

Transmissions continued until the end of 1988 when a decision was made to close down so they could consider applying for one of the licences on offer.

. . . .

Although they did not subsequently return to the air as a pirate they did carry out one broadcast with a Restricted Service Licence in 1992. Today Raiders exists as an Internet radio station at raidersfm.com, primarily targeting Wandsworth and the surrounding area, and still with Mike Summers and Claire Mansfield on its team. Les Gunn, Mark Daniels and Shaun Tilley went on to work in commercial radio.

Sky Radio
Black radio for South East London, 1987-1988

Sky Radio was a black community station broadcasting from the Peckham area between 1987 and 1988. Run by Daddy Big Hat it played predominantly reggae and lovers rock for a slightly older audience, though there were also some specialist shows, such as hip hop, soul and a Sunday morning gospel programme. Some of the DJs had previously worked on Twilight Radio but most were new to broadcasting.

The station became famous for its inventive public service announcements, such as those warning against drug use or promoting safe sex, which Starpoint memorably spoofed in its own ads. Daddy Big Hat was very proud of the high power transmissions they put out on 91.6 FM, which at times were over a kilowatt in power.

Time Radio
Black radio for North West London, 1987-1990

Time Radio began broadcasts in early 1987 from above a shop in Harlesden High St. The station was reported to be the brainchild of Ronald Amanze, who went on to produce and manage a number of black artists.

Time was unusual for featuring a mix of experienced soul DJs from past pirates – CJ Carlos, Graham Gold, Chris Nat, Lyndon T – along with less-known DJs from the local area, who leant more towards reggae and lovers' rock. It was never clear if its ambitions were to be a Londonwide urban music station or a local Afro Caribbean community broadcaster: early in its life it often identified as Time Community Radio while later on DJs often referred to it as Big Time Radio.

In June 1987 there was a split in the station, with many DJs moving to Fresh FM. Although there was talk of Time applying for a licence with help from Graham Gold, they remained on the air into the early part of 1989 with back-to-back music before finally disappearing from the airwaves.

CJ Carlos doing a show in 1988.

Some people in 1987 still broadcast from fields. Photos courtesy of an anonymous Kent station.

Arab Radio London

It's not clear if there were one or two Arabic stations operating at this time as they kept changing frequency. There were test transmissions in February under the name Arabic Community Radio but a station was also heard giving out the name Arab Radio London. Programmes were a mix of music, quiz shows, phone-ins and information, with prayers five times a day. Later they added some Italian programmes too.

Asian Community Radio

Broadcasting to the East End on 94.3 from the summer of 1987. The station had a younger profile, with the emphasis on bhangra and Indian disco music rather than the classical Indian and Bollywood soundtrack music favoured by many of the other South Asian stations in London.

Calibre FM

Calibre attempted a seven day soul music schedule from the summer of 1987, but were only on the air a few weeks. Initial broadcasts were on the crowded 94.5 frequency.

CD1024 / CD93

In the autumn of 1987 jumbled-up rumours of CD1024's launch began to circulate, alleging it was the return of Horizon. Instead, in December CD1024 began taking time every Saturday on TKO for a service of adult-oriented soul and rock. Presenters included Bob Matthews, Barrie Stone, Sammy Jay and former JFM boss Brian Anthony. Returning to the air in 1988 it did Saturdays on 93.2 FM while Starpoint did Sundays. When this arrangement broke down there were reports it was to share with Solar, but instead Sammy Jay went on to launch the more popular Q102.

Chicago '87

Initially launched as Horizon '87, the station was renamed after the original Horizon Radio made complaints. The station played a mix of soul and house (hence the later name) and

broadcast from South East London on 94.5 FM seven days a week.

Digital Radio

A short-lived soul station heard broadcasting in January of 1987.

Radio Embassy

A rock 'n' roll station connected with Radio Memphis which broadcast briefly in the summer of '87 on 106.3 FM.

Elite FM

An early station devoted to house and garage, operating on 103.3 FM.

Fresh FM

A split from Time Radio, Fresh began test transmissions on 14 June and then launched into programmes on 22 June. DJs on Fresh FM included Keith James (breakfast show host), Chris Johns, Mickie D, Doctor Quincy, King Soops, Special K, DJ Blacka, Errol T, Trevor de Costa, Chris Wright, Pat French, J.C., Gemma, Tony T, Doctor D and Lyndon T. Fresh were one of the most consistent stations on the air in London throughout 1988 and later renamed themselves Superfresh.

Funk Force FM

Broadcasting on 105.6 in the autumn of 1987.

Girls FM

After a few test transmissions in January 1987 and some press publicity, Girls FM launched with a seven-day dance music format in August of that year. Transmissions on 96.9 FM were initially a mix of taped music and some

live programmes by an all-female team of presenters. The station had connections with neighbouring Time Radio.

Greek Radio For London

GRFL began broadcasting in January 1987. They were notable for clocking up ten raids in their first two months of operation.

Green Isle Radio

A Turkish Cypriot station from North London, operating on 90.9 FM in the spring of 1987.

Groove FM

Initially a lower-powered station broadcasting to South East London, Groove FM increased their power early in 1988 and began reaching a large audience across London on 89.6 FM. The station played soul and reggae and operated weekends only.

Icehouse

Icehouse, 'your chillin' centre', was a planned all-hip-hop station from Starpoint's former hip hop DJs. It was reported in Parliament to have been raided twice, but few seem to have heard the transmissions.

JFM South

No connection with the original JFM, an occasional pirate heard in the New Eltham area during 1987.

London Music Radio and the New Age Wireless

A ninety minute programme going out at midnight on the first Saturday of each month on 94.5 FM.

London Rock

A second station with this name that began broadcasting in January 1987 to North London on 97.8 FM. Initially London Rock had a mostly AOR format but this widened to play everything from classic tracks to mega-heavy thrash and indie material. The station closed in 1988.

London Town FM

A weekend pop station from mostly former Skyline DJs that began transmissions in the summer of 1987 on the North Surrey / South London borders. After a few broadcasts the people behind it went on to Raiders FM.

Mainline Radio

After two months of test transmissions, Mainline Radio launched in October with seven-day programmes on 89.6 but only lasted a few weeks. Musically they were closer in spirit to the earlier jazz-funk stations.

Melody FM

A soul station operating weekends from the summer of 1987 on 102.4 FM. Presenters included P.J. Bear, Funkenstein T, Mixmaster G, Sterling Steve and T. Whirlwind. Melody was sponsored by Walthamstow's Note For Note record shop and broadcast first from Leyton and then Stratford. The station closed in December 1987 and the team behind it were involved in setting up Dance FM in 1990.

MRS FM

An East London soul station that appeared in the spring. Transmitter issues that resulted in them appearing on multiple frequencies up the band perhaps hastened their demise.

Norwood FM

A spin-off from Direct Line Radio, with weekly programmes on 106 FM for the Norwood area in early 1987.

Power 105

Broadcasting to South East Essex on 105 FM. It left the air in March 1988 after a raid.

Premier Radio

Low power broadcasts to South West London in the spring of 1987.

Primetime FM

Not connected with Time Radio which appeared around the same time, Primetime broadcast from Southall on 90 FM from spring 1987. The station appeared in the press after the owner was in court charged with assault and blackmailing a DJ whom he believed was responsible for tipping off the DTI resulting in a raid on the station. He was found guilty of blackmail and demanding money with menaces, but acquitted of abduction and false imprisonment.

Ram Jam Radio

A short-lived Brixton roots reggae station that appeared at Christmas 1987 on 89.9 FM.

SOL

Broadcasting soul music every Friday night to the North London area from February 1987. Programmes were on tape and ran for just two hours. They later moved to Wednesdays.

Soul FM

The Sound Of Underground London broadcast weekends from the Leyton and Walthamstow area with a jazz funk and classic soul format. The station launched in September 1987 on 91 FM, with a few DJs jumping ship from Melody FM. Soul FM was on much higher power and its later 96.9 transmissions got out across nearby London districts and into Essex and Kent. Presenters included Mixmaster G, P.J. Bear, Sterling Steve, Dave Dupres, and Roger Brooks. It closed in the autumn of 1988 when its owner sold his main business and the DJs decided they could not afford to keep it going by themselves.

South London Sound

South London Sound – aka 'Power 92.8' – appeared in February 1987 and operated for a few months to the immediate South London area.

Southside Radio

A low power station broadcasting to South West London in the spring of 1987 on 105.4 FM. The station returned in the summer of 1988 but did not stick around long.

South West Sound

Broadcasting on Friday nights to South West London on 105.3 FM for a few months from February 1987. John Andersson played rock for the first two hours, Alan Wright (Adam Moore, a producer at LBC) then played funk and soul until the closedown at midnight.

Touch FM

A seven day soul station broadcasting from West London on 96.1 FM. Transmissions began in the autumn.

Traffic Jam

North West London's Traffic Jam began broadcasting at the start of April 1987. While daytimes were predominantly reggae they also had some specialist shows covering jazz and afro beat. Saturday nights featured exclusively female DJs under the tagline 'Ladies in the groove'. The station was unusual in carrying little advertising, though DJs did promote their own events.

WKLR

Briefly broadcasting on 92.8 FM from the North Surrey area in early 1987 on 93 FM. A move to Crystal Palace was apparently planned but their aerial mast was stolen and they never made it to the air afterwards.

WLFM

Another of the North West London pop stations, broadcasting on 106 FM from February 1987.

WNKR

West and North Kent Radio – they dropped the 'A' as it was "less offensive" – began operations in May 1987. Early transmissions were on 91.8 FM from founder Dave Martin's house before they moved to bank holidays only using a local tower block and a studio in someone's house. In 1990 they moved to Short Wave where they remained for many years. Presenters included Rob Marshall and RFL veteran Andy Walker.

1988

Pirate interference

This was the year that the DTI lost control of the FM dial in London. With the media proclaiming DJs were now cool again, everyone wanted to be one. The big pirates had no shortage of people wanting to join but weren't interested unless you were a name – Kiss even got their DJs to vote on new recruits. For most DJs the only way to get on air was to start your own station. Amongst the second tier of pirates there were also inevitable splits as people fell out with each other or those from a particular part of town or playing a particular sub-genre felt they would be better served by doing their own thing.

Previously the main constraint limiting new stations had been the availability of people with the technical skills to get a station on air. Early transmitters needed more careful setting up, the designs were not always so efficient and sometimes components were run at their limits in order to get the maximum power possible so they burned out. By the late eighties the designs had been standardised, the parts were cheaper and more reliable while decent test equipment ensured they were optimally tuned.

Anyone wanting to start a station could now go to one of a handful of companies, set up by the engineers of long-departed stations, who would sell you the kit off the shelf and give you instructions on how to plug it together. For an extra hefty fee, reflecting the additional risk involved, some even provided a turnkey service that enabled a station to outsource all its transmission requirements. Most of these companies had the cover of a transmitter test and development licence from the DTI and legitimate export business, but their bread and butter was still pirate rigs. £400 for a 100W FM transmitter with integrated UHF link receiver, £200 for a UHF link transmitter, £150 for a stereo encoder, £800 for a microwave link.

It was an ideal enterprise: there was a good profit on each unit (reflecting the risk involved and the scarcity of the skills), customers paid cash and thanks to the RIS there was guaranteed repeat custom. Engineers were the ones who got paid no matter what, and some made more than the stations they worked for. As Kiss FM boss Gordon Mac explained, "Without an engineer, you're buying a car without an engine. The DJs are important, but a good engineer has to be treated with kid gloves and kept sweet at every point. They're paid well, but they earn their money."[175]

There were also still hobbyists building equipment for their own small stations and a few people who fell somewhere in-between. If you went to one of the well-known engineers you knew you would get a transmitter meeting a minimum specification and unlikely to cause interference to other services; from one of the other builders you couldn't always be so sure.

Simpler transmitters could drift, so a station might start off at the beginning of the broadcast on 90.6MHz but as it warmed up it would slide down to 90.2, interfering with other services along the way. More common was a problem known as 'sprogging'. Transmitter designs for VHF commonly start with a signal at a lower frequency – say 30MHz – which is then multiplied to get the required broadcast frequency – perhaps tripled to get to 90MHz. This process will generate extra signals at related multiples, so the output after will also contain significant signals at, for example, 60MHz and 120MHz. Additionally, because components in the real world will never behave perfectly, other stages will generate harmonics at multiples of the frequency or – in poor equipment – minor spurious signals at frequencies other than the one that's actually wanted. All these extra unwanted signals are commonly known as 'sprogs' and have to be filtered out.

Sprogging is a particular issue due to the closeness of the aircraft navigation

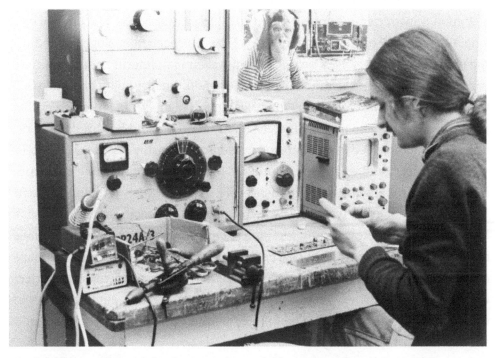

Alice's and Kiss engineer Martin Spencer in his workshop in 1986. Photo by Pyers Easton.

beacon and instrument landing system on 108-118MHz and air traffic control on 118-137MHz. It was interference to these channels that caused pirates on the eastern approach to Heathrow airport along the Thames – such as popular pirate tower blocks in Deptford, New Cross and Brixton – to be more regularly raided. Even so, the Civil Aviation Authority denied that this interference was life-threatening, saying after one incident with Rock 2 Rock, "It was just annoying and should not have been there, but it has been stopped."[176] Luckily such incidents were rare.

Frequency modulation (FM) itself will also generate multiple signals – sidebands – on frequencies up and down the band from the main frequency, high in power close to that frequency then getting lower further away. The maximum 'width' of an FM station will depend on the peaks of its audio; with inadequate filtering and without proper audio limiters or monitoring a station can start interfering with those on nearby frequencies: what's called splatter. Operating correctly, a pirate on 93.1 wouldn't cause problems with Radio Four on 93.5, but unless it was careful then Radio Four listeners, especially closer to the pirate's transmitter, might be irritated by the familiar tsk tsk tsk tsk in the background from the loud beat of the pirate's music.

A good transmitter design will filter out all the extra signals, leaving just one single clean signal on its main frequency. However, each filter stage will reduce the power, so there needs to be a compromise: enough filtering not to interfere with other services, not so much that you need additional amplification to reach the same power output, pushing the price up too high. By 1988 the power that pirates were using had anyway increased: as the VHF band became more congested so stations used more watts to compensate for using less clear channels.

More professional engineers had access to test equipment like spectrum analysers that enabled them to ensure their signals were sufficiently clean. Others might not know what they were putting out, especially outside the VHF broadcast band. A few were also tempted to cut corners, especially during times of heavy action by the authorities when they knew a transmitter would perhaps only last one or two days. Even when equipment left its constructor in perfect working order, out in the wild conditions might be rather different: extreme cold or heat could change how a transmitter operated while rain getting in could short-circuit components and cause havoc.

Even with a good quality transmitter operating in perfect conditions, its sheer power could still overwhelm radios, TVs or other electronic equipment nearby which had not been designed to reject so strong a signal. The owner of one Crystal Palace company wrote to the Evening Standard to complain "My business was nearly ruined by interference on my answerphone. The pirate transmitter was located next to my office and I in fact informed the DTI. Even then it took them three months to act."[177]

The economics of pirate broadcasting

Other aspects of pirate broadcasting were becoming standardised too. New stations knew the mix of music that would attract the audience necessary to satisfy their advertisers. They knew the popular pirate advertisers and the network of go-betweens who would work with businesses to sort out ad production and book time on the stations. They knew which labels would be likely to pay for a powerplay. They knew the venues that would run their events but would not be put off when the RIS inevitably sent letters threatening action for supporting a pirate station.

You could now set up a station for less than two grand. Your first FM transmitter, a UHF link transmitter, a limiter and a stereo encoder might cost you £1,200. If you wanted more safety then it was £500 to use a microwave link instead. As consumer electronics from Japan and Taiwan rapidly fell in price, you could equip a reasonable quality studio with everything you needed for under £500. On average, a station operating seven days a week lost 10-20 transmitters a year and perhaps another two or three in thefts.

Most stations now put their studios in the homes of DJs and their transmitters on top of a tower block rather than renting somewhere. Few bothered with offices if they didn't have other business interests: the boss' mobile phone bill was likely the biggest outlay after equipment costs. Records were either supplied by the DJs or came free from labels. There was the risk of getting caught, but for most stations this was no more than once every six

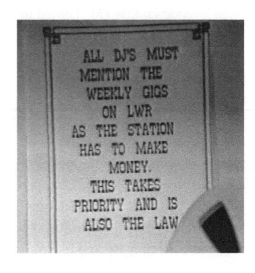

ALL DJ'S MUST MENTION THE WEEKLY GIGS ON LWR AS THE STATION HAS TO MAKE MONEY. THIS TAKES PRIORITY AND IS ALSO THE LAW

months, much less if you were careful. Even when it did go to court, for a first time offence the fine was generally under a thousand pounds with costs – some stations were kind enough to pay the fines when one of their DJs got busted. Rather than raiding a new station as soon as it came on air, the RIS usually waited to gather intelligence in the hope of securing a better conviction down the line, giving newcomers time to establish themselves and build up resources for when they were hit.

Advertisers were typically paying £50-100 a week for ads and most stations could manage at least ten of those. Ads usually came via the station's own network of contacts or called in response to adverts pushing ad sales, so stations didn't even have to pay commission. For a small operation, running powerplays might bring in another £200 a week. For the more popular stations you could double or quadruple all those amounts. In 1988 press interviews, Kiss FM claimed to be making £1,000 a week on advertising but, like other stations asked about their finances, always neglected to mention what the more lucrative club events were bringing in. In just twelve hours on air a well-managed small pirate could make all the money it needed to pay its costs, a major operation in just three. Presenters often had very little visibility of the finances of the stations they worked for. With

MEDINA RADIO
102.2 FM
Straight to the Soul

ADVERTISING RATES FOR 1989
ALL SPOTS 30 SECONDS
PRODUCTION COST'S £35.00 PER TAPE.

MONDAY TO FRIDAY
5x5 (25 PLAY'S)....................................£25
10x5 (50 PLAY'S)...................................£50
24x5 (120 PLAY'S)................................£200
57x5 (399 PLAY'S)................................£300

MONDAY TO SUNDAY
5x7 (35 PLAY'S)....................................£35
10x7 (70 PLAY'S)...................................£70
24x7(168PLAY'S)..................................£168
57x7 (399 PLAY'S)................................£500

SATURDAY AND SUNDAY
5x2 (10 PLAY'S)....................................£20
10x2 (20 PLAY'S)...................................£40
24x2(48 PLAY'S)..................................£100
57x2 (114 PLAY'S)................................£250

SATURDAY'S ONLY
5x1 (5 PLAY'S)......................................£15
10x1(10 PLAY'S)....................................£30
24x1(24 PLAY'S)....................................£75
57x1(57 PLAY'S)...................................£150

POWER PLAY'S
MONDAY TO FRIDAY
5x5 (25 PLAY'S) £250

SHOW SPONSORSHIP
MONDAY TO FRIDAY
1x2 HOUR SHOW....................................£100
5x5 SHOW SPONSOR SPOT'S..................£150
PRODUCTION...£50
TOTAL £300

SATURDAY AND SUNDAY
1x2 HOUR SHOW....................................£300
5x7 SHOW SPONSOR SPOT'S..................£150
PRODUCTION...£50
TOTAL £500

station bosses not about to start sharing the money they were making with their staff, of course the more enterprising DJs did the sums and left to start their own.

As stations clustered around safe, profitable formats it was a long way from the broader mix of music and more experimental programming of the late seventies and early eighties. There was grumbling from some of the older pirates and hobbyist operations, who increasingly found they were shut out of the FM band by the sheer number of copycat stations. Jealousy grew over the stations that had developed sustainable business models, which in a few individuals sometimes tipped over into outright racism.

LWR boss Zak was scathing on his station's new competition: "If one of us got busted, we'd be on the phone telling the others to watch out. Now it's come to the stage where people are shopping each other. A lot of these stations are like a sore, and should be done away with, because they're not doing the cause any good. There's no honour amongst pirates now."[178]

New licences and light-touch regulation

Back in the political world things were finally happening. In February the previous year the government had launched its green paper outlining the options for the development of radio, to which there had been over 500 responses. On 19 January 1988, Home Secretary Douglas Hurd announced plans to move forward with a massive shake-up to the radio system.

He revealed there was to be a new Radio Authority to oversee several hundred new radio stations and that the pirates – once they switched off – would be welcome to apply. "All these services will be free of existing constricting statutory requirements which have applied to Independent Local Radio. They will instead be subject to light regulation designed to protect the consumer rather than direct the broadcaster. The key test which stations will have to pass, to obtain a licence to broadcast, is that of widening the range of consumer choice. They will have to live up to their promises to their audiences if they want to keep those licences."[179]

Only the IBA seemed to be upset by the new plans, with Director of Radio Peter Baldwin telling the papers he had been told the IBA would have its hands too full with satellite and cable television. Behind the scenes there was a government desire to sidestep the IBA, sweeping away the earlier age of public service broadcasting and replacing it with more dynamic market-oriented system. In an editorial, the Financial Times proclaimed "Here is one area, at least, where the Government is taking a modest step away from the centralising, nanny state – something, in fact, to be grateful for in the present climate."[180]

The end of simulcasting

While existing commercial stations were not overjoyed at the prospect of losing their local monopolies, they were placated by being allowed to permanently split their AM and FM services. Capital Radio had been lobbying to do this since 1980. As part of a Home Office experiment from May 1986, it had tried a separate FM adult soft rock service on Sundays called CFM, which proved popular with advertisers targeting London's new yuppies. New research, however, showed that actually 60-75% of ILR listeners were now on FM, so when the split became permanent on 1 November 1988 it kept 95.8 Capital FM largely unchanged while AM became new oldies service Capital Gold.

LBC waited until October 1989 to split its services, with the more downmarket phone-in dominated London Talkback Radio on AM and the more upmarket news service LBC Newstalk on FM. When it became clear neither was working, its owners actively lobbied the IBA to be allowed to replace the FM outlet with a specialist music service – even going as far as to hold talks with Kiss FM – but this move was rejected by the regulator.

The IBA also began to relax the stringent technical rules for independent stations. The most immediate effect was a change to the audio processing that stations used. In order to ensure efficient transmission and improve reception on portables and car radios, medium wave stations compressed their audio, giving less of a difference between the loud and quiet parts of music. However, FM radio, with its hi-fi pretensions, had a signal very close to the original source material. With the cosy duopoly between the BBC and IBA there had been little incentive to change this, even though the equipment now being used to listen to FM radio had changed.

When stations had been simulcast, if a listener had poor reception on one band then they could always tune to the other instead, but now with separate stations it was important for both to get through as well as possible. Research from the USA also suggested that listeners were attracted to the stations that sounded the loudest (even if they became fatiguing to listen to after a long time) and competition on the dial was hotting up. So it was out with the previous subtler processing and in with a new breed of aggressive audio processors designed to maximise the loudness of a station on what were now its most popular environments: the car, the portable radio and the Walkman. Radio in London was literally never to sound the same again.

It wasn't just commercial radio in London that was changing: BBC Local Radio was in for its own shake-up too. On 26 October Radio London was replaced by the new Greater London Radio, ditching the daytime soul music and replacing it with a new adult contemporary format aimed at a more upmarket audience. Matthew Bannister and his deputy Trevor Dann replaced almost all the presenters on the station, bringing in new names like Emma Freud, Chris Evans, Kevin Greening and Chris Morris alongside radio veterans like Tommy Vance and Johnnie Walker. It retained specialist programmes in the evenings, including former pirates Ranking Miss P with reggae, Dave Pearce with hip-hop and dance music. Among the producers was Paul Leaper, who as Paul James had been a presenter on Thameside and went on to run BBC Radio Kent.

While a hit with people in the media and a source of talent that later went on to big things in radio and TV, GLR was not a big success with listeners at the time. It was a sometimes awkward combination of music and speech, with only a small increase in budget over its predecessor. While Capital and LBC were spending over a million each to keep their listeners, GLR had only £5,000 a year for marketing.

New laws against the pirates

Two weeks after the carrot from Douglas Hurd, junior DTI minister John Butcher announced the stick for the pirates: "We have recently reviewed the resource needs of the radio investigation service. We are currently strengthening manning levels in the London area and are investing some £400,000 in new equipment which should assist in the tracing of unlicensed radio operators. At the same time we are implementing new strategies to deal with the enormous tasks facing the service."[181]

One of these new strategies was employing a former Metropolitan Police officer to work full-time on the business aspects of pirate stations. There was a raid on the office of London Greek Radio, taking away many documents in connection with the station, and a subsequent court hearing confirmed that the RIS had the legal right to seize such documents for their investigations. LGR was fined a record-breaking £25,000 including costs. It was followed by a raid on the office of Faze1 in Stockwell, making many suspect big operators like LWR or Kiss – whose offices were equally well-known – must be next. Phonographic Performance Limited, who had previously limited themselves to minor grumbling in the press about the pirates not paying copyright fees, circulated a letter to all the record companies with a list of 83 pirates and a warning that "any assistance given (e.g. supply of records) to any of these stations may result in prosecution under the Wireless Telegraphy Act 1949."[182]

Unfortunately at this point what had started as a sensible, joined-up plan by the government began to go fall apart. It turned out that there wasn't actually sufficient parliamentary time for the passage of the new legislation. On 21 May it was announced that work on the new Broadcasting Act would be delayed until the following year. Two years on from the chaotic cancellation of the community radio experiment it was not what the sector needed. Knowing they had to do something, the government instead announced that they were exploring new stations being licensed by the IBA under existing legislation and in September the IBA put forward a proposal for twenty 'incremental' stations. To avoid the need for new legislation, these would have to broadcast in existing areas and be complementary to existing services. It was another messy compromise, typical of the way radio had been handled by successive governments over the years. On the bright side for those broadcasting without a licence, it did delay proposed new anti-piracy laws.

Mr Butcher's hope that "unlicensed broadcasters will voluntarily stop broadcasting since they, with other interested parties, may soon have an opportunity to make applications to establish legal stations"[183] had little immediate effect on the number of pirates. In the autumn, the last-ever edition of Radio Today was published. It listed a record fifty-three unlicensed stations operating in the London area. On 2 November Douglas Hurd issued a written statement to Parliament approving the IBA's proposal and clarifying that anyone convicted of unlicensed broadcasting after 1 January 1989 would be banned from working on a licensed station for five years. Now he had the attention of the pirates.

The incremental radio scheme

On 13 November the IBA placed advertisements in the press inviting organisations to register their interest in applying for twenty new stations. Early the next year at a meeting of applicants organised by the Community Radio Association, the IBA's head of radio programming, Paul Brown, gave more details about their expectations. There were to be two Londonwide stations, one on AM, which they expected to be shared by several ethnic broadcasters, and one on FM, which was likely to be a specialist music service. There would also be three low-power FM services for individual areas, with two of those expected to be for ethnic services.

Paul Brown sounded a note of caution to applicants: for the third time commercial radio's expansion coincided with a time of economic recession and the outlook for existing independent stations was already of concern. However, entrepreneurs rarely go into business doubting that they will succeed and after waiting so long for a chance at a licence the applicants were not going to be dissuaded now. He was more upbeat about what they hoped to achieve with the scheme: "We need new people doing new things on the radio, as many of them as possible, and as many new sounds as possible."[184]

Among the pirates there was considerable confusion and misinformation about the new licences. While big stations like Kiss FM and London Greek Radio involved people who crossed over into legal radio or into campaigning groups such as the Community Radio Association, most of the smaller broadcasters had no such connections. Many didn't seem to know what licences were going to be on offer where or how they would go about applying. The proposed ban on working in legal radio was confused with the other anti-pirate proposals being suggested for the forthcoming Broadcasting Act. The biggest panic came over rumours that the DTI would now be able to seize DJs' entire record collections from their homes.

As the end of the year approached and larger operators like Kiss announced that they were to close down, so several smaller operations decided to follow suit. Not all were convinced, however. Rock 2 Rock told their local paper "The government will only allow you to broadcast to a small area. You just couldn't stay in business. It's not worth coming off the air in January to then find they don't give out licences until the January after."[185]

On New Year's Eve, London said goodbye to Kiss FM, LWR, London Greek Radio, Time Radio, JBC, Starpoint, WNK and more. The following January the DTI announced in a press release that in 1988 there had been 444 raids against unlicensed radio stations throughout the UK, 355 in London. 117 people had been prosecuted and fined a total of £79,500.

On The Air

Sunrise FM
House pioneers, 1988-1990

Launched in April 1988 from East London, Sunrise took to the airwaves on 88.75 FM playing a mix of soul, funk, house, rare groove and a little reggae. Initially on the air weekends only, early presenters included Steve 'Bad Boy' West, Andy 'Milk Tray' M, Greg Richards, Mad Axe, Matthew B, Peter Stapleton, Captain Ska-let, Chris Marks, Maniax Paul, Tony 'Crucial' White and Judge Jimmy.

Later in the year the hours increased to include weekday evenings and it began full seven-day broadcasts not long after. With the announcement of the new licences Sunrise considered their options but decided to continue broadcasting. Bad Boy West explained "Of course we want to get a licence. But our main aim is to make people happy and that is what we do. Now we have started we can't let people down. We are giving the people what they want. We are playing the sort of music that does not get played on the commercial channels. What's wrong with that?"[186]

As acid house began to take over it increasingly featured on some of the DJs' shows, especially after the launch of the 24-hour rave stations in the summer of 1989 and an influx of ads for raves. House DJs joining the station included Ellis Dee, Ratpack, DJ Seduction and Action Anderson.

From the start of 1990 the station had more pressures over its broadcasts. Some of the later DJs had split to form Future FM and Hardcore FM and keeping up regular broadcasts from a team of volunteers in the face of heavy raids was not easy. For a time Sunrise was forced to reduce hours again to weekends only. Sunrise finally left the air in the summer of 1990.

The original team now runs an Internet radio station at sunrisefm.co.uk.

Swinging Radio England
Vintage soul, 1988-1989

Taking to London's airwaves in the summer of 1988, the retro-flavoured mod station moved from initial weekend broadcasts to five days a week on 1611 AM. Help in getting the station on air came from a station of the same name in

Liverpool and there were plans for others around the UK too, although it's not clear if or for how long any of these broadcast.

Presenters included Harboro' Horace, who compiled the soul reissues for the Kent label; Tony Class and Dom Perignon, two of the leading DJs on the mod scene; Gaz Mayall, host of the legendary night Gaz's Rockin' Blues, as well as Jon Buck, Ian Jackson and Tim Wells. Station manager Mark Johnson declared "Our bias is towards popular music with strong tinges of ska, R&B, soul, psychedelic, Latin, jazz and the blues."[187]

On air the station identified as Radio England, opting for AM rather than FM because they felt they would have less trouble from other stations and the DTI. It also gave them more of the sixties 'boss' sound that they were seeking. SRE is believed to have remained on air until late 1989.

WNK

The pirate behind London's first legal black community station, 1988

WNK – it stood for Wicked, Neutral and Kicking – is now an almost forgotten footnote in London's commercial radio history. Founder Joe Douglas had been involved with the Afro Caribbean programming at Radio London in the early seventies, returning to radio on LWR in 1985, where he presented a weekly reggae and soca show. In the spare time from his job as a telephone engineer at BT he was involved with setting up Tottenham's RJR with another local DJ in early 1987. In the autumn he split to form WNK, though in terms of programming there was very little difference and for a while they continued to share a mailing address.

WNK's studio was in a flat on Tottenham's Broadwater Farm with the 104.4 FM transmitter nearby. The breakfast show was presented by Luther Wilson, who after he finished at 10am would open his grocer's shop on the estate. Programmes were aimed at an older Afro Caribbean audience, with reggae, lovers' rock, soca, calypso and gospel. Community information was mostly limited to plugs for helplines or events, though it did also carry cricket scores for matches where teams from the West Indies were playing. The station was very successful in attracting local advertising, with clients including hairdressers, record shops, a car dealer and a health food shop. At the end of 1988 it closed down to apply for one of the new incremental radio licences.

Legal but sharing

The IBA had planned that the North London FM licence should go to an ethnic minority station and they encouraged applicant groups to work together until more frequencies were available. London Greek Radio and WNK took them up on this idea and were successful in winning the 103.3 frequency. However, the specifics of who would broadcast at what times were more complicated to agree and so the stations ended up switching every four hours, with WNK taking 4-8am, 12-4pm and 8pm-12am. This meant there were two stations with fully-equipped studios and offices plus their own separate management and ad sales teams existing on only fifty percent of the revenue of a normal station.

WNK returned to the air legally as London's first black radio station on 6 November 1989. There were problems from the start. Joe Douglas brought in former JFM DJ Marc Damon as programme controller, who gave it an initial sound closer to the soul-styled JFM than the cross-generational black community station the IBA thought they were getting. He left after only four months following disagreements over the station direction. Joe Douglas temporarily took over, bringing in first Dixie Peach as a consultant and then Greg Edwards, Capital Radio's original soul show presenter, as replacement programme controller. He was to quit a year later, complaining that black radio was being held back by station owners and the Radio Authority.

Early presenters on the legal WNK included former TKO boss Louie St Clair on early breakfasts as well as James Anthony from Solar, Danny Mac from TKO, and DJ Mistri from Rock 2 Rock, who became assistant programme controller. In its short time on air it also served as a training ground for several young presenters and producers who went on to careers at Choice FM and 1Xtra.

It became clear very early on that listeners were not tuning in. Surveys among the local Afro Caribbean community found that they did not think WNK was black enough and they preferred the pirate alternatives on air 24 hours a day.

Rather desperately, WNK began programming music after the switchovers from LGR that it hoped would keep Greek listeners with the station, while its sales staff began targeting advertisers on LGR with cheaper deals, leading to a breakdown between the two stations. WNK also came under criticism for including only minimal speech content aimed at their community, having in their application promised greater community involvement and some cultural programming.

In June 1990 the IBA announced that it would soon have a new AM frequency available for use in North London that perhaps might be suitable for LGR. However, the clash over 558 AM between Spectrum Radio and Radio Caroline meant that it was temporarily in use as a second frequency for Spectrum. After the Radio Authority came into existence it explained the channel couldn't legally just be given to an existing station and would instead be advertised in 1992 when all the other incremental stations reapplied for their licences. In the meantime, WNK staggered on with increasing cutbacks. After losing their major outside investor, Midland Radio, it managed to find new funding in March 1992, which included the original backers of Fame FM.

WNK goes bust

WNK finally went into liquidation at Easter 1993 with debts of £28,000. In their last two weeks they were playing royalty-free music as they owed money to the music licensing agencies that they could not pay, at which point their licence was revoked. The Radio Authority insisted that the station's failure was not of their making, with Head of Development David Vick later insisting "If the black community had got behind WNK a bit more instead of listening to pirates then it might still be on air."[188]

· · · · · · · · · · · · · · · ·

WNK's premises near Wood Green Shopping City were taken over by the newly-licensed London Turkish Radio, who had previously taken an hour a day of time on WNK.

Radio Argus

A rock service launched by Bert Bridges in the summer of 1988 on 1611 AM, briefly adding 92 FM transmissions the following year until LWR returned. Argus continued on medium wave into the nineties.

Boys FM

A gay station playing hi-nrg and dance music along with news and information from the gay scene. The station involved former members of South West Sound.

Britannia Radio

An Asian music station broadcasting on 95.5 FM to South London from the summer of 1988. The station was raided and one person subsequently prosecuted after Capital Radio complained it was interfering with their transmissions.

BRL

Bangla Radio for London, broadcasting from the East End on 91.7 FM in the summer.

City Radio

City Radio was a split from Tottenham's RJR, serving an audience closer to Hackney. They began operating in the spring of 1988, moving straight into seven day programming.

Classic Radio

Launched in January 1988, Classic – sometimes known as CCR: Classic Community Radio – broadcast seven days a week to the Afro Caribbean community in North London on 105.5 FM. Daytimes carried mostly soul and some reggae. Sundays were more varied with shows featuring gospel, sixties soul and jazz. Presenters included Max Reinhardt, now on BBC Radio 3, who presented a Tuesday night show called The Global Juke Box showcasing music from around the world. A number of presenters on the station later joined Powerjam.

Radio Concept

Launched in December on 106.2 FM.

Crystal Radio

Broadcasting on 92.4 in the autumn of 1988 to North West London. The station shared some presenters with WLR and Medina Radio.

Eurojam

Launched in April 1988 with a mostly reggae format from the Finsbury Park area on 89.5 FM. The station operated seven days a week.

EZ Radio

Briefly on the air on 92.4 FM in the summer of 1988 with a reggae service in South East London.

Flight FM

A reggae station specialising in dancehall from East London on 94.2 FM in the summer.

Friction FM

A dance music station that took to the air in the autumn on 91.05 FM. Friction appeared on and off into the nineties.

Radio Galaxy

A South East London soul station which appeared out of nowhere to begin seven day programmes in January 1988 on 103 FM. It's not clear if this was connected to the earlier station from that area.

Good FM

Soul, hip hop and house on weekday evenings for a few months from March 1988 on 88.7 FM. Good FM returned early 1989 but again did not last long.

Greek Community Radio
Launched in summer 1988 on 104.4 FM.

Harp FM
Emerging on 88.4 FM in December playing dance music.

Ice FM
Ice took to the air in February 1988 with a soul and reggae format on 102.8 FM.

Radio Jennifer
Following the departure of founders Dave Fuller and Claire Mansfield from RFM they returned first in February 1988 with DFCM on 105.5 FM, sharing facilities with Hits FM. In the summer they decided to go it alone under a new name, Radio Jennifer, broad-casting every weekend on 89.5 FM. Other presenters included Dana Jay with indie music and Barry Morgan with the latest heavy metal. They moved to 819 AM in August 1990 when part-time broadcasting on FM became almost impossible due to the number of stations.

JSM
A Sunday-only soul station that launched in the summer of 1988 on 88.7 FM in North London.

LNO
London's Number One broadcast evenings and weekends on 98.3 FM in the autumn of 1988.

Radio Lola
Broadcasting in South Essex on 105.3 FM.

London FM
Playing half soul, half reggae, London FM took to the airwaves on 94.5 in December.

London '88 Greek Community Radio
Not the easiest of names for a presenter to get their mouth around, the station began broad-casts in the spring of 1988 on 96.1 FM.

London Irish Community Radio
Broadcasting seven days a week with a mix of Irish country and western and middle of the road music on 89.5 FM. The station launched in the spring of 1988 and primarily targeted the large Irish community in Hanwell in West London. Presenters included Jimmy Smith, DJ Don and Dicey Riley. It closed following a raid in May, with the on-air DJ fined £400 plus £295 costs.

Magic FM
In the winter of 1988 Raiders FM briefly changed its name to Magic FM before going back to the old name.

Maze FM
Broadcasting in the autumn on 96.8 FM.

Meridian Radio
Broadcasting soul music to South East London on 90.0 FM from December, though only to last a few weeks.

Middlesex Music Radio
After a spell on Radio Caroline, Tim Allen found himself back on land working for HMV's in-store radio in Oxford Street but not on the actual airwaves. He finally reappeared under the name Steve Brown doing taped shows on Middlesex Music Radio in May 1988. Programmes were a return to his style on Radio Duck, promising sixteen hits every hour with 'The best of the old and the best of the new'. What little time that remained each hour was packed with jingles. MMR returned again for another stretch of broadcasts in February 1990.

Pioneer Radio
A soul station launched in the autumn. Pioneer was raided after interfering with British Gas communications.

Playback FM
Soul every evening and weekend to Watford on 93.2 FM in the spring of 1988. Three of

their staff were caught in May 1988, which took the station off the air permanently.

PRS FM
The People's Radio Station, launched in early 1988 playing hip hop, soul, jazz and reggae for South London on 90.4 FM.

Ram Jam Radio
A reggae station broadcasting daily on 89.6 FM in early 1988.

Reflection Radio
A reggae and soul station that launched in the winter of '88 on 89.8 FM. Vanishing after only a few weeks, it returned again in June 1990. It is unknown if there is any connection to previous Radio Reflection.

Roots FM
Roots FM broadcast music from the roots of black music: reggae, R&B, African and gospel. The station launched early in 1988 and was put together by LWR's Fuzzy Dee. With its 93.2 frequency interfering with BBC Radio 4 it was soon targeted and removed from the airwaves not long after.

Sangam Radio
Sangam Radio was an Asian station broadcasting to Southall and the surrounding area of West London on 90.6 FM right alongside Sina Radio. It was described as playing Asian film and classical music plus sewing tips and recipes.

Radio Sarah
A soul and reggae station operating from the Streatham area on 105.45 FM in the early summer.

South London Radio
'Clutter-free pop' to South London every weekend on 103.2 FM. The station launched in the summer of 1988 and ran for around a year.

Stage FM
A soul music station broadcasting in the autumn on 98.2 FM.

Stomp FM
A Romford soul station that launched in April 1988 on 105.4 FM. There were major raids in the summer of 1989, hitting them shortly after they came on each week. The station closed down in November 1990 after announcing that with the new laws making it difficult to keep in contact with their listeners or fund the station with advertising they did not see how it could continue. Stomp is now an Internet radio station at stompradio.com.

Switch FM
A short-lived black music station that launched on 98.1 FM in December 1988 and featured some of the Faze 1 jocks.

TDK Radio
Heard with test transmissions of easy listening music in the autumn of 1988.

Veronica Supergold
Having founded North London's original Radio Veronica in 1980, Garry Stevens resurrected the name in June 1988 for a new oldies service. Hits FM had recently fallen apart but Garry was keen to return to the air and began working with Steve Roberts and Brian Smith. Soon the rest of the Hits FM DJs wanted to join and Veronica Supergold began transmissions each Sunday with an all-day schedule. After its name attracted the attentions of Bedfordshire's Chiltern Radio, who were launching a service coincidentally named Supergold, they changed the name to Veronica 102. The team were later involved with The Music Machine and Big L before Veronica was restarted once more in 1991.

WLIB
WLIB launched in Hackney in the summer of 1988 with a mostly reggae format on 90.9 FM. The station broadcast seven days a week.

1989

House music and the second summer of love

With the previous generation attempting to go legal it was time for another revolution in London's pirate airwaves. Popular histories of the rave era might have you believe that house music was non-existent – or perhaps just a northern phenomenon – until a bunch of DJs went to Ibiza, dropped ecstasy and came back to invent the acid house party. It wasn't quite like that. House had been played on London's pirates since 1986, often meeting less resistance on the radio than in the clubs at the time. The sparser, raw sound of the early Chicago releases initially held back its popularity but the more soulful tracks that emerged when labels targeted radio in that city – and house's New York garage relative with its Gospel-influenced vocals – picked up plenty of play on London's pirates too.

Early on there simply weren't enough releases for an all-house show, so it played as part of a mix with electro and contemporary boogie on programmes from Jazzy M and Jasper the Vinyl Junkie on LWR and Steve Jackson on TKO, while on Kiss FM Colin Faver was mixing up house with electronic dance tracks from Europe. They still found it hard to push the new music: Jazzy M remembers "A lot of people were saying to me 'why are you playing this hi-nrg' and it was hard work but people were starting to get into it."[189] By 1987 as the trickle of releases became more substantial, Jazzy M had his Tuesday-night Jacking Zone on LWR, "getting 40-50 letters a week" and Steve Jackson had moved to Kiss with his House That Jack Built.

It needed the arrival of ecstasy in London's clubland in early 1988 for house to go to the next level and it took just a few short months for it to then upturn everything. The previous year there were a handful of trendy West End and gay clubs playing house as part of a wider mix. Now the music went to new nights at massive venues like The Astoria and Heaven. These played only house and ditched clubbing's previous exclusivity and dress codes in a new spirit of openness. Kiss FM might have been largely responsible for the rare groove boom and those residencies were still paying the bills, but it was house that helped take it to its widest audience and was now a staple of shows from Danny Rampling, Judge Jules, Matt Black and Colin Dale as well as pioneers Colin Faver and Steve Jackson.

East-end rave radio

House music's move to East London was responsible for its biggest break on the pirate airwaves. Police in places like Hackney were already used to the blues parties going on in the Afro Caribbean community so they were initially uninterested in the new acid house parties appearing in disused warehouses and run-down venues, especially as their E'd-up punters didn't cause trouble. Local gangs took rather more interest and soon made it clear any illicit activity on their territory was not going to take place without their involvement. One party organiser described his experience with the Inter-City Firm, a notorious group of West Ham FC supporters that police suspected of involvement in protection and drug dealing: "The East End is their manor and they run it. I would not put on a party in Canning Town or Plaistow."[190]

Bow's Sunrise FM was the first of the new generation of pirates to take an interest in house. A multicultural operation, it began in the summer of '88 playing soul, rare groove and a little reggae, but by the new year several DJs had switched to house. It helped that it shared a name with the biggest rave promoter. On the May Bank Holiday 1989, the first dedicated house station, Centreforce, was launched by Andy Swallow in nearby Plaistow. Now running a house night every Saturday at Echoes by the Bow flyover, Andy had been prosecuted some years before for involvement with the ICF but was cleared and had since moved out to Essex. Coming on the air at almost the same time was Obsession FM from Tottenham, its launch bankrolled by a member of a Jamaican family who were involved in weed distribution – if you were young and from a council estate your choices for funding a business opportunity were limited.

These new stations were stripped-down and functional. The music was what mattered and they delivered a mix of seamlessly-blended tunes that only stopped for the ad breaks. Though the media labelled them as acid house stations, earlier on they were closer in spirit to the Balearic origins of the rave scene, mixing US house imports with Italian disco, Belgian new-beat, up-tempo electro, hip-house and early British releases. European dance music that had previously been ignored by London club and pirate radio DJs in favour of more 'authentic' black dance music from the USA was suddenly rediscovered by DJs when its influence on house and techno was identified.

At the start there was only a small cross-over between the DJs playing the big raves and those on the house pirates, although over time this changed as promoters realised how important the stations were in building rave's success, resulting in the two establishing a symbiotic relationship. Unlike the DJs from the jazz-funk era, it was now technical skill on the turntables that mattered and the long shows on the pirates enabled DJs to hone their beat-matching abilities. Talking was mostly limited to occasional lists of tracks they had played, plugs for events and shout-outs to the listeners that had paged-in, though the on-air personalities of DJ Hype and DJ Rap certainly helped them break through to wider success against their peers.

The pager quickly became a station must-have. People would call the pager company – BT's 840 7000 page number became ubiquitous – dictate their message to an operator and then it would be sent over the air and displayed on the pager screen for the DJ to read out. At times DJs received so many that new messages would overwrite the old ones before they could get to them. Stations quickly got to know the tracks that listeners wanted hear and could evaluate how new DJs were going down with their audience, giving them feedback of what listeners wanted, not just what was working in the clubs where DJs played out.

As the summer rave season of 1989 got underway, the big promoters began moving away from the inner city and out to the countryside. Wanting to reduce the vulnerability of having cash on site and looking to open up new channels for sales that took the effort off them, promoters switched to selling tickets in advance through a network of distributors. Pirate stations were soon taking advantage of this as a new source of income, with ads giving the numbers of their own agents. Flush with cash from events, promoters big and small were also shelling out growing sums for ad time on those rave stations that could maintain a reliable presence on the air.

To try and escape the rapidly-increasing attempts by the police to shut down parties, rave organisers implemented tight security over where their events would be held, even using decoy and backup locations. They needed to get the maximum number of people to the real location in the shortest possible time to avoid the possibility of being shut down first or the police setting up roadblocks preventing people getting there. Alongside telephone information lines, pirates soon became a part of this plan, giving out meeting points for raves and directing people to those already underway. After a ban was introduced on using phone lines for raves, pirate radio became even more important. As Radio One and Capital were pushed into clamping down on any tracks with drug references it only served to drive more listeners to the illegal alternative.

The government was now in a huge tabloid-fuelled panic. The security being used to defend events and the presence of big open-air raves in quiet home-counties locations were leading to serious public disorder. Chief Superintendent Ken Tappenden of Kent Police's Pay Party Unit made clear the scale of the perceived threat: "Acid house is not quite as big a headache as the miners' strike but it's getting there."[191] With raves making so much money, promoters were now finding themselves threatened with violence if they didn't hand over a percentage of the take in return for protection. Drugs were also being distributed and consumed on a previously unheard-of scale, making involvement in criminal activity a norm for young people. Pirate radio was seen as complicit in all this criminality, with some stations now finding themselves targeted not just by the RIS investigators but by the police as well.

The pirates go legal

Over in the legal radio world, things were moving fast. On 10 January the IBA advertised the first London licence, for Hounslow, with the other four London licences following at monthly intervals. However, alongside the excitement came increasing concerns about just what kind of radio was going to be licensed under the new scheme. Smaller operations that served audiences previously fulfilled by the pirates worried that they were going to be pushed out by those with the cash to mount a more effective application.

The Londonwide FM licence was the most at issue. By now this had attracted interest from groups including Virgin, Time Out, the Hanson conglomerate, Andrew Lloyd-Webber's Really Useful Group, Financial Times owners Pearson and existing radio operators including Capital Radio and Liverpool's Radio City. Despite the IBA's protestations that it would consider all applicants on their merits, it seemed increasingly unlikely that former pirate radio operators would have any hope of a licence. An editorial in Broadcast Magazine in March complained "Community radio is being sold out to businessmen and consortia with stakes in independent radio stations. Many of the proposals for the first incremental contracts are as close to the community and ethnic groups they purport to serve as [Capital FM breakfast jock] Chris Tarrant is funny."[192]

On 24 April the first of the new licences were announced, with former pirate Sina Radio winning the Hounslow licence for its South Asian station. In April the news that London Greek Radio and WNK had jointly won the licence for Haringey increased hopes that former unlicensed stations without massive backing could still compete. As expected, the Londonwide FM licence was the most hotly-contested, with 32 applications arriving at the IBA for the 5 June deadline. However, listeners hoping for a dance music station like Kiss FM were to be disappointed when on 12 July the IBA announced that London Jazz Radio were the winners. The IBA's head of radio, Peter Baldwin, said the station "Offered the prospect of the best radio service to increase the choice available to listeners in London."[193]

In the context of licences for black community stations being given in South London to what was to become Choice FM and in North London to WNK, it no doubt made sense to the IBA that they should be balanced with a markedly different format. At a time of recession, the station that was to become Jazz FM was also very well-funded – spending £50,000 just on its application – while its board and advisory panel were packed with establishment figures. However, real jazz was always going to be a minority taste for a predominantly older generation, while attempting to broaden the format for popular consumption made it more of a second-best choice rather than one that fulfilled listeners' core musical passions. The IBA did, however, say that they hoped to issue more licences as soon as new frequencies became available.

Since October 1987, Radio One had used a temporary 104.8 FM frequency in London to avoid losing audience in this important territory. With it now launching a national FM network on a newly available sub-band, Kiss began a campaign for 104.8. In just a few weeks they gathered over 3,000 letters in support, which were delivered to Home Secretary Douglas Hurd. In August the Home Office announced that two more Londonwide frequencies had been found. This time there were forty applications, which included Kiss FM and a group of former Solar Radio DJs led by Clive Richardson, who revived Solar's name for their application.

THE WIN OR LOSE PARTY

AT THE WAG 35 WARDOUR ST., W1
WEDNESDAY 27TH DECEMBER 1989; £10
2 FLOORS OF MUSIC FROM 10 UNTIL LATE.
DJ'S WILL INCLUDE: PAUL ANDERSON, TREVOR MADHATTERS, COLIN FAVOR, JUDGE JULES. TEE HARRIS, COLIN DALE, STEVE JACKSON, HEDDI, GORDON MAC, JAY STRONGMAN, LINDSAY WESKER AND MANY MORE KISS DJ'S!

Kiss fm

On 16 December the winners of the two new licences were announced: Lord Hanson's easy-listening station Melody FM and Kiss FM, promising dance music for a rather younger generation. In a sign of the issues that were to come over whether black community stations should be defined by more than their music, Patrick Berry, MD of South London licence winners Choice FM, said he was "Totally flabbergasted at the decision and appalled at the weak rationale ... We are not even on air yet and the IBA have done this. What chance have we got for competing for an audience or advertising against a London-wide black music station?"[194] The IBA's Peter Baldwin responded "Any intention by these two stations that they would simply be black dance stations is misguided. They must appeal to all age groups in their local ethnic community."[195]

The excluded return to piracy

Over the course of the year, many of the pirates that had switched-off returned to the air. LWR, Time Radio, JBC, RJR, Fresh, Twilight, Starpoint and others all came back as pirates – several after only a few weeks off air. The majority quickly realised that they had no chance of getting a licence under the system as it stood and saw a risk to their existence by staying off any longer. The DTI reported that during the first five months of the year raids were up 50%.

Robert Atkins, the minister now in charge of shutting down the pirates, was not going to let up in the crusade. Presenting the latest figures for the Radio Investigation Service back in January he had attacked the BBC for its new Lenny Henry comedy featuring a pirate station called the Brixton Broadcasting Company and Lenny for accepting an honorary position of president at Kiss FM. Mr Atkins also complained about the wrongful portrayal of its officers in a recent episode of Emmerdale where a pirate station's equipment had been smashed up in a raid.

In its annual report, Capital Radio chairman Richard Attenborough demanded tougher action be taken against illegal broadcasters. Showing how much they had been a training ground for legal radio during the eighties, the station at the time employed five presenters who had worked on pirates in the previous five years.

The end of the year saw some of the heaviest raids of 1989. On one weekend, two teams of RIS officers toured London taking at least twelve stations off the air. Others managed to remove equipment before it was their turn. The unlucky ones were the subject of studio raids and several people were arrested.

On The Air

Centreforce Radio
The first seven-day rave station, 1989-1990

Sunrise FM might have set the template with its early acid-house shows and Fantasy FM might have gone on to bigger success, but Centreforce was London's first seven-day all-rave broadcaster.

The station was set up by Andy Swallow, who co-ran a venue called Echoes Nightspot in Bow doing Saturday nights as DJ Pasha while Tony 'Balearic' Wilson, a friend of Paul Oakenfold, did Fridays. When acid house parties took off, Andy cannily saw an opportunity for tying together his interests in music promotion with a pirate station. Echoes acid house nights were already proving very successful and DJs were recruited from there and other East London clubs and record shops.

Party season launch

Centreforce took to the air on 8 May 1989, just before the peak of the summer party season, and was an immediate success with listeners. Especially in the earlier days, it had a fairly rough-and-ready broadcasting style, but as the only place you could hear rave music at any time of the day nobody seemed to particularly mind. Transmissions usually came from the top of the Balfron Tower in Poplar, linked from nearby studios in empty flats in Poplar or Canning Town.

For the most part presenters got on with delivering a non-stop mix of music with just the occasional interruption for shout-outs read off a pager and a block of ads at the top of the hour for raves and club nights. Musically it was more populist than the stations that followed, reflecting the broader approach of the earlier big raves. Summer Saturday nights were peak times, with party-goers tuning in for directions to the meeting points for events. Amongst the presenters were DJ Randall, Kenny Ken, Jazzy J, DJ One, Keith Mac, DJ Hugs, DJ Danielle, Mr Music and Dave Corporation.

The acid house panic

Bad press, however, began to haunt the station, mixed in with a general media panic about raves and drugs. The newspapers eagerly reported the police saying that they considered both Centreforce and Echoes to be fronts for notorious West Ham gang, the Inter-City Firm. On a Thames TV investigative report, one former DJ alleged he was assaulted after he quit and it was claimed another had his Walthamstow record shop smashed up.

Centreforce mounted a pre-emptive publicity exercise to try and convince people that it was not how it was being portrayed in the media. DJ Gary D was adamant "We do it for fun. People get the impression we're some sort of gangsters, but none of the DJs get paid – they do it for love. That applies to everyone involved here. There is no 'Mr Big', no organiser. Centreforce is a family affair, my two boys play shows when other DJs can't make it and my wife plays too. We charge £150 to run an advert but it all goes out on running the station. We just upgraded the decks, bought a half-decent mixer, then there's the £750 phone bill and the three transmitters we've had nicked. No-one here is coining it in."[196]

The police, however, were certain that there was a major drug dealing network run by the ICF that was centred on Centreforce and Echoes. Detective Sergeant Craig Stratford, one of the leaders of the investigating team later said "It certainly appeared that drug dealing was taking place in the requests of the punters as well as the people who were running it, the DJs."[197] On Friday 20 October the police simultaneously raided Centreforce's Plaistow studio, the Echoes club and a dozen houses and arrested 35 people. However, nothing of significance was found and the two DJs on air were not charged. The police's surveillance activities had already been spotted by the station, who had also noted a recent lack of DTI raids compared to others on the air. DS Stratford admits "You can either blame the non-success of the raid on their intelligence, or on us being unlucky or totally wrong."

Andy Swallow denied all the allegations: "I haven't been to a football match in years, I couldn't even tell you who West Ham are playing next week. Obviously, as most people know, I have been in trouble in the past, but that was when I was a kid. When people say that Centreforce is the ICF they couldn't be more wrong. We are not into extortion, we don't go around demanding percentages of other people's parties; we are in the business of running a radio station and a couple of clubs. As for DJs who leave our station to work for someone else, we put absolutely no pressure on them. As a matter of fact we have helped several of the pirates in many ways, especially Fantasy FM who are supposedly our main rivals."[198]

Centreforce returned one week after the raid but was hit again almost as soon as they came back on the air. After laying low for a short while they returned to regular broadcasts but the raids did not let up, resulting in ever-longer gaps between broadcasts. In early 1990 several of the DJs defected to a new station, Dance FM, and Centreforce itself vanished from the dial in May. The police were still convinced that they could make a case on conspiracy to supply drugs but in court much of the evidence was ruled inadmissible by the judge and the prosecution eventually dropped the case.

• • • • • • • • • • • • • • • •

Andy Swallow went on to run a successful garage label producing acts like The Artful Dodger and Miss Dynamite. The name was revived in the late 2000s using both the Internet and a block of shows on Romford's Time FM. While lasting longer than the original pirate Centreforce, these came to an end in 2008 when Time FM's station manager (and former Radio Jackie station organiser) Peter Stremes left.

Fantasy FM
The biggest of all the rave stations, 1989-1991

In August 1989, Mystery Man launched London's second big rave station, Fantasy FM. In just a few months Centreforce had already demonstrated the huge demand for the music that people were hearing at raves, but the quality of their jocks was rather varied. Fantasy established deeper links to the DJs and pro-moters involved in the emerging scene. From the start they had big plans, as DJ Shadowfax explained: "We have a nucleus of really diverse DJs who specialise in presenting, scratching, mixing... but we've got entrepreneurial type business minds. We're hoping to get sponsored by Nissan."[199]

When they first came on air Fantasy were broadcasting on 98.6 FM from

Fantasy FM's studio in 1990.

East-End tower blocks. Early in 1990 they moved to 98.1, where they remained until the station closed. DJs played house, techno, acid house and the growing number of UK rave releases, some of which can now be seen as the first roots of hardcore and jungle. An early recruit was DJ Hype, who had both fantastic deck skills and an impeccable ear for the tunes that were going to be big. Others included DJ Rap, DJ Spice, The Rhythm Doctor, DJ Krome, Evil O, Shadowfax, Cool Hand Flex, DJ Tek, DJ Vibes, DJ Massive and DJ Tricks. There were guest shows from Baby Ford, Mr C of The Shamen and Aphex Twin under the name DJ Ace.

As one of the more permanent features on the dial, Fantasy were soon charging £200 or more a week to advertise. Later they hooked up with a company that leased 0839 premium service lines to rave promoters and began their own helplines, dating lines and other services, bringing in another revenue stream. In 1990 Fantasy began working with Wayne Anthony's Genesis organisation to run events, though their first party had operational problems and was closed down by the police. Fantasy also ran their own events and became particularly known for their massive all-nighters at the Astoria in Charing Cross Road which had followed on from Nicky Holloway's The Trip at the same venue.

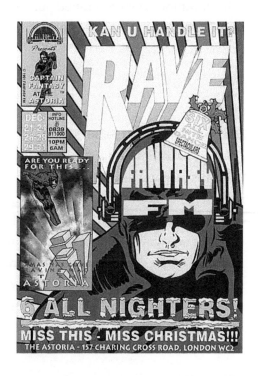

Fantasy FM closed down in 1991. The station had plans to broadcast legally via cable or satellite radio but these seem to have come to nothing. Several of its DJs went on to success in music or in later radio stations, with DJ Hype becoming one of the longest-serving DJs on Kiss 100 FM.

Obsession FM

Early ravers, 1989-1990

A rave station launched at a similar time to Centreforce on 104.2 FM, Obsession was typical of the multicultural nature of the early days of UK house: founders Roy and Savas came from Chinese and Greek families respectively and it was backed by Otiz F. Angel, whose parents were from Jamaica. DJs on the station were mostly friends rather than well-known names.

Members of Angel's extended family were involved in the weed distribution business and then diversified into ecstasy as the scene took off, which led to Obsession being cited as proof that organised crime was moving into pirate radio in order to shift product. In his memoir, Angel recalls "Running an illegal radio station wasn't that hard for me; in fact it was business as usual. I mean, instead of weed customers we had advertisers and sometimes it was still a problem to persuade them to pay us our money, but if the boys at the station couldn't handle it, we sent members from The Firm who had their own way of persuading people to pay up. And just like the dope business, every once in a while we had to flee from the police. Running down the stairs of a huge block of flats carrying transmitter equipment was always an annoying experience."[200]

In December 1990 combined police and DTI activities resulted in ten raids in a month and the arrests of two people, after which Obsession decided to close down.

Q102

Xfm's indie forerunner, 1989-1990

Sammy Jay (Sammy Jacob) had been a soul DJ on Horizon Radio while still in his teens. Later he'd moved to Solar Radio, helping out behind the scenes in its second pirate incarnation, and had then been involved in the adult soul and rock formatted CD93. In 1989 he began a station that was to take him in a different musical direction. Q102 first took to the air on New Year's Day. When it started it was very much a follow-on to CD93: the early broadcasts featured rock during the day while night-times were devoted to soul and jazz. After a few months the soul side was axed and Q102 became more of the indie station that it is remembered as today.

Leyton's finest

Q102 broadcast on Saturdays only, with a studio in Sammy's house in Leyton linking to a transmitter on a tower block in nearby Leytonstone using equipment built by former Solar engineer Keith Renton. Later they moved the studio to Sammy's mum's house in Clapton. Early DJs included Sammy Jay, Donald Johnson and Bob Matthews (Bob Mower), most recently on CD93 and earlier Jackie and Caroline. However, with the introduction of DJs like the NME's Steve Lamacq (under the name Andy Hopgood), Adrian Gibson and Joe Walker a more credible indie format emerged, if less angular and less political than the early eighties equivalents. Jingles came from one of the many Q102s in the USA and seemed to be used ironically rather than because of any fit with the programming.

Most of the funding for the station came out of Sammy's pocket. Steve Lamacq remembers "The DJs paid £10 each, every week, to keep it going (although the envelope where you were supposed to leave your money was always full of IOUs)."[201] There were no real ads on the station, although as usual record companies were happy to support it with promos. Its broadcasts seem to have attracted only minimal attention from the authorities. There were occasional unannounced visitors as Bob Matthews recalls: "I remember sitting in a small backroom in Leyton doing the show when the next presenter arrived (Alison Mitchell?) with Johnny Walker in tow. Got the shock of my life!"[202]

Xfm

In September 1990 goth band The Cure announced they would start a pirate radio station to launch their new album. In the event the station never made it to the air, but they did make contact with Q102 and guested on the station. This cemented a relationship between Sammy and The Cure's label, Fiction Records, who went on to invest in his legal broadcasting plans after Q102 closed later that year.

• • • • • • • • • • • • • • • •

Sammy Jacob began campaigning for a legal indie service in London, running a series of Restricted Service Licence stations in London and at festivals under the Xfm name. In 1997 Xfm won the last of the Londonwide FM licences, but financial problems resulted in a takeover by Capital Radio the following year. In 2007 he went on to launch NME Radio with a format similar to the original Xfm, though in 2010 that also closed.

Aquarius FM
Launched in August on 105.8 FM, Aquarius broadcast soul to South East London but had vanished by the winter.

Breeze FM
A dance station that began in January on 96.9.

Broadway FM
A dance music station that launched in early 1989 and closed not long after following a raid in which one person was arrested and taken away for questioning. They were later fined £2,000 plus £450 costs – high for a first offence.

CBN Radio
Broadcasting on 100.4 FM.

Chillin' FM
Launched in November on 92.6 FM with a house and dance music format.

City Weekend Sounds
Briefly on the air to North West London from May 1989.

Climax Radio
A rave station that took to the air in August on 95.4 FM. Despite not having the big names of some of the other rave stations of the time, Climax still picked up a loyal audience. Presenters included Mr Climax, Jam Easy, Maniacs Paul, Adrian H, Dem 2, Marvellous Mad Max, Vinyl Mac and Micronaut.

Community Radio Network
A black music station launched in January on 90.8 FM.

Crush FM
A short-lived dance music station that launched on 96.1 FM in October.

Radio Free North Kent
Broadcasting a rock service on 101.2 FM from August 1989.

Future FM
A rave station launched by former Sunrise FM jock DJ Seduction in May 1989 on 105.5 FM. The station did not last long as according to him it was "too time consuming and too risky!" Other presenters included DJ Babyface, Paul Jackson and Man Incognito.

Gremlins FM
Broadcasting on 106.5 FM.

GRQ
GRQ apparently stood for Get Rich Quick. Launched in October, it broadcast on Monday nights on 105.4 FM, but had vanished by the following year.

The Home of Good Baking
Unbelievably, not a wind-up. Starting in August it broadcast for a few weeks on 95.4 using the jingle package from the in-house radio station at United Biscuits that broadcast back in the seventies.

Hotwire
Broadcast on 105.4 FM from just outside London.

Injection Radio
A weekend-only dance and rave station launched in October on 93.1 FM. It is only believed to have lasted a few months.

Juice FM
Launched in November with house music on 105.3 FM but wasn't to last.

KAOS FM
Launched in November playing house music on 91.9 FM. Later it began identifying as RKL – Radio Kaos London – and switched to 100.5 FM.

Kick FM
A rave station launched in November on 104.2 FM.

Laser Radio

Right after Kiss FM relinquished 94 FM, Laser Radio took over their spot with a seven-day service playing a mix of soul, house and rave from a transmitter on the Chingford Hall estate in North East London. Several DJs came from Soul FM and included Lenny Grooves, Ritchie B, Mike Scott and Chris Jackson.

Friends FM

A rave station launched in December 1989 on 100.7 FM from East London. Friends had a reputation for playing the rougher breakbeat style that began coming in at that time. Set up by Mad B (aka Formula 7), who later ran Quayside Records, DJs included Nicky Blackmarket. He later reminisced on the Drum and Bass Arena website "The whole procedure from setting up a studio to positioning the aerial was all part of the fun, you will never get that back now. I used to do the Sunday evening show in my pyjamas and dressing gown."

Lightning Radio

Lightning was initially an offshoot of Passion Radio and picked up a number of DJs from that station when it eventually closed. Musically it played across the reggae spectrum and with some soul shows too. Lightning was accused of interfering with aircraft communications when frequencies used by jets coming into Heathrow were jammed on multiple occasions. This resulted in it being raided eleven times in the first four months of 1990. The station returned after long break that August and remained a regular on South London's airwaves.

London Independent Radio

A short-lived reggae station from South London on 93.8 FM.

Meantime Radio

Launched in March 1989 in the North West London area on 92.9 FM.

Medina Radio

Launched in April 1989, Medina was a dance music station broadcasting to North West London. Some of the DJs had previously been involved with Crystal Radio and WLR. Amongst them was Jack Smooth, one of jungle music's pioneers, later on Green Apple.

Mega FM

A soul station launched in May on 95.5 FM.

Nova FM

Briefly on the air in August 1989.

Prophecy FM

Launched in November 1989 on 100 FM. Prophecy closed in February after a raid and subsequent court case, accusing the DTI of singling them out for harsher treatment.

Rush FM

Hackney's hardcore Rush FM began broadcasts in June on 106.2, initially just evenings and weekends but before long going 24 hours. As it was increasingly targeted by the authorities it reverted to weekends only and changed its name to Weekend Rush. The station became notorious after barricading and booby-trapping the doorway of the top floor flat of the tower block where its transmitter was housed, station members abseiling down from the roof above to gain access. The station closed in 1996. Presenters included DJ Trip E and DJ Cutly.

SLR

After WNK closed down to apply for a licence, several of the DJs jumped ship to SLR which began broadcasting in Tottenham on WNK's old 102.9 frequency. The station remained a regular on the airwaves.

Soul City Radio

A Sunday-only soul music station broadcasting on 93.3 FM from the Enfield area.

Space FM

Space FM launched in December on 99.7 FM and was alleged to be Centreforce operating under a different name in the hope it might give them less hassle from the DTI and police. It was raided soon after and did not return to the airwaves.

Star Radio

A black community station launched in 1989, though it was off the air for much of the winter. It returned in May 1990 but again did not seem to last long.

Strong Island Radio

A weekend dance music station broadcasting on 96.8 FM. Its young presenters included DJ Wildstyle and DJ Cream.

 CAUTION: RADIO·ACTIVE!!

STRONG ISLAND RADIO
★ 96·8 FM ★
(WEEKENDS)
THE HOTTEST STATION AROUND!!

Supreme Radio

An earlier incarnation of Station FM, the first broadcasts from Supreme went out in April 1989 from Hackney. Presenters included DJ Keithley, Dub Bug, Hector Selector, WJ, Good Grooves and Lady J. Station FM has continued ever since, with boss DJ Keithley racking up thousands of pounds in fines and several hundred hours of community service for unlicensed broadcasting. He also won a gong at the British Reggae Awards for best radio DJ.

Tropical Radio

A largely reggae station launched in January on 105.2 FM and broadcasting for most of the year.

WIBS

WIBS apparently stood for the West Indian Broadcasting Service, though the name might have been influenced by WIBS in Grenada back when they were still called the Windward Islands. It broadcast a mostly reggae format to North London.

WLR

A black community station from North West London, WLR initially carried more soul music than those broadcasting to similar audiences in other parts of town. It featured several former Time FM DJs including Chris Nat and Sean Lewis. After many months off, the station returned in December 1990 saying they were determined to ride out any problems with the authorities. The station is a direct ancestor of Unique FM, which has broadcast in the area into the new millennium.

XERB

Launched in October 1989 with oldies on 105.2 Sunday afternoons. It later renamed itself Wurlizer Radio.

1990

Goodbye needle time, hello incrementals

For the first time since its inception, commercial radio looked like it might finally have the edge over the pirates.

At the end of 1989 the needle time restrictions were finally lifted following an investigation by the Monopolies and Mergers Commission: now BBC and independent stations could play music all day if they wanted to. However, the percentage of a station's revenue that needed to be paid in copyright fees to the music publishers and record companies remained at the same high level of 10.75% for new stations, rising to 17% over five years. It wasn't until 1993 that a more realistic deal set at 5% of revenue was achieved, providing a better balance between what was undoubtedly the main attraction of most stations and what was also the primary promotion tool for the record companies.

London's new incremental stations were now coming on air. Sunrise Radio – the new name for Sina – had launched the previous November along with London Greek Radio and WNK. In March Choice FM took to the airwaves from Brixton, featuring DJs from several former pirates including LWR's Daddy Ernie and DJ Elayne. Radio Thamesmead, which had previously only been available as a community station on the cable TV network in its local area, also launched that month and again included a few former pirate DJs from pop and soul stations. In June it was the turn of the multi-cultural cooperative Spectrum Radio, having beaten a joint bid by LBC and Capital for the medium wave licence.

Unfortunately, none of these stations had a great start. Sunrise spent over fifty percent more on its launch than it originally planned and had to return to its investors for additional funding when revenues were not as expected. It also received criticism from Capital Radio for its pop-based English-language breakfast show, considered by Capital to be rather too close in format to theirs. Both LGR and WNK were seriously constrained by the time sharing agreement that they had reached. Losses began mounting at London Greek Radio, and the following year it held a fundraising drive from listeners; WNK fared even worse, becoming increasingly desperate in its attempts not to go under.

Choice FM found that the transmitter power it was allowed to use meant reception was poor for many of those in its target area – although it was also hoping to maximise its coverage. While the IBA had made clear that WNK and Choice were black community stations serving all age groups – not black music stations – both concentrated on playing mainstream soul and reggae with little of the other community programming that they had promised in their licence applications.

Spectrum Radio had a problem in even being heard by potential listeners when it was assigned the 558 AM frequency used by the offshore Radio Caroline. The authorities and Caroline both refused to give way over the channel, with Spectrum given a temporary second frequency as the two transmitters battled it out on 558. Spectrum's transmitter was based at the Lots Road power station in Chelsea, used for powering the London Underground, which had also been the original home of Capital and LBC. This gave the additional problem that when coal was delivered at high tide the transmitter was forced to close down in case the coal dust ignited. Aside from any difficulties receiving it, Spectrum's mix of programmes for different ethnic communities did not prove popular with listeners. It also had to compete with a new Community AM service launched the same month by the BBC, using GLR's medium wave transmitter each evening for programmes for the Afro Caribbean, Asian, Arabic and Irish communities of London.

Jazz FM, thought by the IBA to be able to ride out the recession due to the deep pockets of its main investor, turned out not to be so capable. In September 1991 it radically changed format, dumping the more serious jazz output in favour of smooth soul and light jazz. Presenters Chris Philips and Jez Nelson, who had made their names on the pirates, found themselves out of the station overnight, only learning the news from a club doorman who'd read the next morning's papers. To outsiders it seemed clear that Jazz FM had breached the programming obligations in its contract – its 'promise of performance' – but the Radio Authority preferred to give in than to see a station go under. The promised 'light-touch' regulation of the new Authority turned out in practice to still be quite interventionist when it came to ensuring services remained on air.

More successful in finding an audience was Kiss FM when it launched in September. The first research figures gave it 1,078,000 listeners, a massive achievement in only four months on air that vindicated the need London

Gordon Mac launches the legal Kiss FM.

had for such a station. Internally there were problems, however. The launch had been expensive and the impressive listener figures were not translating into advertising sales, while its investors – many new to radio – were pushing its largely inexperienced management team to deliver them an impossible return. Two years later, lead investor EMAP had taken full control of the station, the majority of its pirate DJs had been shown the door and its music policy was edging it closer and closer to Radio One.

The huge growth in dance music during this time – much of it more European in lineage rather than owing a direct debt to black music from the Caribbean or USA – meant Kiss came into a rather different musical environment than a black music station might have done had 1985's community radio experiment gone ahead. Dance music was now a significant part of the charts and backed by the major record labels. In March 1990 Radio One began adding more dance tracks to their daytime playlist after research suggested they were losing out to other stations due to their policy of avoiding music meant for the dancefloor. Capital Radio was making similar changes to its music policy.

The new anti-pirate laws and the rave crackdown

While finances were an issue, Independent stations did, however, have hope that the government might be about to get on top of the pirate problem. The new Broadcasting Act, which was to introduce the new commercial radio regime under a light-touch Radio Authority, also contained a series of measures aimed at cracking down on unlicensed broadcasting. Its press release announced six main changes:[203]

- to extend the offence of broadcasting without a licence, mainly to tackle the problem of prosecutions which fail because there is no firm evidence that the defendant was actually operating the equipment, as opposed to having it available for use.
- that an owner or manager of premises should be guilty of an offence if he knowingly allows unlicensed broadcasting to take place from those premises.
- to make it an offence to advertise on, or supply certain goods and services to, an unlicensed broadcasting station. This would make it easier to take action against those who manage and finance unlicensed stations, and those who sustain them by advertising on them or making recordings for transmission on them.

- to ensure that the records and tapes of pirates become liable to forfeiture, and that other items, such as record players, turntables, amplifiers and microphones, are also included.
- to strengthen the present, inadequate, search and seizure powers.
- that the offence of broadcasting without a licence and the new offences should be triable either way, and that on indictment the maximum penalties should be two years' imprisonment, or an unlimited fine, or both. At present cases can only be tried before magistrates courts and the maximum penalties available are three months' imprisonment and or a £2,000 fine.

Even before the parts of the Act relating to pirates came into effect on 1 November, action against stations was becoming increasingly heavy. Work by the police's Pay Party Unit began to have a serious effect on rave organisers and the number of major events that managed to operate successfully was considerably curtailed. The police also acted together with the Radio Investigation Service on those aspects that involved the pirates. The money flowing into stations to promote monster raves began to be replaced by rather smaller residencies at licensed premises instead.

In an echo of the Free Radio Association's rally exactly twenty years earlier, rave organisers came together for one last-ditch protest in Trafalgar Square as the Freedom to Party Campaign. Put together by promoter Sunrise's Paul Staines (now more famous as conservative blogger Guido Fawkes), it had its own right-wing libertarian backer in the shape of David Hart, an advisor to Margaret Thatcher who ran strike-breaking efforts during the miners' dispute. The rally even had its own pirate station operating from the offices of Hart's Committee for a Free Britain.

The five-year ban on working for a licensed station if you were convicted of unlicensed broadcasting had the most significant effect on the makeup of those involved in pirate radio. For longer-established presenters it was no longer worth the risk when there might be an opportunity on one of the new stations. Illegal broadcasting was now for a younger generation who saw little prospect of ever becoming a part of the legitimate system. Among the engineers who supplied the pirates with equipment – now hoping for a slice of the work on legal stations – several moved out of London to stop the flow of people to their doorsteps brandishing bundles of cash.

Getting rougher on the airwaves

Earlier pirate stations had always been careful to coexist with their legitimate neighbours. Newer operators – now with less to lose – weren't always so bothered. In May there were reports of pirate operators in West London disconnecting the power to mobile phone base stations in order to put their own equipment on the air. Vodafone was particularly badly hit, with engineers reportedly threatened and their vans damaged, resulting in some refusing to work at certain buildings. There were also direct attempts at interference to legitimate services in April, when LBC in North London was blocked again by protest transmissions, this time as part of the campaign against the poll tax.

Far more common were spats between stations. Almost every week there was another story of a transmitter being taken or aerials being damaged because of interference on neighbouring channels or disputes between people who had previously worked together. Pirates were soon going to increasingly elaborate lengths to try and keep their equipment out of the reach of both the DTI and other stations. Transmitters were hidden down ventilation shafts using car jacks or concreted into structures on the top of tower blocks. Rush FM put their equipment inside a fortified flat on the top floor of a block to which access could only be gained by abseiling in.

Stations now didn't dare to leave a frequency for fear of having it taken over by another operator in their absence. Some, like weekend-only oldies service Radio Veronica, used 'throwaway' low-power transmitters running a tape on repeat during the week to discourage others from moving in. Frequency management increasingly turned into a small-scale protection racket run by people who weren't even broadcasting. Try and transmit on someone's channel without paying up and you'd quickly find yourself off air and visited by the owner's representatives. On the other side, people would think twice about stealing a transmitter from someone who was paying 'insurance'.

Having gone legal, former pirates now found themselves on the other side of the fence. In October a South London unlicensed station announced they spotted two people entering the tower block where they broadcast from, one a DJ on Kiss FM. Shortly after they reported their transmitter smashed up and part of it stolen. It was suggested the duo had taken things into their own hands when the neighbouring station interfered with listening to Kiss.

Through the autumn there were increasingly-heavy raids on the unlicensed stations left on air. By October the numbers were down to just the regular stalwarts who refused to give up whatever the circumstances. In December the airwaves were at times almost deserted, though that wasn't to last for long. Just like after Capital Radio launched, the pirates soon realised the limitations of the new services.

The failure to licence a full-time black community station in North London gave an opportunity for Afro Caribbean stations to continue broadcasting in Tottenham and Harlesden. The increasingly chart-oriented newcomer Kiss FM was soon unable to satisfy the demand for more specialist dance music tastes. Post rave and a massive flood of local record releases, pirates were already splintering into specialists for sub-genres: hardcore with its influences from reggae in the east, a more Balearic-derived mix in the north and west, closer in spirit to US garage in the south.

In the first four months of 1990 there were 169 raids on unlicensed stations in London, 14 people were interviewed by investigators and 33 people were successfully prosecuted. Figures for the rest of the year are unavailable. After spending much of the eighties demanding regular figures on how many pirates were raided each year, the arrival of new licensed services seems to have caused MPs to lose interest.

On The Air

Dance FM
East London ravers, 1990-1993

After the police action to try and shut down Centreforce, a number of the station's DJs left to join Dance FM, where they hoped they could simply get on with playing music rather than being at the centre of media speculation and police activity. The station was set up by the people who had previously run soul station Melody FM back in 1987 and broadcast mostly from Lund Point in Stratford. Early on there were reported to be occasional issues with Centreforce, who accused Dance FM of destroying their aerial on one occasion.

Dance FM's studio, apparently in a garage.

Presenters on Dance FM included Bryan Gee, Kenny Ken, Jeff B, Mr C, Rob Atkinson, Linden C, Rob Elliot, Chris Energy and DJ Easy O. After problems at home, sixteen-year-old Easy O ended up moving into to the house housing the studio, covering for other DJs and doing a marathon twelve-hour broadcast one Christmas.

Dance FM closed in late 1993 after an increase in activity against the station, though most of its DJs continued to play out on to later stations.

Green Apple Radio
From West London youth project to Britain's first satellite dance station, 1990-1992

Green Apple launched at the start of 1990, broadcasting a dance music service from Slough to the East Berkshire / West London area. The station was started by Joe Joshi, who wanted to do something for local young people and decided on a radio station as a way of achieving this. Then, according to his wife Geraldine, "as the new music began to filter through to local DJs who were desperate to get on air, passions developed to the extent that the station completely took over our lives."[204]

At the beginning Green Apple split into daytimes playing more of a soul / rare groove sound and evenings that were playing house. Early DJs included Paul Dodd (ex JFM), Paul James, Ian Dee, The XL Boys and musicians Chad Jackson and Jack Smooth, whose early jungle productions featured on his show. Later the house side began to dominate, although Green Apple remained much more diverse musically than its East London equivalents. It was also culturally diverse, with white, black and Asian members.

The station was raided in May 1990 when one person was caught and subsequently charged. By now Green Apple had a large line-up of DJs so the location of its studio was an open secret among young people in Slough. The number of DJs meant that shows took more of a zoo approach rather than being hosted by a single presenter, with often several DJs in the studio at one time taking turns on the decks. Towards the end of 1990 Green Apple left the air to be replaced by Jock's Cafe playing a more hardcore / breakbeat sound, but after a few weeks Green Apple returned again.

As techno began to become a distinct genre it featured on shows from DJ Float and DJ Zap, who played the harder Belgian-style under the 'only for the headstrong' banner. There were also house musicologist DJ Jav, Black Mark, Adrian Long and Ras Kwame, who presented a very polished show and went on to be one of the launch DJs at BBC 1Xtra before joining Capital Xtra.

In 1992 Green Apple moved to satellite radio, leasing time from the Euronet channel every Friday night. Before the days of modern Electronic Programme Guides listeners could not easily stumble across these transmissions. Despite this they still managed to pick up a loyal listenership. DJs like Carl Cox brought dance music to parts of Europe where the style was previously unheard of. The broadcasts finished when Euronet hit financial difficulties and closed down in spring 1993. A group of presenters from Green Apple also unsuccessfully applied for the local licence in Slough that went to Star Radio.

• • • • • • • • • • • • • • • •

Several of the DJs went on to play on Point Blank FM where Paul James, Ian Dee, Nikki Taylor and the Nipper can still be heard.

Bass FM
An exclusively house music station launched in February 1990 on 92.7 FM.

Big L
When Garry Stevens decided to move away from broadcasting for a while, Big L was launched in Veronica's place, run by presenter Ruski 'on the Radio'. Transmissions were on 98 FM every Sunday from Chingford with programmes played on tape over a radio link from Edmonton. The station continued until March 1991 when Veronica was once more reborn.

Classic Rock FM
A short-lived operation that came on the air in October 1990.

Contact FM
A house music station launched in January 1990 on 101.1 FM.

Destiny FM
Launched May 1990 on 98.3 FM with house music.

Elite Radio
Launched in August on 97.75 FM featuring former Tropical Radio presenters.

Emerald Radio
An Irish music station launched in October 1990 on 101.7 FM. The station was only heard for a few weeks.

Radio Fun
Launched in August on 93.8 FM from North London with house and hip hop.

Fusion FM
Launched in March with soul, jazz and house on 101.6 FM.

Hardcore FM
Launched in April with a rave music format on 88.9 FM. At least one presenter was previously on Sunrise FM. The station championed the breakbeat hardcore sound emerging as the decade ended and broadcasts continued into the early nineties.

Jock's Cafe
Launched in December on 99.7 FM, this was mostly Green Apple DJs with more of a breakbeat style. It broadcast the sound of plates and cooking in the background of DJs.

Radio London
Briefly on the air in August on 101.3 FM – and not connected with the other Big L that was broadcasting at the time – or for that matter the former BBC station.

London Sun Radio
Playing reggae, soul and a little house, launched in May 1990 on 100.3 FM.

Lovelight Radio
Launched in June on 104.3 FM.

Megablasters
A dance station in the South London area that surfaced briefly on 105.6 FM.

Radio Mi Amigo
An oldies service operating on 104.2 FM on Saturday afternoons – the time when Capital Gold carried sport.

Moonlight 101
A house music station launched in May on 100.8 FM.

The Music Machine
Not wanting to leave the 101.6 FM frequency vacant during the week when Veronica and Q102 were off the air, Veronica launched a low power continuous music station in the spring of 1990. The station took its name from one of the jingles used. Eventually evening programmes from presenters were added as well, but with continual raids The Music Machine closed after a few months and they

concentrated just on Veronica. The name was used again in 1992 for a station featuring a number of former Veronica and RFM presenters.

Network FM
Playing house music on 101.5 FM.

Ocean FM
Briefly on the air in July on 88.5 FM.

Paranoia FM
Launched in November on 106.9 FM playing house music.

Planet Radio
Broadcasting on 91.6 FM in North East London.

Pleasure FM
Launched in March with a rave format on 89.8 FM, Pleasure FM quickly vanished from the air after a raid. The station returned in August on 99.9 but chose a spot just next to where Kiss were about to appear. They continued operating into the nineties, later with more of a UK garage format.

Power 98.4
One of several stations around the country with the Power name, this one launched playing house music in July 1990.

Powerjack
A short-lived rave station launched in November on 101.8 FM.

Powerjam
Black community station Powerjam launched on 92 FM in July 1990 with several former DJs from Classic Radio. It has continued to operate in South London ever since.

Premier Radio
Launched with a broad black music format in April 1990 on 89.8 FM.

Pulse FM
Rave station Pulse FM began operating in August on 105.5 FM after Friends FM went off air. The station continued operating into the nineties with presenters including Jesse James, Anton, Nicky Blackmarket, Jinx, Helium, Psycho D and former Kiss regular and Music Power Records boss Nick Power.

Q Radio
No connection with the magazine, this one broadcast on 97 FM in early 1990.

Rave FM
One of the biggest hardcore stations, Rave launched in February on 95.3 FM and was run by brothers Noah and Kenny Charlery who also promoted the Living Dream rave events and ran the Kikman label. A few Fantasy FM DJs jumped ship to Rave FM when it started, though some later returned. Presenters included DJ Rap, DJ Randall, Timmi Magic, Mike De Underground and Coolhand Flex.

Ravers FM
A short-lived contender launched in May on 98.5 FM.

Respect FM
Launched in February on 104.3 FM.

Rhythm FM
Operating out of East London, Rhythm FM launched in October on 98.4 FM.

Roxy FM
Launched in January playing soca and calypso on 97.9 FM, but was not to last.

Scream FM
Another rave station launched in November on 101.0 FM.

Smart Boys
A house music station launched in February 1990 on 101.2 FM. Smart Boys had less of

the breakbeat tracks that the East London stations were increasingly playing. Presenters included several DJs who would go on to form Renegade Soundwave, including Alex Angol and Danny Briolett.

Soca Radio
Launched in July 101.3 FM from North London.

South London Sounds
A rock station broadcasting from South East London featuring several former RFL presenters including the legendary Kenny Myers.

Starbase
A short-lived station that appeared on 101.5 FM in August.

State FM
A dance music station broadcasting on 101 FM.

Suburban FM
Briefly on the air in July on 103.9.

Thames FM
Launched in February on 99.4 FM with a mixed format including rock, oldies and house, depending on the DJ's whims.

UK London
Launched October on 104.3 FM with DJs including former LWR presenter Yomi.

WBLS
The second – but not the last – station with that name in London, broadcasting soul on 92.2 FM.

Outro

There are several reasons why this story ends in 1990, some personal, some to do with the development of Britain's radio industry.

The biggest was that 1990 was the year I stopped reporting on the pirates. In November the new Broadcasting Act came into law making it an offence to give support to unlicensed stations, including listing their frequencies or other information. Three weeks later our company received a letter from the Department of Trade and Industry warning us that we would be prosecuted if we continued to give out details about the pirates on our telephone information lines. While the AM/FM phone lines continued to operate with more general radio news I gradually lost interest in radio as I moved into the fledgling Internet industry. Some of the people I knew who had been involved in that era of pirates moved into legal radio, but many like me moved on to other things.

There was also a feeling that with the loosening-up of the radio system and the introduction of the incremental stations the pirates had achieved their main goal. From four BBC national stations, one BBC local station and two Independent Local Radio stations in 1985, London had added an extra nine services by 1990 – with more promised. The Radio Authority was on its way with a new form of lighter-touch regulation. What could possibly go wrong?

In 1988 I did an interview about the capital's pirates with NBC Radio's London bureau for syndication on their news stations in the USA. The reporter asked me how I expected there to remain such diverse services when in America the experience in radio had been very different. Stations there were increasingly part of large corporations who had little interest in the communities they served. Local services were being replaced by networked programming and survival was only guaranteed for the formats serving audiences that were valuable to advertisers. I said I hoped that the regulator would act in favour of diversity and keep stations to the formats they promised. The optimism and hope for the future of radio that I shared with many others proved misplaced.

Many of the people involved in stations licensed in 1989's incremental radio scheme and immediately after had ideals beyond just creating profit-making ventures. They had aspirations to serve their communities, whether they were people in a particular neighbourhood, from a particular culture or simply people who liked a particular kind of music. The new stations, however, had to operate under legislation designed solely for delivering commercial radio: there were no provisions for protecting non-profit operation or community owner-ship and control. As stations hit problems all that the regulator could do was shrug, approve the handover of a licence to one of the established radio groups and modify the promise of performance until the owner felt it was sufficiently profitable. It was ultimately big business that benefited most from the actions of the pirate radio stations that resulted in the deregulation and expansion of the radio system.

In the twenty-five years since, commercial radio has consolidated into just two companies, Global (broadly a successor to Capital) and Bauer (which bought out Kiss investor EMAP). Their specialist music stations no longer play specialist music: now you get pop with a flavour rather than the real thing. The local sta-tions are no longer local: for much of the day the same service is relayed across stations in different areas or seemingly-local programmes may come from a central studio miles away. In 1984, the IBA's Director of Radio, Peter Baldwin, pointed out "The whole ethos of local radio, Independent Local Radio, is to be as local as possible because that is the greatest characteristic, when we do research in our areas, that people value our service [by]."[205] With BBC Local Radio now also running some national shows to cut costs, local radio's most attractive feature has been progressively lost.

There are still some around the edges of the mainstream commercial radio system who have held on with something different. London Greek Radio have evolved their format for a newer generation while, somewhat ironically, Radio Jackie are on the air in South West London with a station that is closer to the ethos of eighties ILR than the descendants of the ILR companies who were previ-ously trying to shut him down. Such stations are, however, very much exceptions in the system. On satellite radio and the Internet, earlier ex-pirates have become heritage operations, with Solar, Starpoint and mi-soul playing music for a gener-ation that were young at the time of their pirate predecessors.

Three decades since the first government report to recommend its introduc-tion, Ofcom finally began formally licensing community radio stations as a dis-tinct, non-profit-making tier in 2004. This has finally led to more experimental legal radio in London, for example from Resonance FM and former pirate Rinse FM. There are now plans that when digital radio listening is sufficiently wide-spread the national services should move off and make way for more of these ultra-local broadcasters.

Then there are the people who never stopped broadcasting illegally. Although electronics continued getting cheaper and new techniques were still developed, by 1990 the big problems in pirate broadcasting technology had been solved and the equipment fully commoditised. The presentation aspects of a station also changed less radically: the growth of MCs was one of the few departures from a DJ in front of a pair of decks with a stack of tunes and a mobile phone for listener feedback. Post-1990 the progression in London's pirates is better told as a music story, not a radio one, as the cutting edge moved on from hardcore to jungle to drum 'n' bass to two-step to UK garage and on to dubstep, grime, UK funky and more.

Legal black community radio has been a failure in London: Choice FM was absorbed into Global and rebranded as the urban music Capital Xtra while WNK and First Love Radio (after several relaunches) went out of business. Instead, pirates have continued to fulfil the needs of what is now an older Afro Caribbean audience. Today, Tottenham's RJR and Harlesden's Unique FM have a direct heritage back to the stations of the eighties in their areas.

Today's pirates are all niche broadcasters, fulfilling the needs of very specific audiences, rather than being able to break out to broader appeal like their forerunners. Music on the airwaves is no longer so scarce, while digital tuners and presets mean far fewer listeners now scan through the wavebands for interesting radio. Today's listeners are far less likely to stumble on illicit broadcasts.

On the other side of the fence, the Radio Investigation Service has become part of Ofcom and continues its work to shut down the pirates. It now has technology that lets it accurately pinpoint the source of unlicensed transmissions in all major UK cities without investigators having to leave the office. However, its pattern of raiding stations remains opaque and those new capabilities don't seem to have translated into making the airwaves any emptier of pirates. Newer laws seem to have been equally unsuccessful in reducing the economic viability of unlicensed broadcasting. The number of raids across the UK rose from 475 in 1991 to 1,438 in 2001. As a long-term minor irritant, Parliament is now largely uninterested in the illegal broadcasting that remains.

While the Internet now fulfils the needs of most of the younger generation of DJs and music fans, as long as there's an FM band there will always be pirates. And even when radio goes all digital and the analogue FM band is finally shut down there will still be those who find a way to broadcast from outside the system.

Credits

People

I am especially grateful to Aleks Wright for his help and suggestions. Special thanks also to Pyers Easton, Lawrie Hallett and Ian Trill.

I would also like to thank the following people who contributed information and photos to the book: Leroy Anderson, Mike Barraclough, Philip Bragg, Ron Brown, Steve Chandler, Steve Collins, Gary Drew, Bob Dunn, Pat Edison, Christopher England, Graham Foy, Bear Freeman, Dave Fuller, Ray Harrington, Andrew Hewkin, Geraldine Joshi, John Kenning, Mike Kerslake, Allan King, Gary King, Graham King, Mark King, Arnold Levine, Claire Mansfield, Alan Maylin, Mark McCarthy, Pete McFarlane, Leon Morris, Bob Mower, Tony Norris, Andy Richards, Keith Southgate, Steve Taylor, Norman Thompson, Roger Tidy and Carl Webster.

In research I drew extensively on the archive of TX / Radio Today and the associated telephone information lines. I am grateful to the many people and stations whose original contributions to those went into this book.

Books

Altered State: The story of ecstasy culture and acid house, Matthew Collin, Serpent's Tail

Radio Jackie: A very English struggle, Colin King, Larks Press

Kiss FM: From radical radio to big business, Grant Goddard, Radio Books

Last Night a DJ Saved My Life: The history of the disc jockey, Bill Brewster and Frank Broughton, Headline

Masters of the Airwaves: The rise & rise of underground radio, Dave VJ and Lindsay Wesker, Every Generation Media

Not the BBC / IBA: The case for community radio, Simon Partridge, Comedia / MPG

Offshore Radio, Gerry Bishop, Iceni Enterprises

Radio Is My Bomb: A DIY manual for pirates, Hooligan Press

Rebel Radio: The full story of British pirate radio, John Hind and Stephen Mosco, Pluto Press

Sounds Like London: 100 years of black music in the capital, Lloyd Bradley, Serpent's Tail

Magazines

Anoraks UK Weekly Report, 1983-1989

Caroline Movement Bulletin, 1979-1985

Free Airwaves, 1980

Free Broadcasting Magazine, 1979

Free Radio Waves, 1985-1986

Media Monitor, 1985-1987

Script, 1972-1975

Touch Magazine, 1989-1994

TX / Radio Today, 1985-1988

Wavelength, 1977

Websites

In researching this book a large number of websites had useful snippets of information. For those interested in the subject these are some good starting points.

AM/FM: www.amfm.org.uk

DJ History: www.djhistory.com

The DX Archive: www.dxarchive.com

Radio Eric: radio.eric.tripod.com

Gunfleet: www.gunfleet.com

The Pirate Archive: www.piratearchive.net

Quotes

1. International Times, Vol. 1, Issue 14
2. Script magazine issue 14, November 1974
3. Rebel Radio, John Hind and Stephen Mosco
4. Script magazine issue 6, 1973
5. LTIR information sheet, 1972
6. Wavelength issue 3, March 1976
7. Radio Kaleidoscope Southend web site
8. E-mail to author
9. Telstar 1 website
10. E-mail to author
11. E-mail to author
12. E-mail to author
13. E-mail to author
14. House of Commons debate 'Radio Jackie', 22 December 1971
15. House of Commons debate, 'Local Commercial Radio Stations', 29 March 1971
16. Daily Mail, 5 May 1975
17. E-mail to author
18. E-mail to author
19. Radio Jackie: A Very English Struggle, Colin King
20. Script magazine issue 7, October 1973
21. LTIR information sheet, 1972
22. Script magazine issue 14, November 1974
23. LTIR newsletter, 1972
24. Sunday Telegraph, 24 January 1988
25. Sounds Good, Radio London, Winter 1983
26. The Guardian, 19 August 1985
27. E-mail to author
28. Rebel Radio, John Hind and Stephen Mosco
29. Time Out, 23 March 1979
30. Sounds, 15 January 1983
31. Nick Catford posting, Radio Jackie Supporters Group, 8 October 2000
32. Report of the Committee on the Future of Broadcasting
33. The London Programme, LWT, 1982
34. The London Programme, LWT, 1982
35. One year on – an examination of Britain's only community-access radio, Christopher England, May 1979
36. What is the point of community radio, Christopher England website, 2012
37. TX Magazine, September 1986
38. What is the point of community radio, Christopher England website, 2012
39. Letter to listener, 1977
40. Rebel Radio, John Hind and Stephen Mosco
41. Evening Standard, 21 January 1982
42. Usenet posting on alt.radio.pirate by Bob Tomalski
43. Kid Johnson interview by Horace Cracksman, former Radio Telstar South website
44. Mike Burnett on Radio Telstar South, Rock Radio website
45. Kid Johnson interview by Horace Cracksman, former Radio Telstar South website
46. E-mail to author
47. Radio Today issue 16, November 1987
48. Radio Today issue 16, November 1987
49. Radio Today issue 16, November 1987
50. E-mail to author
51. Sounds Good, BBC Radio London, Winter 1983
52. Radio Today issue 17, November 1987
53. Bromley Sound page, Radio Eric website
54. Sounds, 15 January 1983
55. The Guardian, 25 April 1985
56. Rebel Radio, John Hind and Stephen Mosco
57. E-mail to author
58. E-mail to author
59. E-mail to author
60. The SLR Story, South London Radio, July 1982
61. The SLR Story, South London Radio, July 1982
62. The SLR Story, South London Radio, July 1982
63. E-mail to author

64. Blues & Soul magazine, November 1984
65. YouTube comment by Thehorizonradio, 2012
66. Evening Standard, 5 January 1988
67. Rebel Radio, John Hind and Stephen Mosco
68. Crowbar Squatters News, April 1986
69. E-mail to author
70. Comment on Streamola Archive web site
71. The Observer, date unknown, 1984
72. TX Magazine issue 9, September 1986
73. Sounds Good, Radio London, Winter 1983
74. Sounds Good, Radio London, Winter 1983
75. Skyline Radio page, Radio Telstar South website
76. The London Programme, LWT, 1982
77. Evening Standard, 19 October 1984
78. House of Commons debate 'Pirate Radio Broadcasters', 20 January 1984
79. Breakfast Pirate Radio, Joly McFee blog, 2010
80. Rebel Radio, John Hind and Stephen Mosco
81. File on Four, Radio Four, July 1984
82. Jazzy B interview, DJ History website
83. Rebel Radio, John Hind and Stephen Mosco
84. The Guardian, 23 July 1984
85. Cyprus Weekly 3 April 1987
86. The Daily Telegraph, 15 May 1989
87. Campaign, 15 November 1985
88. E-mail to author
89. Sounds Good, Radio London, Winter 1983
90. E-mail to author
91. File on Four, Radio Four, July 1984
92. File on Four, Radio Four, July 1984
93. File on Four, Radio Four, July 1984
94. Sounds Good, Radio London, Winter 1983
95. Gilles Peterson interview, DJ History website
96. The Guardian, 1 December 1984
97. Evening Standard, 30 November 1984
98. Today newspaper, 5 May 1988
99. Disco magazine, 10 February 1979
100. Rebel Radio, John Hind and Stephen Mosco
101. Rebel Radio, John Hind and Stephen Mosco
102. Touch Magazine, May 1994
103. Masters of the Airwaves, Dave VJ and Lindsay Wesker
104. Campaign Magazine, 6 November 1987
105. Touch Magazine, May 1994
106. E-mail to author
107. E-mail forwarded to author
108. TX Magazine, September 1986
109. TX Magazine, September 1986
110. Campaign, 19 May 1989
111. Media Week, 14 July 1989
112. The Guardian, 14 August 1989
113. E-mail to author
114. Record Mirror, 13 July 1985
115. Kiss FM's Written Word issue 4, February 1989
116. Home Office press statement, 23 January 1985
117. File on Four, Radio Four, July 1984
118. The London Programme, LWT, 1982
119. House of Commons debate, 6 February 1981
120. IBA press statement, 25 July 1985
121. The Guardian, 19 August 1985
122. The Guardian, 19 August 1985
123. The Guardian, 19 August 1985
124. Deadline magazine, December 1988
125. Cleveland Anderson interview, Electrofunk Roots website
126. House of commons debate 'Pirate Radio', 23 May 1985
127. City Limits, 20 October 1988
128. Tosca profile, mi-soul website
129. Evening Standard, 27 December 1989
130. Soul Survivors magazine, June 2013
131. Observer magazine, date unknown, 1985
132. Gilles Peterson interview, DJ History website

133. Profile, TX / Radio Today issue 13, February 1987
134. Mail on Sunday, 11 May 1986
135. Mail on Sunday, 11 May 1986
136. House of Commons written reply, 30 June 1986
137. The Sunday Times, 6 July 1986
138. House of Commons debate, 30 June 1986
139. Sounds Good, Radio London, Winter 1983
140. Making Waves, Discovery Channel, 1984
141. E-mail to author
142. Unattributed statement in Essex newspaper
143. File on Four, Radio Four, July 1984
144. Radio Today issue 16, November 1987
145. Media Monitor issue 50, 27 April 1987
146. E-mail to author
147. Network 21 website
148. E-mail to author
149. Enfield Advertiser, 4 June 1987
150. Letter to magazine
151. File on Four, Radio Four, July 1984
152. Evening Standard, 10 July 1987
153. Evening Standard, 10 July 1987
154. NME, 8 August 1987
155. The Guardian, 29 July 1987
156. The Guardian, 29 July 1987
157. Daily Telegraph, 29 July 1987
158. Angie Dee profile, Sound Women website
159. Masters of the Airwaves, Dave VJ and Lindsay Wesker
160. Campaign magazine, 6 November 1987
161. Touch magazine, May 1994
162. The Nation's Favourite, Simon Garfield
163. The Guardian, 5 May 1986
164. The Black and White Pirate Show, Channel Four, 1987
165. Sounds Like London, Lloyd Bradley
166. City Limits, 5 November 1987
167. City Limits, 5 November 1987
168. Deadline magazine, December 1988
169. Evening Standard, 3 January 2002
170. Fabio interview, DJ History website
171. Radio Today issue 18, September 1988
172. City Limits, 20 October 1988
173. E-mail to author
174. E-mail to author
175. The Face, January 1988
176. London Daily News, 18 April 1987
177. Evening Standard, 23 October 1984
178. The Face, December 1988
179. House of commons written answer, 19 January 1988
180. Financial Times, 20 January 1988
181. House of commons written answer, 1 February 1988
182. PPL letter to members, 15 April 1988
183. House of Commons written answer, 1 February 1988
184. Kiss FM: From Radical Radio to Big Business, Grant Goddard
185. South London Press, 8 November 1988
186. The Independent, 9 November 1988
187. Letter to author
188. Touch Magazine, May 1994
189. DJ magazine, December 2003
190. The Sunday Telegraph, 29 October 1989
191. The Sunday Telegraph, 29 October 1989
192. Broadcast magazine, 31 March 1989
193. Letter from IBA to Kiss FM, 11 July 1989
194. Music Week, 6 January 1990
195. Media Week, 5 January 1990
196. i-D magazine, October 1989
197. Altered State, Matthew Collin
198. Rave Magazine, February 1990
199. Rave Magazine, December 1989
200. Rave Story, Otiz F. Angel
201. Going Deaf for a Living website
202. Comment on AM/FM website
203. Home Office press release, 4 July 1989
204. E-mail to author
205. BBC TV News, date unknown, 1984

Index

Lightning Source UK Ltd.
Milton Keynes UK
UKHW021849270520
363925UK00016B/4414